Gopher Glory

100 Years of University of Minnesota Basketball

Gopher

■ 100 YEARS   OF UNIVERSITY OF

Glory

MINNESOTA BASKETBALL

Edited by
Steve Perlstein

with assistance from
Mark Moller

Layers Publishing, LLC
Minneapolis, Minnesota

Copyright © 1995
Layers Publishing, LLC

Permissions Department
Layers Publishing, LLC
2 East Franklin Avenue, Suite 8
Minneapolis, MN 55404

Jacket and interior design by David J. Farr, *ImageSmythe*.

Front cover art © 1995 Terrence Fogarty, used by permission of the artist.

Prepress by Clarinda Color, St. Paul, Minnesota

Printed in Korea by Sung-In Printing.

Cataloging in Publication Data

Gopher glory : 100 years of University of Minnesota basketball / edited by Steve Perlstein
    p. cm.
    ISBN 0–9646918–9–2

    1. University of Minnesota--Basketball--History. I. Perlstein, Steve, 1965– ed.

GV885.43U65G67 1995
796.323'63'09776579
QBI95–20298

Acknowledgements

The publishers wish to thank the following people and institutions for their help and advice essential to the creation of *Gopher Glory*:

Carin Anderson, Pat Forceia, Nancy Hagenson, and the Men's Athletic Department's Marketing Department; Mark Ryan, Mark Moller, Erik Sandvick, Karen Zwach, Bill Crumley, and the rest of the Men's Athletic Department's Office of Media Relations; Wendell Vandersluis; the University of Minnesota Archives; Margaret Carlson, Bob Burdett, Al Anderson, and the University of Minnesota Alumni Association; Clem and Yevette Haskins; Kevin McHale; Clarinda Color; David Farr and *ImageSmythe*; Julia Williamson; Charles Falk and Sung-In Printing; The Bookmen; Tom Leigh; Jim Dutcher; Bill Musselman; John Kundla; Townsend Orr; Kevin Lynch; Trent Tucker; Marc Wilson; Marvin "Corky" Taylor; Ron Johnson; Eric Magdanz; Lou Hudson; John Wooden; Glen Reed; Jerry Kindall; Ray Christensen; Walter Chapman; George MacKinnon; Don "Swede" Carlson; Louis Brewster; Warren Ajax; and Sam Petersen and Janean Selkirk of Petersen Selkirk Public Relations.

Photo Credits

Wendell Vandersluis, University of Minnesota: v, vi, vii, 61, 62 (4), 63, 64, 67, 68, 69 (2), 70, 71, 72 (2), 73 (2), 75, 77, 78, 79, 80, 81, 82, 86, 92 (2), 93, 101, 102, 103, 106-107, 109, 111, 113, 115, 116, 122, 123, 124, 125, 126, 127, 128 (2), 129, 131, 132 (2), 134, 135 (2), 137, 140, 141, 143, 145, 146, 147, 148, 149, 150, 151, 152, 154, 156 (2), 157 (2), 158 (4), 159 (2), 160 (2), 161 (2), 163, 164, 166-167, 168, 169.

Kevin Gruye, University of Minnesota: ii-iii, 121.

Courtesy of St. Paul Pioneer Press: 85, 87, 88, 90, 94, 97, 99.

Courtesy of the University of Minnesota Department of Men's Athletics Media Relations Department: 3, 6, 7, 9 (2), 12, 13 (2), 15 (2), 16 (2), 20 (3), 21 (4), 22 (2), 23 (4), 24 (2), 26, 27, 28 (2), 29 (3), 30 (4), 31, 32, 35, 36, 37, 38 (2), 40 (3), 42, 44, 45 (4), 46 (2), 47 (2), 48 (2), 49, 51, 53, 55 (2), 56, 57, 58, 60 (2), 63, 64.

Courtesy of the University of Minnesota Archives: 4 (3), 5.

Courtesy of Glen Reed: 44.

Contents

Foreword

By Clem Haskins

When I decided to accept the offer to become head basketball coach at the University of Minnesota, I knew a few things. I knew I was taking over a program that had gone through some controversial times in recent years. I knew our team would take some serious rebuilding to make it into a Big Ten contender once again and to win back the support of Gopher fans. I also knew I was moving to a hockey state: When Yevette and I were looking for houses, we didn't see basketball goals in the driveways, but we saw hockey sticks in the garages.

Once I got here, though, I learned a few things about what I thought I knew. The basketball tradition at the University of Minnesota is a powerful thing. It makes players—especially players who grew up in Minnesota—want to play here, and it makes them want to excel once they get here. And I learned that Minnesota is indeed a basketball state. Minnesotans might play plenty of hockey, and they even watch their fair share, but when the Maroon and Gold takes to the raised floor at Williams Arena, there is no doubt this is a state populated by serious basketball fans, up to and including the governor. Neither my players nor I have ever experienced anything like standing on the floor while the sold-out Barn shakes from the shouts of 15,000 wild Gopher fans. We never had to win these people back; we just had to show them that we were willing to work hard and put a competitive team on the floor every night.

We did work hard. It took a couple of years, but that work paid off, and we have enjoyed success for most of my years here. We confounded the skeptics with consecutive appearances in the NCAA Tournament, making it to the Sweet 16 and the Elite Eight. We won an NIT championship. And I am proud to say that our five players who were seniors in 1994-95 participated in postseason play for each of their four years.

But I am proud of more than what we have accomplished on the basketball court. I am proud of the fine young men who have decided to play basketball at the University of Minnesota during my tenure here. Not only are they outstanding athletes, but they are good, hard-working students, and they are assets to their community. I am honored that so many of Minnesota's best basketball players—people like Chad Kolander, Kevin Lynch, Sam Jacobson, and John Thomas—elected to stay home and play for the Gophers.

That's a reinforcement of the level of commitment and support I have felt from the citizens of Minnesota, from Winona to Thief River Falls, and Luverne to Grand Marais. I remember one incident early in my time here at Minnesota. We were traveling to Canby for an intrasquad game. We arrived several hours before game time, and as our bus passed the gym, we were stunned to see thousands of people already lined up around the block to make sure they got a seat in the gym to meet us that night. Not bad for a hockey state.

Yevette and I have spent nine years in Minnesota. It has become our home, and we have felt more welcomed and supported than we ever could have imagined, from the governor to folks we pass on the street. Our players, whether they are from Minnesota or somewhere else, have all felt the same way. That's a credit to this state and to its people, and we are proud to be a part of that.

Preface

By Kevin McHale

When I was a kid growing up in Hibbing, the only place I wanted to go to school was the University of Minnesota. I remember I always used to go to the Hibbing library because they got the *Minneapolis Tribune* there, and it was the only place in town where I had access to the *Tribune*. I would go the day after every Gophers game and read about the Gophers, look at the color photos the *Trib* ran of players like Jim Brewer, Corky Taylor, Ron Behagen, and Clyde Turner competing in their maroon and gold uniforms, and I'd think about how great they looked.

As I got older and began getting people's attention as a basketball player at Hibbing High School, Coach Jim Dutcher and his staff contacted me about playing at the University of Minnesota, and I was just thrilled to death. I got other calls, and other schools tried to recruit me, but after I got that scholarship offer from the U, I just hung up the phone. I wasn't interested in talking to anybody else. I never wanted anything other than to go to the University, get an education, and get a chance to play basketball. Of course, basketball was a part of my experience at the U, but it wasn't everything for me there by any stretch of the imagination. I had a great time while I was there, I got an excellent education, and I met a lot of very special people in addition to having a superb basketball experience. Coach Dutcher remains one of the great influences in my life today, because of what he taught me about myself as a person and as a basketball player. I will forever be grateful to Coach Dutcher and to the University of Minnesota for that.

Now that Gopher fans have voted me Player of the Century, I feel a little strange. It almost doesn't seem right being honored by the University; I feel like it should be the other way around, like I should be honoring the U because of all that it gave me. I got to play in the Big Ten, which was always a very competitive league that helped me develop a strong work ethic. But I also got to play in pickup games with some of the football players during the winter in the Bierman gym and during the summer in the stifling temperatures of Williams Arena with the sun's heat being magnified by the metal roof. I remember those times just as fondly.

But most of all, I remember the thrill I felt representing the State of Minnesota. On the Iron Range, when people said "The U," everybody knew what they meant. There's only one U. If a kid from the Range went to the U as an athlete—whether it was for basketball like I did, hockey like the Michelletti brothers did, or anything else—people were proud of you. If you went to the Twin Cities and played for the U, it was a great thing. I never spent much time thinking about it—about which school I would attend, about having an NBA career. I wanted to play basketball and I wanted to play it at the University of Minnesota.

As we celebrate 100 years of basketball at the U, those memories have come back to me as clearly as ever. That tells me the importance of the traditions that were laid down before I came to the University of Minnesota, and that have continued since I moved on. I can tell you that not many Universities have a legacy like that, and it is one about which we should all be proud.

Gopher Glory

100 Years of University of Minnesota Basketball

SECTION 1

At the dawn of the 1890s, America was undergoing a tremendous wave of social, political, and economic changes that would thrust the nation into the 20th century. Minneapolis and St. Paul were part of this change and growth, expanding to a combined population of 300,000 as they became centers of the milling and railroad industries. During this time, baseball, boxing, and football were the sports that captured the attention of Americans, but there was an athletic void during the winters—especially in the upper Midwest, where the end of the college football season brought an onslaught of bitter cold and heavy snow until baseball began in the spring.

Into this gap stepped an unassuming Canadian of Scottish descent named James Naismith. The game he created would not only fill the winter void in the sporting life of the United States, but it would become an integral part of the nation's culture and a popular export around the world. The elements of peach baskets, a soccer ball, and a bored gym class that led to the formation of the game of "basket ball" are well known. The spread of the game from its primitive roots in the winter of 1891 is remarkable. In January of that year, the *Triangle*, the school newspaper of the Springfield Training School, published the thirteen rules and Naismith's instructions for the new game of basket ball. The *Triangle* was distributed through the network of YMCAs,

■ *Albert Varco played for the Gophers in the early 1900s.*

and the tremendous growth of the game had begun.

In Minneapolis, a new YMCA building at 10th street and Mary Place (now LaSalle Avenue) was completed in March 1892 and the gymnasium and swimming tank were proving to be great attractions. The gymnasium was home to several teams, and the physical director, Dr. J.C. Elsom, had scheduled regular contests on Tuesday and Saturday evenings after 9:00.

While the game's initial popularity and rapid spread were due to the YMCA, the true development of and lasting foundation for basketball was on college campuses. In 1893 and 1894 several former Springfield students brought the game to Stanford University, Yale, Geneva College in Pennsylvania, Haverford College, the University of Toronto, and Vanderbilt University. Amos Alonzo Stagg, eventually a Hall of Fame football coach, brought the game to the University of Chicago.

In St. Paul, Raymond P. Kaighn, one of Naismith's original students, organized what is considered to be the first intercollegiate basketball game between his Hamline University and a team from the School of Agriculture of the University of Minnesota. The School of Agriculture—now known as the St. Paul campus—and its students were mainly the sons of farmers from around the state who came to learn agricultural techniques and animal husbandry during the winter months, when there was

■ *James Naismith, the inventor of basketball and the mentor to L.J. "Doc" Cooke, the father of Gopher basketball.*

not much work to be done on the farm. On February 9, 1895, the strapping farm boys met the Pipers in a basement handball court—with some difficulty due to the nine-foot-high ceiling. The game was played nine-on-nine and the Ag boys won 9-3. The rules at the time awarded three points for a field goal and three points for a free throw; it is unknown who scored and how. A month later the Ag boys won again, 9-6, and could claim an undefeated "season" of collegiate basketball.

The direct connection of the spread of basketball to the University of Minnesota is not clear, although there was a branch of the YMCA on the Minneapolis campus, and certainly many students could have picked up the game at the Minneapolis or St. Paul YMCAs. As early as February of 1894, the *Ariel*, the University newspaper, published an editorial calling for the construction of a gymnasium on campus and recognizing the absence of sufficient wintertime physical activity as a detriment to the student body: "... Students of the University of Minnesota are compelled to lapse into a state of total athletic desuetude, all from the lack of a gymnasium."

The *Ariel* was not only concerned with the physical health of the students, but in a remarkable parallel to today's headlines, it continued to argue for a gymnasium because, "Athletic entertainments not only revive and sustain interest in sports, but they replenish the treasury of the Athletic Association."

In March and April of 1895, the *Ariel* pleaded for support from the student

body for the Athletic Association and gave a financial report that concluded the Association was in debt by the count of $145.25. In November 1895, the *Ariel* reported that basketball had become very popular on the Ag campus and that a basket ball league had formed with teams from the Minneapolis YMCA, Macalester College, Hamline University, State Military Company A, a Minneapolis campus team, and the Agricultural School.

The Ag school, however, continued to be the leader in the new sport. The November 23, 1895 edition of the *Ariel* carried a detailed description of a contest between the Ag seniors and a team of alumni at the Drill Hall in St. Paul. "Long before the game was called the balcony was crowded with excited spectators. The Cadet band was out and the music was fine. The Senior class, with canes and colors proudly flying, took possession of the seats on the north side of the balcony....The Senior team were the first to enter the hall, closely followed by their opponents. As they entered they were greeted with showers of applause from the gallery."

While the Ag school had fully embraced basketball, the Minneapolis campus was less enthusiastic. In the December 7 issue, the *Ariel* reported that the game was to be introduced to the first meeting of the "University Gymnastics class" which was to be directed by D.F. Grasse of the Medical Department. In the same issue, the Ag school reported that they had beaten St. Thomas College in a practice game, 4-3, on November 27.

■ *The exterior and interior of the cramped Minneapolis YMCA, where the Gophers played many of their early games.*

By January 1896, the Minneapolis campus had finally organized a team to play in the Twin City Basket Ball league, independent of the financially ailing Athletic Association. On January 13, 1896, a basketball team from the Minneapolis campus of the University of Minnesota played its first game. The *Minneapolis Journal* gave the following account of the contest in its January 17 edition:

"The University team surprised the basket ball cranks by taking the game from Company A in the last half by the score of 5 to 4. Company A, with aggressive work maintained a good lead until near the close of the first half, when she 'broke' and practically gave the game to the university team by fouling. Capt. Grasse, of the 'U' team did some very creditable penalty goal 'shooting.'...(the gym) was filled with a large and appreciative audience composed of both factions, who yelled themselves hoarse until the close of the game."

The team roster included team captain D.F. Grasse, Edmund Sheldon, a law student from Minneapolis, George Montfort, a law student from Litchfield, William Kehoe, William Mann of Minneapolis, Robb Lincoln of Fergus Falls, and Deidrich Grusendorf of New Ulm. Officials for the game included Dr. Louis Cooke, the physical director at the Minneapolis YMCA. While the U team barely escaped with a 5-4 victory, the Ag boys continued to excel by beating Macalester 18-2.

The University team met the Agricultural squad for a league game on January 21 and fell by a score of 5-3. The *Ariel* reported, "The game was quite rough and it was difficult for some in the balcony to keep from yelling 'Second down and no gain—line up quick.'"

Basketball's popularity at the Agricultural school seemed to be unmatched. In the February 1, 1896 edition of the *Ariel*, the Agricultural section published a description of its game with the Minneapolis YMCA given by the *Minneapolis Tribune:* "Fully 200 Minnesota boys came over with the team to cheer them on to victory and they brought a band with them. The boys formed a parade after the game and marched down Nicollet with torches blazing and the band playing, and they made the air ring with their triumphant college yell."

By the end of the inaugural Twin City Basket Ball season, the U team had won three games and lost five, while the Ag team finished 6-2 in second place to the Minneapolis YMCA. Despite the older age of the U team, the Ag boys maintained a decided advantage.

The fall of 1896 was an important time in the development for University of Minnesota basketball, when the University Armory Building opened. At the time of its construction the Armory was not only the largest building on campus but one of the larger armories in the nation. The September 12, 1896 edition of the *Ariel* reported: "In style it is like the turreted castles of the Middle Ages and is built of buff-colored pressed brick, with Kasota stone trimmings. The main floor is divided by a long corridor ...across the corridor is the main assembly and drill hall, 80x140 feet...extending clear around the main floor is a large sloping balcony, suspended from roof trusses, leaving the main floor clear; at the ends of the hall there are two squad drill rooms, 36x95 feet with a balcony. The three rooms can be thrown together by means of movable

■ *The campus armory, used as it was intended — housing troops.*

partitions, giving a total seating capacity of over 3,000."

Finally, the growing campus had its all-purpose gymnasium; the Armory would become the home court for University of Minnesota basketball for the next 30 years.

In the winter of 1897, a second key development in University of Minnesota basketball occurred. The University was in need of someone to direct the new gymnasium and manage the physical education department. It turned to the physical director of the Minneapolis YMCA, Dr. Louis Cooke, to attend to the duties on a part-time basis. Cooke, who had refereed the first basketball game by a team from the Minneapolis campus, can rightly be described as the father of University of Minnesota basketball.

Louis Cooke was born on February 15, 1868, in Toledo, Ohio, just three days before the state legislature of Minnesota acted to enable the opening of the University of Minnesota. After two summer sessions at the YMCA Training School in Springfield, Cooke went on to the University of Vermont, where he received

his M.D. in 1894 and was a star pitcher for the Vermont baseball team. He was physical director at YMCAs in Toledo, Ohio, Duluth, and Burlington, Vermont, before coming to Minneapolis in 1895. Dr. Cooke's impact was immediate and long-lasting, not only on the athletic facilities, but on the students with whom he became immensely popular.

Despite the presence of the new gymnasium in the Armory, basketball continued to struggle on the Minneapolis campus. Although it was now a regular part of the gym class curriculum, the Athletic Association had not chosen to take the lead in organizing a varsity squad. By December, a group of underclassmen had formed a basketball club, but their efforts were hampered by lack of a proper ball—they were using a football—and a lack of baskets. By the fall of 1896, the game began to undergo changes. The teams were limited to five men when the playing space was less than 1,800 square feet, seven men when the space was 1,800-3,600 square feet, and nine men when over 3,600 square feet. The A.G. Spalding Co. was now producing an official ball, a round rubber bladder, weighing between 18 ounces and 20 ounces, and goals were to be hammock nets of cord, 18 inches in diameter.

Without the backing of the Athletic Association, the U's efforts to field a team in the winter of 1897 stumbled on until finally the first game was played on February 6, when a team traveled to St. Paul to play the Ag boys. The team was made up of seven inexperienced freshmen. The experienced Ag team routed the U 25-1. With the sting of defeat still fresh, and with the Athletic Association treasury in mind, winter sport manager William Brown put out a call for basketball tryouts in the February 20 *Ariel*:

"Candidates for positions upon the 'representative' University basket ball team are urged to hand in their names immediately. The season is already so far advanced that things will have to be done with a rush as far as basketball is concerned. Dr. Cooke is now prepared to take hold of the work and with his coaching the 'U' ought to turn out a team to be proud of....Management hopes to aid substantially in paying off the A.A. debt by arranging a series of games with neighboring teams and charging an admission fee of 10 or 15 cents to each game."

In the span of just three years basketball had arrived on campus to fill a void in the winter sporting life, and had now become an economic necessity for balancing the Athletic Association's books.

Six teams were formed to play a tournament for Dr. Cooke to choose the best U players. On March 6, a U team met the YMCA Triangles and lost 18-6. But at the University Armory on the 13th, with fewer than 60 spectators who had handed over 10 cents each looking on, the U beat the YMCA Triangles 11-5 in what was the first official game between a University basketball team and another institution at the Armory.

Despite Dr. Cooke's attempts at organization, more than one squad from the Minneapolis campus competed that year, and the other squad lost to the YMCA Alphas 23-6 on March 9. The representative U team included Paul B. Arnell, right forward; P.A. Johnson, left forward; Michael Kiefer, right guard; R.B. Stephens, left guard; and several reserves. The organization of basketball as a regular sport continued with this report in the April 10 edition of the *Ariel*: "Suits have been ordered for the team and the boys expect to play the last three or four games of the year in somewhat better looking garments than cast-off football 'duds.' The new uniforms will consist of a maroon sleeveless jersey, maroon baseball pants and stockings and gold belt."

The U team fared better, as they finished the 1897 season. After an 11-7 win over the YMCA Goalites, the U tied the YMCA Picked Team 5-5, lost to the YMCA Alphas 13-6, and the YMCA Basketites 15-5, but triumphed in the Armory over the Scots from Macalester College 11-9. Despite a late start, and with the help of Dr. Cooke, the U finished 3-6-1 in its first year of organization under the Athletic Association.

The following fall proved that basketball had finally taken hold at the Minneapolis campus. There were more than 20 men trying out for the team and Dr. Cooke had again agreed to coach the squad. By this time, Cooke had been named Director of the University Gymnasium and was working full time with all the U teams except football. The U again competed in the

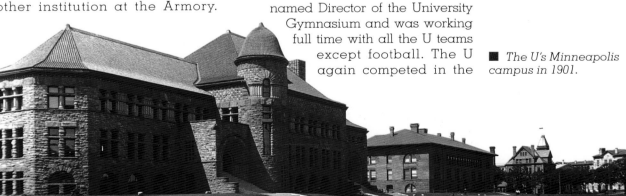

Twin City Basket Ball League and opened with a narrow loss to the Ag boys at the Armory, 8-7, in early January. The team consisted of R.B. Stephens, P.A. Johnson (captain), Herbert Jones, Glenn Robertson, and Michael Kiefer. The U team finished the 1898 season at 3-4, with wins coming over a Faculty team led by Doc Cooke (14-6), Macalester (12-2), and the Minneapolis YMCA (14-13).

The U continued to improve in 1898-99. With veteran forward Charles Olson and guard Michael Kiefer, the U finished with a 5-5 record, including big victories over the St. Paul YMCA (28-5 and 23-9) and their first victory over the Ag boys, 20-9.

The 1899-1900 season was the beginning of an extraordinary run for the University of Minnesota basketball team—one that established the program as a national power in collegiate basketball's first decade, and allowed the rise of Minnesota's first star players. From 1899 to 1907, over a span of 115 games, Minnesota compiled an amazing 89-27-1 record for a .765 winning percentage. The 1899-1900 season began with veterans Bruce McGregor, Michael Kiefer, and Daniel O'Keefe at guard, Henry Holden at forward, and captain Charles Olson at center with freshman William Deering of Fargo, North Dakota, at forward. Deering was to become the U's first star player; the *Ariel* gushed about his abilities in the December 13, 1899 issue: "(Deering) has about the easiest and prettiest way of dropping the ball in the basket ever seen on the floor."

Despite a season-opening loss to the Minneapolis YMCA, the U reeled off three straight wins over Minneapolis Central High, led by a tough, young center named George Tuck; the Fargo YMCA; and St. Cloud Normal school. The U team had become quite adept at the passing game, moving the ball around for a good shot and keeping their less experienced opponents grasping. On February 3 at the Armory, Minnesota played its rivals to the south for the first time and triumphed over Iowa 30-4. A week later the *Ariel* reported that the Iowa University paper had determined that the Hawkeye's defeat came because the Minnesota players held an unfair advantage by playing with "rubber shoes with suction spaces," although the *Ariel* maintained the Maroon and Gold wore ordinary tennis shoes.

On February 17, Minnesota again played what would become an historic rival when the Wisconsin Badgers came to the Armory. Though the Minnesota players would later complain bitterly about fouls called by the referee from Wisconsin, the U came away with a hard-fought 18-15 win. The team finished the 1899-1900 campaign with a 10-3 record and two sweet victories over rivals Iowa and Wisconsin, and they outscored their opponents 235-125. The following fall the U again had a veteran squad and opened the season with six straight wins, including two wins over their old rivals, the Ag boys from the St. Paul campus. These contests were the last between the School of Agriculture team and the Minnesota Varsity.

After a win at West Superior Normal school on February 1, the Normal players refused to play the next day unless a new officiating crew was found. On the 2nd, West Superior won 14-12 but the *Minnesota Daily* cast some doubt on its victory in the February 5 edition: "The Normalites seemed to meet with better success under the supervision of the new officials who brought up some new and interesting points of basketball playing."

The Maroon and Gold was led by William Deering, who had played at the Fargo YMCA and Fargo College before beginning his U career and was a strong shooter; captain Daniel O'Keefe of Red River Falls, Wisconsin, practiced daily at the Armory; Roy Ireland at center was particularly adept at tapping the ball towards the opponent's goal on the center jump; and veteran guard Michael Kiefer was fast and a good ball handler. After the dubious loss at West Superior Normal, the U returned home to wallop the Iowa Hawkeyes 38-5, sweep a set of three games in Fargo by a combined score of 87-17, and trounce the Badgers at the Armory 42-15 to finish the season at 11-1.

Following the regular season, Minnesota made an historic trip to Chicago for a national tournament directed by the University of Chicago's Amos Alonzo Stagg, an old acquaintance of Cooke's from the Springfield Training School. The tourney was held at the national sportsman's show at the Chicago Coliseum and featured the Ravenswood YMCA; Company E of Fond du Lac, Wisconsin; West Side YMCA of Chicago; the University of Nebraska; Company I of Kenyon, Ohio; the Toronto YMCA; Minnesota; and the "Silent Five", a team of deaf players from New York City. The U team lost to Ravenswood 20-12 and to the "Silent Five" 24-20. In a 1936 feature for the *Minneapolis Tribune*, Doc Cooke recounted the trip: "To set off the basketball court from the countless exhibits displayed all around the building, it was necessary to put up a low fence, with nets extending up from the sides, making it an enclosed court. Teams from all over the United States competed and Minnesota made a surprisingly good showing although she did not win. The Ravenswood YMCA of Chicago was the tournament winner, a team which Minnesota had held to a close score."

The trip was an extraordinary development, since most college teams of that era rarely traveled beyond their immediate area for games. Once again Minnesota had been a part of an historic basketball happening.

The 1901-02 season would prove to be the most successful in the short history of the program. With the return of William Deering, now team captain, veteran guard Michael Kiefer, Roy Ireland, and Henry Holden, and the addition of center George Tuck from Minn-

■ *George Tuck, Minnesota's first All-American, in 1902.*

■ *The 1901-02 national champions.*

eapolis Central High, the Golden Gophers had an experienced team and a presence underneath the basket.

After the success of the 1900-01 campaign, Minnesota could lay claim to being the best team in the West. Yale had finished 10-6 that year and claimed the championship of the East. With no head-to-head matchup to determine a national champion there was some doubt about who was really the better team. In December of 1901, the Elis set out on a westward trip that would mark the first collegiate basketball contests of a national, rather than regional, flavor. Their tour included stops at Duquesne in Pittsburgh, the University of Cincinnati, the University of Wisconsin, and Minnesota. Fans awaited the game with much anticipation in the Twin Cities. Seating prices were raised from 35 cents to 75 cents for a front row seat, 50 cents for the second and third rows, and 35 cents for general admission.

Yale arrived on the heels of a 35-20 win over the Badgers in Madison and was confident of a win, but Kiefer made several key steals and Tuck's work at center pushed the Gophers to a 23-13 lead. With shouts of "Rah! Rah! Rah! Yale!" from several Eli alumni in the crowd encouraging them, the Elis made three goals and a foul shot to close the gap briefly, but baskets by Deering, Tuck, and Ireland led to Minnesota's 32-23 triumph. The win over Yale sent the Gophers blazing through the rest of their schedule. Minnesota won four games at Fargo by a combined score of 213-44 before returning home to beat in succession Nebraska (52-9), Wisconsin (30-10), and Iowa (49-10). In all, the Gophers won 15 games and lost none by a combined score of 542-141, and with wins over eastern powerhouse Yale and the three best teams in the West in Wisconsin, Iowa, and Nebraska, Minnesota laid rightful claim to being national basketball champions. Under the leadership of its founder, Bill Schroeder, the Helms Athletic Foundation made retroactive selections of national champions for the years 1901-1937 when the National Invitational Tournament began. Yale was named Helms Foundation National Champion for 1901 and Minnesota received the honor for its undefeated 1901-02 season.

The 1902-03 season was nearly as successful. Again Minnesota went the entire year without a loss, compiling a 13-0 record and dominating opponents by a combined score of 540-116, including season-ending victories over Wisconsin and Nebraska at the Armory. Alas, the lack of an interregional opponent such as Yale the year before prevented the Gophers from claiming a repeat national title.

Minnesota's consecutive undefeated campaigns had earned it national recognition as a collegiate basketball power, and during the 1903-04 season Doc Cooke arranged an historic eastern trip of a grueling nine games in 11 days. The schedule included stops at Chicago, Purdue, Ohio State, Cornell, and other colleges, a high school, and a match with a professional team in Schenectady, New York. With Deering as team manager, the team still relied on guard Michael Kiefer and center George Tuck, along with Albert Varco at forward, the Leach brothers, Helon and Hugh, Ernest Pierce, and Randolph McRae. Despite the travel, the Gophers finished the trip 7-2 with the only losses to the West Side YMCA of Chicago (36-26) and the Schenectady professional team (21-18). In the February 28, 1936 *Minneapolis Tribune*, Doc Cooke tells of an early morning incident:

"While playing in Chicago on that trip, the team was quartered at the Chicago Beach Hotel. The boys, being unaccustomed to such luxurious quarters, and correspondingly excellent meals, satisfied their palates to such an extent they became logy and temporarily out of condition, so I immediately put them on a strict training regime. When we reached our modest hotel in Lafayette, the boys were sent to bed at half past nine and awakened at 6:30 the next morning for a calisthenics drill. This was conducted in a hallway on the second floor of the building. The boys were dressed in their night shirts and pajamas. So concerned was I in getting these boys back in condition, I had given no thought of consideration for the other guests of the hotel. We first came to the realization that we were awakening the others from their early slumbers when doors all along the hall were opened, heads popped out and in indignant voices were heard: 'What the hell is going on here!'"

The Gophers finished the 1903-04 campaign at 10-2 after sweeping

THE BOYS WERE SENT TO BED AT HALF PAST NINE AND AWAKENED AT 6:30 THE NEXT MORNING FOR A CALISTHENICS DRILL. THIS WAS CONDUCTED IN A HALLWAY ON THE SECOND FLOOR OF THE BUILDING.

Nebraska (41-21), the North Dakota Aggies (33-15), and the West Side YMCA (23-13), all at the Armory. Again Minnesota could claim to be a national basketball power and several prominent easterners agreed. In the February 25 edition of the *Minnesota Daily* there appeared a reprint of an article by Myron W. Townsend of the *Rochester (N.Y.) Herald* in which several prominent basketball experts of the East proclaim Minnesota's superiority:

"I asked Dr. J.H.W. Pollard, famous in the East as a football and basketball coach, what he thought of the relative ability of the Columbia and Minnesota teams, the leaders in the two sections. He had no hesitancy to declare that the Gophers would defeat the New Yorkers without any trouble. Pollard's opinion should carry much weight in comparing the merits of the teams. 'Minnesota would most certainly win the match,' he said. 'The Gophers play much cleaner, faster ball, and do not stoop to any of the rough house methods of the New Yorkers. I refereed the Cornell-Minnesota game, and I never saw as fast basketball play as I did in this contest. The westerners played in whirlwind fashion and satisfied me that they outclassed any team in the East. They play fairly, and squarely, too.' "

The following year the Gophers again headed East after suffering their first loss to Nebraska at the Armory, but they did not fare as well, going 2-5-1 with a tie at Dartmouth and a loss at future conference rival Chicago. That loss was avenged with a 33-22 triumph over the Maroons at the Armory to close the 1904-05 season at 7-7-1. That season was the final one for Ernest Pierce, George Tuck, and the perennial guard, Michael Kiefer. The three players had been a part of Minnesota's first national title, back-to-back undefeated seasons, and two historic eastern trips. Pierce, an excellent shooter, would go on to become the alumni and field secretary for the U for many years while Tuck would become a manufacturer in San Francisco and would later be named by the Helms Foundation as Minnesota's first All-American. Michael Kiefer was certainly a unique player in Minnesota history. Later a doctor in Sleepy Eye, Minnesota, Kiefer began playing as an undergraduate in 1897 and continued to play for the next eight seasons while attending medical school.

In the fall of 1905, representatives of six of the Big Ten colleges formed the Western Inter-Collegiate Basketball Association. Wisconsin, Chicago, Minnesota, Northwestern, Purdue, and Illinois would play a conference schedule to determine a champion of the West. The Gophers continued to dominate western collegiate basketball, compiling a 13-2 overall record and a 6-1 conference mark with the only loss at the hands of the Badgers in the Gophers' first game at Madison. The Gophers were led by Garfield Brown. The guard

■ *Many early Gophers teams posed for group photos poised to travel. This is the 1904-05 squad.*

averaged 6 points per game and came off the bench battling pneumonia to help beat Chicago 20-17 at the Armory. The first ever conference championship went to Minnesota, and the following year Minnesota tied Chicago for the conference crown and finished 10-2 overall.

In 1907-08, Minnesota slipped to fourth with a 2-6 conference tally, and was swept by co-champions Wisconsin and Chicago as well as the Illini, but the Gophers did take two games from eastern power Columbia at the Armory. Doc Cooke recounted some peculiar oddities encountered against Nebraska in the 1908-09 season in the March 1, 1936 edition of the *Minneapolis Tribune:* "In 1909, we played Nebraska four games, two at Minneapolis and two at Lincoln. When we went on the floor at Lincoln, we found one of their baskets attached to the end wall of the gymnasium, while at the other end of the court, the basket was attached to what looked like a big barn door, doubled board thickness and suspended from the roof trusses by chains. It was our poor luck to draw this basket in the first half. The game no sooner got under way when our boys noticed that every time they took a shot at the Nebraska goal, one of the opposing players would push the big door and it would start to swing, compelling us to shoot at a moving target. However, at the start of the second half, we had the other basket, of course, and it wouldn't require any intelligence test to know what our boys did under the circumstances. Either we were better barn door pushers or better shots, I was not sure, but we won both games."

After a fifth place finish in 1908-09, the Gophers rebounded with a 10-3 campaign in 1909-10, finishing second to Chicago with a 7-3 conference mark after heartbreaking defeats to Purdue and Chicago. The Maroons were the Gophers' nemesis in the early years of conference play. After winning three of the first four games against Chicago, Minnesota dropped six of the next eight as Chicago won or tied for four of the first five conference championships.

The 1910-11 season returned the Gophers to the top of the conference standings, where they finished tied with Purdue at 8-4. Led by team captain and guard R.M. Rosenwald and forward Frank Lawler, who averaged nearly eight points per game, Minnesota swept

■ *Minnesota All-American Frank Lawler in 1912.*

Wisconsin and Iowa, but split with the Maroons and the Boilermakers and fell twice to Illinois. Lawler followed George Tuck and Garfield Brown as Minnesota's third All-American choice by the Helms Foundation. Despite Lawler's return the following year, Minnesota fell to fourth place at 6-6 in the conference with a 7-6 overall mark.

Beginning in 1911-12, Minnesota would finish no higher than fourth place in the conference for five consecutive years. The Gophers' first losing season in 14 years came in 1912-13, and from 1911-22 the Gophers lost ten consecutive games to the conference-dominating Wisconsin Badgers, who won or tied for 4 titles from 1911-12 to 1915-16.

The string of lower division finishes was finally broken with the 1916-17 season. The Gophers swept through a pre-conference slate that included Minnesota colleges St. Olaf, St. Thomas, and Gustavus, and entered conference play 7-0. Minnesota was a veteran team led by captain Addison Douglas, Arnold Wyman, Chas Partridge, and, after a two year absence, Francis Stadsvold. The first conference game was with the Badgers, who had not lost at the Armory since 1911. With Stadsvold pouring in eight points and Harold Gillen leading the way with 10, the Gophers beat Wisconsin 33-25. Minnesota followed with wins over Illinois, Northwestern, and Ohio State. After a 3-1 road trip, the Gophers returned to the Armory with victories over Chicago and Iowa, during

■ *The 1911-12 Gophers team.*

which Gillen scored 14 of Minnesota's 31 points. After a crushing loss at Madison, Minnesota defeated Northwestern at home to clinch a tie with Illinois for the conference crown. While Gillen received much praise for his shooting prowess, Francis Stadsvold was widely regarded as the best player for the Gophers—both would later be named Helms Foundation All-Americans.

The following year, Minnesota slipped to second in the conference race at 7-3, 9-3 overall, but the 1918-19 Gophers would become known as the "1.000 Percent Team." That squad featured captain and guard Erling Platou, who would later be named Helms Foundation College Player of the Year and All-American with an extraordinary 11.8 points per game average. Platou was all-conference along with teammates Arnold Oss, who averaged 9.4 points per game at forward, and center Norman Kingsley, who added 7.4 points per

game. Kingsley, Oss and Platou's unusually high scoring averages came in an era without a shot clock, and with a center jump after each basket. The Gophers offense was a force to be reckoned with after scoring 40, 50, and 68 points in preseason contests. The onslaught continued with conference wins over Indiana, Wisconsin, and Illinois by an average of more than 22 points. Minnesota finished the conference season with four road wins, including the final victory of the season, a 26-21 win over the Purdue Boilermakers at Lafayette, Indiana. Minnesota was only the second Big Ten conference winner to finish the season undefeated, and its 13-0 overall record would eventually earn them a second Helms Athletic Foundation National Championship.

The loss of Platou, Kingsley, and veteran guard Joel Hulktrans in 1919-20 proved too much to overcome, and the Gophers tumbled from first place to eighth, finishing 4-9,

■ *The 1916-17 Big Ten champions.*

■ *Two-time All-American Arnold Oss, a member of the great 1918-19 team.*

The Gophers in action during a 1924 game at the University Armory, the season before the team moved to the bigger Kenwood Armory.

8-9 overall. In 1920-21 Minnesota improved with a 10-5 overall mark and a 7-5 conference record, good enough for fourth place. Senior Arnold Oss continued to star for the Gophers. He led the Big Ten with 3.67 field goals per game and a 7.5 points per game scoring average, while teammate Neal Arntson finished third with 3.33 field goals and 8.8 points per game. Oss was named first-team All-Big Ten and All-American.

The 1921-22 season was notable for an opening 31-11 loss to Hall of Fame Coach Phog Allen and the University of Kansas. With Oss now an assistant coach, the Gophers tumbled to eighth. Minnesota slipped to ninth in 1922-23 with a 1-11 conference mark and improved only to eighth with a 5-7 record in 1923-24.

In the fall of 1924, the father of Minnesota basketball stepped down after 28 years as the head coach of the Gophers. Doc Cooke had been a part of every major basketball event in the University of Minnesota's history. He had officiated the first game played by a team from the Minneapolis campus and had raised basketball from a gym class activity to a major sport with overflowing crowds and basketball heroes. Cooke's impact on the game went beyond Minnesota, though—he was an original member of the national basketball rules committee, and he helped guide the development of the game from its early stages to a more modern version.

"I wanted to bring one more Big Ten title to Minnesota before giving up the job, and I felt sure at the start of the season that last winter was the year. But we got a lot of bad breaks and I had to close the story without a happy ending," Doc Cooke said upon his resignation.

Cooke had guided Minnesota to two national championships, five conference championships either won or shared, and he finished his coaching career with a remarkable 245-137-2 career record (.641). After his retirement from coaching, Doc Cooke continued to serve the University as a professor of physical education and assistant athletic director until his retirement in 1936. In 1938, the new athletic administration building was named Cooke Hall in his honor. Cooke mused on the changes in basketball he had witnessed over his 28-year coaching career: "The rules have changed a great deal and the game has developed just as any other game has developed. It is all for the betterment of the game, but I sometimes laugh when I think of the game as we first played it back in 1897."

Dr. Louis J. Cooke died at the age of 75 in 1943. Members of the famous "1.000 Percent Team of 1919" acted as pallbearers at his funeral.

With the end of the Cooke era, the Gophers faced new challenges and a new coach. Harold T. Taylor succeeded Doc Cooke for the 1924-25 season after a year as an assistant. Taylor had been a high school coach in Aurora, Minnesota. His first team had several excellent players including captain and guard Vic Dunder, guard Eldon Mason, forward Maurice Merickel, and Ray "Black" Rasey, a flashy dribbler and scorer at forward. Taylor and the Gophers began the season with a promising three-win streak over North Dakota (30-15), Notre Dame (25-12), and Creighton (29-25). The Gophers faced the Irish and Coach Knute Rockne on a break before their New Year's Day bowl game. The Irish were led by fullback and 1925 basketball All-American Noble Kizer, but Black Rasey scored 15 and Dunder's tight defense gave Minnesota the win. By late January, the Gophers had swept a pair from the Badgers and were 3-2 in the conference with Ohio State coming to Minneapolis.

In the early days of Gopher basketball Doc Cooke had charged 25 cents for a seat and 10 cents more for the dance that followed. It was a way of drawing crowds to the unfamiliar sport. By February of 1925, however, crowd support had overcome the capacity of the University Armory, so Athletic Director Fred Luehring made the decision to move the remaining home games to the Kenwood

Armory in downtown Minneapolis. The decision was an economic one; Minnesota had been hampered by the Old Armory's seating capacity of 2,000. The Kenwood Armory, standing where the Guthrie Theater is today, had a large drill hall that since its dedication in 1910 had held auto shows, dances, boxing matches, and state high school basketball tournaments, and now it was the home of Gopher basketball. With a seating capacity of 6,000, Luehring did not have to worry about turning people away for lack of room, and Minnesota's attendance continued to grow. While the increased attendance made the move appear to be a step in the right direction, the Gopher players were not particularly enamored of the new accommodations. Walter Chapman, a Gopher forward and guard from 1926-28, recalls the Kenwood Armory: "In those days I lived at home in the Kenwood section of Minneapolis. I would take the streetcar from campus down to the Armory for practice and then walk the two or three blocks home. On game days everyone was

■ *Vic Dunder, captain of the 1924-25 Gophers squad.*

■ *Mally Nydahl (left) and Ray "Black" Rasey.*

■ *Eldon Mason (left) and Roger Wheeler*

responsible for getting to the Armory on their own and it was always easy for me being so close. We always had great crowds and the lighting was OK, but it was really a terrible place to play. The floor wasn't level, it seemed to have little mounds to it in places, and the ball didn't bounce right."

After the Gophers lost their first game at Kenwood to Ohio State (32-20), they bounced back by pounding the Purdue Boilermakers 36-16, with Black Rasey pouring in a then-conference record 20 points for Minnesota. The Gophers went 2-3 in their final five games, including a 38-17 drubbing of their old rival Chicago, but they finished the conference season at 6-6, six places behind the champion Buckeyes.

The 1925-26 season appeared promising with the return of team captain Black Rasey, Mason, and regulars Herb Wolden, Roger Wheeler and Mally Nydahl. By now, Rasey had established himself as a star player for the Gophers. George MacKinnon, then a freshman player and future three-year letterman in football and track remembers, "He was an excellent scorer and a great dribbler. Black Rasey was the best basketball player I ever saw at the University."

Despite the presence of Rasey, the Gophers struggled, finishing 6-10 overall and slipping to seventh in the conference at 5-7. The following year the Gophers' season was a disaster. With Rasey gone, the squad was in the hands

■ *An architect's sketch of the planned Minnesota Fieldhouse in 1926.*

of captain Eldon Mason and promising young players like Mally Nydahl, George Otterness, Johnny Stark, MacKinnon, and Chapman. Minnesota struggled all year and only won one game in conference play to finish ninth in the Big Ten at 1-11, 3-13 overall for 1926-27. After the season, the Athletic Department announced that Harold Taylor would not be offered a contract to continue as head coach.

With demolition beginning on campus in preparation for a new fieldhouse, the pressure to win had grown. In quick succession Doc Cooke retired, the team abandoned the University Armory for downtown's Kenwood Armory, and Harold Taylor was fired for not producing enough wins. With these changes, the University of Minnesota closed the door on the first era of its basketball history. With the construction of the huge new University Field House underway, Minnesota ushered in a new era of huge crowds and big-time college basketball.

SECTION 2

"MacMillan has plenty of good sound basketball and should develop a good team in due time," Doc Cooke noted upon the hiring of Dave MacMillan as the University of Minnesota's third head basketball coach. Like Cooke before him, MacMillan would dominate an era of the game and more than 20 years of Gopher basketball.

Unlike his predecessor, Harold Taylor, MacMillan's experience was not limited to coaching in the high school ranks. "The Canny Scot" came to the University in 1927 with a notable basketball pedigree. A native of New York City's East Side, MacMillan grew up playing on a team from the Madison Square Church House and the 23rd Street YMCA. MacMillan was an all-around athlete who excelled at baseball as well as basketball. He attended Oberlin College for two years before returning to New York in 1912 to join the first great professional basketball team, the New York Celtics. The Celtics, with such stars as Johnny Beckman, Chris Leonard, Pete Barry, Dutch Dehnart, and Nat Holman, dominated pro basketball's early years in the teens and 20's, and MacMillan's experience with the Celtics set the standard by which his Minnesota teams would become known: a tight, ball-control game with strong defense and lots of passing in order to obtain the best possible shot. After MacMillan's stint with the

■ *Jim McIntyre, a two-time All-American in 1948 and 1949.*

original Celtics, he returned to Moscow, Idaho, to coach at the University of Idaho. In seven years, MacMillan's Vandals compiled a 93-35 record, including a 19-1 campaign in 1921-22. His .727 winning percentage is still the highest for any Vandal head coach with a tenure of longer than two years. Although Minnesota considered former Gopher great Francis Stadsvold, then coaching at West Virginia, MacMillan's basketball resume was impressive and he began his career at the University of Minnesota in the fall of 1927.

The MacMillan era did not get off to a promising start. The Maroon and Gold opened the 1927-28 season with losses to Cornell and Notre Dame, and wins over North Dakota and Marquette. There was considerable questioning of the new coach's tactics, but MacMillan was unfazed. "If it's good enough for the world's greatest professional basketball team (the Celtics), it's good enough for me."

Walter Chapman, a member of the 1927-28 squad and later the long-time principal at Marshall High in Minneapolis, remembers some of the players on MacMillan's first squad: "Mac's first year we were respectable. We should have done much better with the players we had. Mally Nydahl was a great all-around athlete and a letterman in football, basketball, and baseball. Robert Tanner was a heck of a

■ *From left, George MacKinnon, John Stark, and George Otterness.*

football player and a solid reserve. George Otterness was an excellent player, a good shooter and also a great track man. George MacKinnon was a three sport star in football, basketball, and track. Johnny Stark was one tough little basketball player, he was an excellent defensive player."

After winning the Big Ten opener over Iowa 33-32, MacMillan and the Gophers lost to the Badgers in the final game at the Kenwood Armory and dropped two in a row at Northwestern and Chicago. The trip to Chicago was a relatively easy matter compared to other Big Ten trips of the time. George MacKinnon remembers: "We would leave on the train out of the old Milwaukee Railroad Depot in Minneapolis on Thursday night, play a game Saturday night and Monday night and then return Tuesday. That year we had one of our longer trips when we traveled to Columbus and West Lafayette. I didn't mind the long trips too much though, because I was in law school and I would bring along my typewriter and brief cases." Those long hours on the train paid off for MacKinnon, who would later become the United States Attorney in Minnesota during the Eisenhower administration and was named a federal district judge for Washington, D.C., in 1969.

Upon their return from Chicago, the Gophers were 1-3 in the conference and struggling with the demands of MacMillan's system, which would be tested further against the Buckeyes of Ohio State

in the dedication game for the new University Field House.

The Field House dedication was the culmination of several years of planning, with the Board of Regents giving an initial authorization for $500,000 in November 1926. The location, at the intersection of Oak Street, University Avenue, and 4th Street SE, was right across from still-new Memorial Stadium and was to be home for several Gopher sports including off-season football and baseball, tennis, and, of course, basketball. Minnesota architect C.H. Johnston designed the enormous structure and construction began in the spring of 1927. At the time of its completion, the Field House was the largest building of its kind in the United States at 446 feet long by 236 feet wide and 104 feet high, higher than a nine-story building. Permanent double-decked seating was installed at the Oak Street end with a 9,500-person capacity. The basketball court was laid on a cinder foundation, and, unlike the cramped old University Armory, the court had at least 10 feet of out-of-bounds space. Several years later, the court was made more permanent and was elevated three feet. On either side of the baskets there were tennis courts and beyond those lay a vast open space of dirt for football practice and a 220-yard circular track. Temporary bleachers were set up over the tennis courts for basketball games, which pushed capacity to 15,000. The lighting was provided by fixtures using 86,000 watts of electricity, and a tunnel con-

■ The construction of the University Field House (left, and below left and right) in 1927 and 1928 was a massive project.

■ The finished Field House, ready for use (right).

nected the Field House and Memorial Stadium underneath University Avenue. In all, the Field House cost $650,000 and would become a tremendous home-court advantage for the Gophers for years to come.

The dedication game against Ohio State on February 4, 1928 was quite an event. Several prominent dignitaries came to see the engineering and architectural marvel, including J.L. Wilson, athletic director at Northwestern, and the Canadian who had invented basketball some 37 years before, Dr. James Naismith, who later spoke about his attendance as a guest and the honorary referee: "It is no little satisfaction to me to see this vast assemblage out to witness a basketball game. It carries me back to the time when in a little gymnasium, 35-by-45, I stepped out on the floor to put the ball in play in what was the final test as to whether the game that we had prepared in the office would stand the test of practical experiment. It took only a few moments to convince me that the game would be a success. Within the life of a single individual it has spread into almost every nation and the rules have been translated into seven languages. I wish to congratulate the University of Minnesota as being one of the pioneers in the development of basketball under the direction of my life long friend, Dr. L.J. Cooke. I wish to express my appreciation of this visit and assure you that I shall follow the fortunes of your basketball team with more interest and enthusiasm for this personal contact with your institution."

With a state-record crowd of 11,000 looking on, the Gophers and Buckeyes put on a display that surely made Naismith proud of his creation. With a see-sawing lead in their favor at 32-27 late in the second half, it appeared Minnesota would christen its new Field House with a win. Ohio State battled back, though, and the team managed to tie the game at 32-32 at the final gun. Each side scored four points in the first overtime period, with Ohio State being awarded a basket when Minnesota center Glenn Williams' hand was caught in the net as he went up to block a shot. After Walter Chapman pushed the lead to 40-38 in the second overtime, the Buckeyes tied the score. George MacKinnon describes the result of a one-handed shot by Buckeye center Van Heyde with time winding down:

"Ohio State's fellow shot a ball at the basket with one hand. It bounced up and lit on the top of the rim and balanced there. It started rolling towards the middle of the backboard. When it got there it fell over into the net and won the ballgame."

After the loss to Ohio State, Minnesota would have to wait a few weeks to obtain its first win at the Field House with a 30-18 victory over the Chicago Maroons. It was their final win of the season and despite the new coach and new home court, the Gophers finished ninth in the Big Ten for the second consecutive year. The following year

■ *Glenn Williams in 1928.*

■ *The brand-new Field House, sold out for its inaugural game on February 4, 1928.*

was no better, although the Gophers had a great scorer in George Otterness and veterans Robert Tanner at guard, Glenn Williams at center, and Fred Hovde, who would become the longtime president of Purdue University, at forward. Despite winning only one conference game, the Gophers continued to pack the Field House. Team manager Mort Skewes recalls one of the special players that year: "Harold Scheie was a reserve from 1928-30 and was in medical school. He never had any money because he was working his way through school and in those days there was no aid for players and he was always eating crackers instead of full meals. Scheie would get in from time to time just to take a pot shot or two because he could sink them from way out on the floor. Coach MacMillan would shove him out on the floor for only a short time because he was too small to play defense, but he sure could shoot."

In 1929-30 the Gophers began to improve. Minnesota opened the season by going 5-0 in the preseason, but dropped its first four conference games. They eventually finished seventh in the Big Ten and were swept by conference champion Purdue. The Boilermakers were led by their center, Stretch Murphy, and a young guard named Johnny Wooden, who scored a total of 23 points in the two games against the Gophers.

Led by veteran forwards Earl Loose and Harry Schoening, center Don Bondy, and guards Mike Cielusak and Virgil Licht, the Gophers began 1930-31 with a six-game winning streak before losing a heart-breaker at Chicago. The Gophers outshot the Maroons from the field, but Chicago nailed 12 of 14 free throws to squeak by with a 32-31 win. The Gophers won three straight to push their record to 4-1 before they headed to Evanston for a showdown with even-

tual conference champ Northwestern. The then-undefeated Wildcats won by nine, but Minnesota bounced back by whipping the Badgers 42-15 at Madison. Despite nine points by Wooden, the Gophers beat Purdue and then Ohio State, and they had a chance to claim a share of the conference title but lost consecutive tilts to Northwestern at the Field House and Purdue at Lafayette. Minnesota finished second in the conference at 8-4 for Dave MacMillan's best finish.

With all-conference players Schoening and Loose gone, Minnesota turned to team captain Mike Cielusak and Virgil Licht to lead the 1931-32 campaign. Again the Gophers opened undefeated, running to a 7-0 start before losing to Michigan. Minnesota reeled off four more wins. With their conference record at 5-1 and their title hopes high, the Gophers dropped two straight on a road trip to Indiana and Illinois. Despite winning their last four games, Minnesota finished tied for second in the conference with Northwestern at 9-3. The Big Ten championship went to Coach Piggy Lambert's Purdue Boilermakers with All-American and National Player-of-the-Year John Wooden leading the way.

After two years near the top of the Big Ten, Minnesota's basketball fortunes turned sour. For the next four seasons, the Gophers struggled to escape the Big Ten cellar, finishing ninth twice and seventh twice. The few highlights included a 43-41 overtime win over Moose Kraals and Notre Dame at the Field House at the end of the 1934 season, and Minnesota's appearance in its first post-season tournament since Doc Cooke and the 1901 Gophers went to Chicago. After the 1935-36 campaign, Minnesota again headed to the Windy City for the District Olympic Tournament. The tournament was to determine who would go on to New York for the national Olympic Tourney. Players would be chosen from that tourney for the first Olympic basketball team to compete for a medal at the 1936 Berlin Olympics.

■ *Fred Hovde (left) and David MacMillan (below).*

■ *Virgil Licht (left) and Michael Cielusak*

■ *A tipoff during a 1932 game at the Field House.*

■ *Gordon Spear.*

Minnesota won two home games over Caroll College of Montana and Drake University to win District 6 before heading to Chicago to face District 5 champion DePaul for the right to advance to New York as the Midwest representative. Despite a strong scoring effort by forward George Roscoe (20 points over two games), the Blue Demons swept two from the Gophers.

With the Gophers' ninth place finish in 1935-36, prospects for the following year hardly seemed bright. But 1936-37 would prove to be the best season for the Gophers in nearly twenty years. After whipping Carleton 41-11 to open the season, Minnesota dropped three straight before finishing the preseason with a pair of wins at the Field House, including a 34-25 revenge win over DePaul in which sophomore phenom John Kundla scorched the Blue Demons with 18 points.

Kundla was a great scorer and part of a well-balanced attack for Minnesota. Kundla, of

Minneapolis Central High, and Gordie Addington held down the forward positions, floor leader Marty Rolek and Dick Seebach were at the guards, and Bob Manly of St. Paul Cretin High was at center. Reserves Butch Nash, Earl Halvorson, Grant "Spike" Johnson, and Gordon Spear provided help off the bench. Johnny Kundla, eventually head coach of both the Minneapolis Lakers and the Gophers, remembers his teammates well: "Bob Manly was only 6-foot-3, but he was a great defensive player at center. Although they didn't call it a point guard then, Marty Rolek was essentially a point guard and he ran the plays and was a very calm, cool floor leader who passed well and was a tough defender. We called Dick Seebach 'Two Flat' because he had two flat feet. After games he would have the trainer tape his ankles so he could go out dancing. Gordie Addington had terrific spring to his legs. We had a set play where he would tip

■ *The Gophers beat Ohio State 31-14 on the way to win a share of the Big Ten title in 1936-37.*

the ball right to me on the jump ball right after each basket; we scored once or twice a game with that play."

After splitting their first two conference games, Kundla, Rolek, and the Gophers won nine of their last 10 Big Ten games, losing by only one point at Purdue. That loss at Purdue was no surprise; Minnesota had often struggled at the tiny high school gym where the Boilermakers played. "Purdue was always a tough place to play. Their crowds were right on top of you in that little gym and when you took the ball out of bounds they would tug on your shorts just enough to annoy you," remembers Earl Halvorson, a Gopher forward from Minneapolis West High School.

A season-ending loss at powerful Notre Dame could not dampen the spirits of Minnesota's first Big Ten championship team since the "1.000 Percent Team" of 1919. The Gophers shared the

crown with Illinois at 10-2. Kundla recalls how the Big Ten title relieved pressure on Coach Dave MacMillan: "Mac didn't have a very good record at that point and when the season began he was receiving a lot of pressure from writers for the *Minneapolis Tribune* and the *Minneapolis Journal*. They didn't like his deliberate slow-down style of play and were increasingly critical. I remember one time when Marty Rolek came into the huddle during a game and said 'Let's show that Johnny Johnson (of the *Minneapolis Journal*) how to play basketball!' We probably saved Mac's job by winning the championship that year."

With a veteran team returning, the Gophers hoped to challenge for the Big Ten crown again in 1937-38. After a quick 4-0 start, Minnesota headed East for a Christmas break trip to New York and Washington, D.C. Kundla remem-

Another look at the 1937 Ohio State game.

bers the big crowds and the excitement of Madison Square Garden in its heyday of college basketball doubleheaders.

"I recall that on the train trip out to New York, Marty Rolek asked Mac if he could order anything on the menu in the diner car. Mac said sure, order anything and Marty, thinking it was alcoholic, promptly asked for a shrimp cocktail. With his roots in New York and his playing days with the New York Celtics, Mac was in his glory in New York and he toyed with the famous New York press by telling them that we all had really

strong wrists from milking cows. It was everyone's dream to play at Madison Square Garden. After we scrimmaged against Mac's old Celtics teammate Nat Holman's City College of New York squad, we played in back to back doubleheaders at the Garden in front of 18,000 people."

In the first contest, the Gophers beat Long Island University 56-41, with Kundla adding 10 points to the trio of Gordon Spear, Gordie Addington, and Paul Maki, who each had 12 points. The following night, Kundla and Addington

The 1936-37 co-Big Ten champions.

combined for 15 points as Minnesota beat New York University 36-31. From New York, the Gophers headed to Washington, D.C., where they fell 35-27 to guard Red Auerbach and George Washington University. Minnesota returned home to avenge the previous season's loss to Notre Dame, but the Gophers opened conference play with three straight losses. The chances for repeating looked slim with an 0-3 conference mark, but Minnesota won its last nine games and finished second to Purdue at 9-3, including a season-ending 35-28 win over the Badgers in front of 13,000 at the Field House. During the streak, Kundla averaged 7.5 points per game. Earl Halvorson recalls Kundla's playing days: "Johnny Kundla was a

great scorer and rebounder. He was the best player on our team and contributed more to our success than anyone else. John and I had played together when we were 14. We played at West Lake Church across from the old Minneapolis Auditorium. John was a Catholic and I was being confirmed as a Lutheran, but three of four Sundays we had to go to West Lake and John and I played on a team that won the city championship for boys 14 and under."

With the return of co-captains Kundla and Addington, scorer Paul Maki, Gordie Spear, and Johnny Dick, the 1938-39 season looked promising. The Gophers raced out to a 7-0 start, including wins over N.Y.U. at Madison Square Garden and over Temple at Convention Hall in Philadelphia. Overall, Minnesota now had a 16-game winning streak heading into Big Ten play. But the Gophers could not maintain the pace and slipped to a fourth place finish at 7-5. In the season-ending win at Iowa City, Johnny Kundla scored a team-high 16 points and finished as the career leader in points scored for the Golden Gophers. Basketball at the University of Minnesota also reached new heights when 15,800 packed the Field House to see the Gophers fall 31-30 to Ohio State.

The following year, Minnesota reversed its usual travel plans and headed to the Pacific Northwest and took two of three from the Washington Huskies in Seattle, but slid to seventh in the Big Ten. Illinois center Bill Hapac set a Big Ten scoring record when he poured in 34

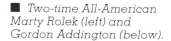

■ *Two-time All-American Marty Rolek (left) and Gordon Addington (below).*

■ *The Gophers' 1937-38 starting lineup.*

points against the Gophers on February 10, 1940. For the 1940-41 season, Minnesota returned to the East, but they lost for the first time at Madison Square Garden to New York University and fell to the Colonials of George Washington. After a 50-38 win over the Illini on February 8, 1941, Minnesota was tied for third place and appeared to be improving, but a 3-3 mark down the stretch left Minnesota at 7-5 and tied for third place behind conference champion Wisconsin. Following the conference season, the Badgers went on to become the second consecutive NCAA Tournament champion from the Big Ten after Indiana's win in 1940.

That was the first year of play for a young forward from Minneapolis Edison High School, Don "Swede" Carlson, who remembers playing for Dave MacMillan and his teammates in the early 1940s: "I am honored that Dave MacMillan was quoted as saying that I was the best all-around ball player he ever coached. My role was to go into the game and guard the 'hot-shooting' player at the time. I think that all the teams that I played on at the U tried as hard as they could to win games and everyone worked very hard. We also had many players that excelled at certain parts of the game. Jack Young was a great passer and John Dick had an excellent court sense, and I think Willie Warhol was an excellent player as well. Mac was a great coach to play for. He knew basketball so well and he always stressed fundamentals and discipline. He was well-liked by all of his players because he wanted to win just as badly as we did."

In 1941-42, Minnesota improved its conference mark to 9-6, good enough to tie Purdue for fifth place behind champ Illinois. By the end of the season, Dave MacMillan had been head coach of the Gophers for 15 years, compiling a .545 overall winning percentage (159-133) and leading Minnesota to a shared Big Ten title in 1936-37 and four second place finishes. At the age of 53, the Canny Scot stepped down as head coach. In August of 1942, Dr. Carl Nordly was named to replace MacMillan as the Gophers head coach. Nordly had been a professor of physical education at the University since 1935 and had earned both his Master's and Ph.D. from Columbia University. A graduate of Red Wing High School in 1919, Nordly had been a star athlete at Carleton College, where he earned 11 letters and was all-conference in football and basketball. While at Carleton, Nordly played first under Everett Dean and then Osborne Cowles, who would go on to coach Minnesota. Nordly's coaching style was an abrupt departure from the passing game favored by MacMillan.

"The style of play we use will fit the material," Nordly said then. "If they're fast, we'll run their legs off. If they're heavier and a bit slower, we'll concentrate on a powerful defense and maybe a few more shots. And if the boys show they can hit from the floor, they'll be allowed to hit from the floor."

The freedom to shoot was the most dramatic departure from MacMillan's style. Despite Nordly's extensive athletic background, he had only refereed basketball and had never been a head coach. With several players called into the service for the war, Nordly's team was young but not without talent. The Gophers were led by forwards Wes Windmiller and Dave Ruliffson,

■ *Carl Nordly (at right), who coached the Gophers in 1942-43 and 1943-44.*

■ *Donald Carlson (right).*

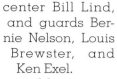

center Bill Lind, and guards Bernie Nelson, Louis Brewster, and Ken Exel.

Minnesota won four straight to open the season before dropping a 47-38 contest to Ozzie Cowles' NCAA runner-up Dartmouth team at the Field House. Minnesota finished a disappointing sixth in the conference at 5-7. Again with the loss of several players to the service, the Gophers slipped to eighth in 1943-44, winning only two conference games.

After two years of disappointing results, Nordly stepped down as head coach, and in January of 1945 he left Minnesota for Paris to serve as Civilian Consultant on Athletics, U.S. Army, European Theater of Operations. With Nordly's departure, the University of Minnesota turned to Weston Mitchell. Mitchell had coached John Kundla at Central High in Minneapolis. His tenure was brief and unsuccessful, as the Gophers finished a distant sixth at 4-8

and 8-13 overall. In three years Minnesota had gone 25-36 overall, and finished no higher than sixth in the conference. Attendance had dwindled to fewer than 5,000 per game, and Minnesota needed a reversal of its basketball fortunes.

The decline of Minnesota basketball during this period does not rest squarely on the shoulders of Carl Nordly and Weston Mitchell, who were experienced basketball men attempting to maintain high standards of basketball excellence while many of their greatest players were fighting for their country in World War II. Louis Brewster, a guard from Wahpeton, North Dakota, and a Gopher in 1942-43 and 1945-47, recalls the unusual circumstances the war presented him and his teammates: "I have often thought back to my playing years at Minnesota with some regret because I never felt that we accomplished as much as we should have, but in recalling my playing days I realize that those were unusual times and conditions. As a sophomore in 1942-43, most of the upperclassmen from the previous season were already off in the service for the war. We had several sophomores and many walk-on players. I remember we had Ken Exel, who was an excellent defensive player as well as a great playmaker and a very steady, heady ballplayer. My fellow sophomores, Dave Ruliffson and Wes Windmiller, were quick, good shooters and good defensive players. In 1945-46, myself and several others returned from the service changed. We had grown, and some players now had wives and families. There were also underclassmen who had stayed and played during the war who were younger, and new freshmen like Jim McIntyre. With the return of Dave MacMillan as head coach there was a lot of adjustment and it took nearly the whole year for the team to come together. I remember that year we took a trip down to play Iowa State and Nebraska. Mac could get really excited during games sometimes and during a flurry of second-half action in the Nebraska game he hollered down the bench, 'Windmiller, come here!' Well,

■ *Louis Brewster (left) and Wes Windmiller (below).*

■ *Weston Mitchell (left) who coached the Gophers for one season, 1944-45.*

after another call or two, our trainer Lloyd 'Snapper' Stein said, 'Mac, Windmiller didn't make the trip!' "

In the summer of 1945, Minnesota turned once again to the Canny Scot and reappointed Dave MacMillan as head coach. MacMillan benefitted from several promising newcomers and the return of several war veterans. Minnesota opened the 1945-46 campaign with returning players Warren Ajax, Louis Brewster, Max Mohr, Tony Jaros, and Don "Swede" Carlson, along with newcomers Jim McIntyre at center and Ed Kernan at guard. The Gophers whipped South Dakota (71-27) and South Dakota State (78-25) to open the season, and headed into a New Year's Eve contest with defending National Invitational Tournament champion DePaul at the Field House. The Blue Demons were led by future Minneapolis Lakers star George Mikan. Although Mikan was a consensus NCAA first-team All-American from 1944-46 and had a career scoring average of 19.1 points per game, the Gophers held him to 11 points and won 45-36 behind 17 points from Ed Kernan. Then-assistant coach Johnny Kundla remembers the strategy laid out by the Canny Scot for containing Mikan:

"We had Jim McIntyre overplay Mikan. George is right-handed and when he'd turn back to his left away from McIntyre we'd have Tony Jaros or Don Carlson bottle him up. He just never got off an easy shot that night."

Don "Swede" Carlson, whom Dave MacMillan would call the best all-around player he ever coached, recalls that the game stuck with Mikan later in his pro career, because Carlson made it stick. One of the first Minnesota players to play professional basketball, Carlson first played with the Chicago Stags of the Basketball Association of America, and then spent five years with Mikan and the Minneapolis Lakers of the BAA and then the NBA. "I played with George on the Lakers and I would always bring up that win over DePaul," remembers Carlson. "I'd remind him of how we shut him down and what a great game it was."

After the DePaul win, Minnesota won six straight and was 4-0 in the conference, but the Gophers went 3-5 down the stretch and finished fifth.

In 1946-47, the Gophers returned sophomore guard Ed Kernan of Two Harbors, Minnesota, Jim McIntyre, and Louis Brewster while adding Marshall High School prospect Wally Salovich, Jack Young, and a promising 6-foot-3, 190-pound football player from Superior, Wisconsin, named Harry (Bud) Grant. The 1946-47 campaign became a showcase for the first in a long line of dominant big men from Minnesota to play for the Gophers. At 6-foot-9, 235 pounds, Jim McIntyre was easily the tallest player Minnesota had ever had. At Patrick Henry High, McIntyre had led his team to the Minneapolis City and Minnesota State titles in 1944 and 1945, and he had scored a combined 100 points in the three state tourney games of 1945. After scoring 86 points as a freshman reserve, McIntyre erased Tony Jaros's season scoring record with 314 points for the 1946-47 season, averaged 15 points per game, and was a unanimous all-conference selection. Minnesota improved, finishing in fourth place, 7-5 in the conference, including a record-setting 81-point performance against Purdue at the Field House.

The road was not a friendly place for the Gophers that year, however. In Bill McGrane's *Bud: The Other Side of the Glacier*, Bud Grant recalls a particularly nasty incident in Iowa City: "I was a sophomore, and I was moving on defense past their big man, Noble Jorgenson. I suppose the official was looking the other way, because when I went by Jorgenson I hit him in the chest with a left hook.... I was paying him back for the elbows to the head I'd been getting. It staggered him because he hadn't seen me, and I gave him a pretty good shot. But because I was on the move, I was past him before he knew who had slugged him. He looked around and the closest Minnesota player he saw was Bill Pepper, who had just come into the game and had nothing to do with what I'd done. Well, Jorgenson hit Pepper with a haymaker and broke his jaw."

With McIntyre, Grant, Kernan, and Young leading the way, the popularity of the Gophers surged and fans set

■ *Jack Young.*

attendance records with 16,519 against Iowa and 132,949 for the season. Despite the return of Grant, Kernan, and McIntyre, the Gophers slipped to 5-7, 10-10 overall, and a seventh place finish for the 1947-48 season.

In March of 1948, Dave MacMillan released a statement: "I have requested of Frank McCormick, director of athletics at Minnesota, that I be assigned to other duties within the department to be determined by McCormick at a later date. Because of the pressure attached to Big Ten coaching, it has affected my health and therefore I believe it is to the best interests of the University that the head coaching job be turned over to someone else."

McCormick responded with his own statement: "It is my belief that MacMillan is one of the finest basketball coaches in the nation. Dave has made many noteworthy contributions to basketball, not only at Minnesota, but within Western Conference and national intercollegiate circles, as well."

Without exception, the players who played under MacMillan at Minnesota call him a tough but fair coach who knew a great deal about the game and imparted that knowledge to his players. His loyalty to his style of play was both an asset and a detriment, but without question, his players were always well-prepared and disciplined. MacMillan's popularity was never more evident than when more than 300 people, including players from his days at the University of Idaho, gathered for his 1948 retirement dinner. MacMillan finished with an overall record of 197-157 (.556) in 18 seasons at the Gophers' helm. His tenure began with the Roaring Twenties and the construction of the Field House, and it ended in the era of the post-World War II boom.

SECTION 3

In 1948, for the third time in seven years, Minnesota was searching for a new head coach, and the job looked like it would go to an old Gopher nemesis. John Wooden had been a three-time All-American at Purdue in the early 1930s, and after the end of World War II, he was interested in returning to the Big Ten as a head coach. The coaching legend who would become the "Wizard of Westwood" recalls the events then: "It was early April of 1948 and I had already been offered the head coaching position by Frank McCormick, Minnesota's Athletic Director. He had offered me the position but he wanted me to keep Dave MacMillan on as my assistant. Well, I liked Dave and I knew his record well but I felt that our coaching philosophies and techniques were so different that it would not have been in either of our best interests for him to be my assistant. I told Mr. McCormick that I wanted to bring my own assistant along. One day, Minnesota was set to call me with their answer at 5:00 and UCLA, which had also been pursuing me, was to call at 6:00. They were willing to let me bring my own assistant and they wanted a definite answer when they called. Well, 5:00 came and went and I didn't hear from Mr. McCormick. When UCLA called at 6:00, I accepted the position. An hour later Frank McCormick called to let me know that he had arranged to let me bring my assistant but I told him that I had already

given my answer to UCLA. Apparently a snow storm had knocked out phone service and that's why Minnesota couldn't reach me at 5:00." Whether Minnesota's basketball history would have included 10 NCAA championships and four 30-0 seasons had Wooden come to Minneapolis is merely speculation, but one cannot help but wonder about what might have been.

Having missed out on Wooden, Minnesota turned to 47-year-old Browns Valley, Minnesota, native Osborne Cowles. "Ozzie" Cowles had been a star athlete at Carleton College, where he earned 11 letters in football, basketball, and baseball, and was an all-conference selection for three years in basketball before he graduated in 1922. He returned to Carleton as head basketball and baseball coach from 1924-1930. Later, after a stint at River Falls State Teachers College in Wisconsin, Cowles headed to Dartmouth, where he led the Green to seven Eastern Intercollegiate Conference (now Ivy League) championships and the 1942 NCAA Tournament finals against Stanford. He then spent two years in Ann Arbor, winning the conference championship for Michigan in 1947-48, before returning to Minnesota in the spring of 1948.

With Cowles installed as head coach and the return of Grant, McIntyre, Salovich, and Duane Baglien from the 1944 team, plus sophomore forward

■ *Harry "Bud" Grant, who was a Gopher basketball great before he worked his way into the Pro Football Hall of Fame.*

Myer "Whitey" Skoog, Minnesota's prospects for 1948-49 were bright. The Gophers opened the season with wins over Western Illinois and Nebraska, with McIntyre stunning the Cornhuskers with 30 points and Whitey Skoog, the forward from Brainerd, adding 17. At Chicago Stadium, the Gophers whipped DePaul for the fourth straight year in a game with 54 fouls called and another 18 points for McIntyre. Minnesota continued its streak with wins over Navy, St. Mary's of California, Dartmouth, and Drake, the latter two wins giving Minnesota its first in-season tournament crown at the Corn Bowl tourney at Des Moines, Iowa. After opening the Big Ten season with a win over defending conference champion Michigan and four more conference wins, the Gophers had won 13 straight games, and they ap-

peared ready to contend for their first Big Ten title since 1936-37. Despite 15 from McIntyre and 13 from Skoog, the Gophers lost a heartbreaker at Illinois, 45-44. Minnesota split its next two games and then reeled off four straight and headed into Madison with a shot at tying for the Big Ten conference crown. The Badgers triumphed in a thriller, 45-43, as two late shots by Skoog just wouldn't fall. The Gophers settled for second while Illinois claimed the title.

Although the team fell short of winning the Big Ten title, there were notable individual accomplishments. After four years at Minnesota, Jim McIntyre had rewritten not only the school's record books but the conference's as well. McIntyre set Western Conference records for most points for four years in all games (1,223), most points for four years in con-

■ *Wally Salkovich.*

ference games (648), and most points for three years in conference games (580). In 1947-48, McIntyre had been a consensus NCAA All-American, was first-team All-Big Ten, and he was again an All-American in 1948-49, the first back-to-back All-American picks for Minnesota since Marty Rolek in 1937-38. McIntyre's career scoring mark would not be surpassed for another 11 years, and nearly 50 years later he is still in the top 20 on Minnesota's all-time scoring list.

After a new roof had been added to the Field House in 1948, the summer of 1949 saw extensive remodeling for the 22-year-old building at a cost of just over $1 million. The Field House was divided into two separate amphitheaters. The east end would continue to house the basketball court, permanent seating was added on either end of the baskets, and the floor was raised another two feet. Seating for basketball was listed at 18,025, but during the coming decade that figure, much to the consternation of the fire marshal, was often surpassed. The west end was devoted to a new indoor ice rink with a seating capacity of nearly 7,000. At halftime of the Min-

nesota-Wisconsin basketball game of March 4, 1950, the Field House was officially rededicated to honor Dr. Henry L. Williams, head football coach at Minnesota from 1900-1921.

The loss of McIntyre would prove to be a tremendous challenge for Minnesota despite the return of Skoog, Salovich, and guard Gerald Mitchell,

■ *The 1948-49 Gophers listen to first-year coach Ozzie Cowles.*

■ *Richard Means.*

because not one of the 1949-50 Gopher players was taller than 6-foot-4. Bud Grant skipped his senior season for the Gophers when he went professional in December, signing with the Minneapolis Lakers. After a sensational all-conference sophomore season, the scoring and team leadership burdens fell to Whitey Skoog. Like the previous season, the Gophers started fast with an 8-1 mark that included close wins over Stanford and California at the Cow Palace in San Francisco. After dropping the conference opener at Northwestern, Minnesota trounced Purdue at the Field House 67-40, only to lose a close game to the Badgers at Madison. The Gophers led 54-53 with nine seconds to play, when Wisconsin's Danny Markham hit a long-range shot and added two free throws to hand Minnesota a 57-54 loss. Dick Means, a transfer from the University of Nebraska, led the Gophers with 19 points. After winning at Michigan and Michigan State, Minnesota had a 3-3 conference mark but struggled the rest of the way, going 1-5 to finish 4-8 and in sixth place. Another highlight came in January when 18,025 packed Williams Arena for the Ohio State contest. In his junior season, Skoog set a new school record for scoring, with 374 points in 22 games, and finished fourth in conference scor-

ing with 201 points. Skoog was named All-American, All-Big Ten, and the team's most valuable player.

Skoog again led Minnesota as team captain in 1950-51 as a senior, and the Gophers improved to fourth in the conference with a 7-7 conference mark and a 13-9 overall record that included a runner-up finish at the Big Seven Tournament in Kansas City. In the opening tournament game against Colorado, senior forward Maynard Johnson of Plainview High set a new Minnesota single-game scoring mark with 38 points. Johnson finished a close second to Whitey Skoog, averaging 14.4 points

■ *The Gophers take on Iowa (above left). Two-time All-American Whitey Skoog drives past a defender (above right). Jim McIntyre scores over Geoge Mikan's head (at left).*

■ **Opposite** *Williams Arena underwent extensive renovations in 1950 (top). After the work was completed, notice the netting that surrounds the court. This is where the term "cagers" to describe basketball players comes from (bottom).*

Glen Reed (left), Bob Gelle (right).

Ed Kelafat.

per game, and forward-center Bob Gelle added an 8.1 average. Skoog finished his career with the Gophers with first-team all-conference honors and a third-team All-America selection.

Glen Reed, from Superior, Wisconsin, was a Gopher forward from 1950-54, and an assistant coach under Ozzie Cowles from 1956-59. Reed recalls his teammates and playing days at Minnesota: "I was a very average Big Ten player even though I was a starter most of my career. I didn't score a lot but played good defense, had intensity, and set up my teammates well. I remember I was having a great game at Iowa versus Deacon Davis and Carl 'Sugar' Cain in 1954, when I scored 16 points in the first half, but I ended up fouling out early in the second half. I had the privilege of playing with several good athletes at Minnesota. Ed Kalafat was a steady player who used his 250 pound bulk well under the basket, and, of course, Dick Garmaker and Chuck Mencel were excellent ballplayers. When Mencel wasn't shooting from the outside and (Charles 'Buzz') Bennett and I weren't feeding Kalafat in the pivot, Garmaker used his strength and quickness to drive to the basket for the short shot. I remember one road trip where I had been assigned to room with big Ed Kalafat and Bob McNamara (Gopher football All-American). We were assigned twin beds and one mini roll-away bed. Well, we all arm-wrestled for the good beds, and of course this skinny left-hander ended up with the roll-away."

The loss of Johnson and Skoog to graduation and, for Skoog, a career with the Minneapolis Lakers, did not send the Gophers tumbling into the conference cellar, though. That's because Minnesota welcomed two sensational freshman to the veteran mix of Dick Means, Bob Gelle, John Wallerius, Ken McGonagle, and Gerald Mitchell. Eau Claire, Wisconsin native Charley Mencel and Anaconda, Montana native Ed Kalafat began their Gopher careers in 1951-52. Mencel was a 6-foot guard and Kalafat was 6-foot-6. The two would dominate the Gopher scoring column all season. Kalafat, playing at center and forward, averaged nearly 16 points per game and grabbed just over seven rebounds per contest. Mencel added 13.6 points while Gelle and Means contributed a little over nine points per game. Both Mencel and Kalafat made second-team all-conference as the Gophers compiled a 15-7 overall record and a 10-4 mark in the Big Ten for a third place finish. The highlight of the season came with the biggest upset by a Gopher squad since the win over George Mikan and DePaul in 1945.

At the close of the 1950-51 season, Williams Arena had played host to the NCAA championship game, when Adolph Rupp's Kentucky Wildcats beat Kansas State 68-58 for the title. Rupp

■ *The Gophers in action in 1952.*

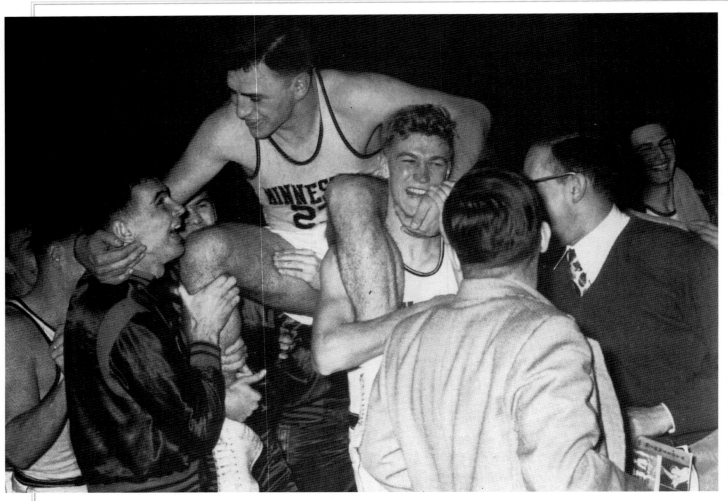

■ *The Gophers lift Ed Kalafat to their shoulders after he scored 30 points to beat top-ranked Kentucky in 1951.*

■ *Jerry Kindall (at right).*

and Kentucky returned to Minneapolis in December 1951 to take on the Gophers. Despite having their All-American center, Bill Spivey, recovering from knee surgery, the talented Wildcats took a 33-27 halftime lead. But the Gophers, and particularly Ed Kalafat, were not to be denied. Minnesota rallied to beat the nation's top-ranked team 61-57 behind Kalafat's 30 points.

The Gophers repeated their third place conference finish with an 11-7 mark in the Big Ten's expanded conference schedule of 18 games for 1952-53. Mencel's scoring average surged to 18 points per game, and Kalafat continued to dominate the low post with 15.5 points and 8 rebounds per game. Senior Bob Gelle also improved his scoring average to 12.8. For the third straight time, the Gophers finished in third place in 1953-54, with a 10-4 conference mark. Despite the presence of Kalafat, Dick Garmaker, and Mencel, the Gophers finished behind either Illinois, Indiana, or Iowa each year from 1951-52 to 1954-55.

During a 1953 preseason game at Xavier University in Cincinnati, starting guard Charles Bennett unwittingly gave

the Xavier crowd a special glimpse. Teammate Glen Reed remembers: "Buzz Bennett got a big laugh at Xavier. When he dropped down his warm-up pants for team introductions, Buzz discovered he was missing his game shorts. You would say today that he unknowingly 'mooned' the entire crowd!"

Jerry Kindall, from St. Paul Washington High, was a forward on the Min-

nesota teams of 1954-56. Kindall, a member of the College Baseball Coaches Hall of Fame and the head baseball coach at Arizona for more than 20 years, re-calls his playing days in Gold Country:

"I was a good defensive player, and for only 6-foot-2 I could rebound well. I was pretty quick and had a fair 15-foot jump shot, but I was easy to defend because I couldn't go to my left. I remember that Chuck Mencel was a great player who could bring the ball down the floor and was a deadly long-distance shooter; he'd score a lot of threes today. Dick Garmaker had a great pull-up jumper too. Doug Bolstorff was an intense player. Before games he would have to lie down to bring his emotions under control. I can still picture him virtually asleep on the bench, but when the tip went up he was fired up from start to finish, and his intensity made him a great defensive player. Playing basketball at Minnesota also gave me my first airplane trip when we went to Stillwater, Oklahoma, on a North Central Airlines DC-3. Ozzie Cowles was a good coach who always

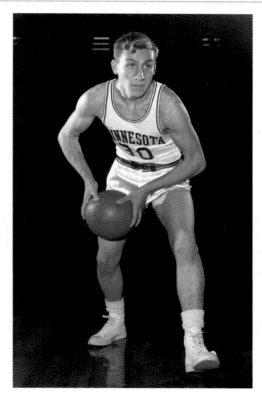

■ *Chuck Mencel.*

dressed so dapper with those bow ties of his. He really stressed fundamentals and man-to-man defense. I'll never forget the game at Ohio State in 1954. The

■ *The Gophers in 1954.*

Buckeyes played at the Hippodrome at the state fairgrounds. It was old and very drafty and cold. Ozzie put me in late in the first half and I was stiff and cold. I fouled a guy right away and Ozzie yanked me right out. I pled, 'Please let me stay in until I get warm!' but he brushed me off, saying, 'That's a baseball player's excuse!'"

The 1954-55 Gopher team faced the loss of Ed Kalafat after a stellar career, but returned senior co-captains Chuck

Minnesota bounced back from a 94-93 overtime loss to DePaul in the season opener at Chicago Stadium, where they set another team scoring mark. They avenged the loss by beating the Blue Demons (94-84) a week later at Williams Arena, with Garmaker scoring 24 and center Bill Simonovich adding 20. In late December, the Gophers hit the Tobacco Road with wins over Wake Forest and Duke before losing to North Carolina State in

■ *Chuck Mencel goes up for a jumper in 1954.*

Mencel and Hibbing native Dick Garmaker. Garmaker was all-conference in 1953-54 when he burned up the league with a 24.6 conference scoring average and seven rebounds per game. He had come to Minnesota after leading Hibbing Junior College to the National Junior College Tournament in 1951. Before the 1954-55 season, Coach Ozzie Cowles remarked on Garmaker's skills: "I personally feel that Dick Garmaker is one of the greatest basketball players I've had play for me. He can do everything on the outside that a small man can and also play in the pivot with equal skill. He's also a fine rebounder."

the finals of the Dixie Classic in Raleigh, North Carolina. The holiday tournament was the first excursion into the deep South for a Gopher basketball squad. The Gophers' title hopes looked strong when they raced out to a 10-2 conference mark. Included in the run was another team scoring record of 102 set against Purdue, another Purdue victory in six overtimes, and a 26 point drubbing of Ohio State. The six overtime game was a then-college record, and was the result of a lot of ball holding and conservative offense. The game had ended in a 47-47 tie at the end of regulation. After Purdue held the ball and missed its only shot in the

■ *Dick Garmaker (left), Bill Simonovich (right).*

first four five-minute overtimes, each team finally scored in the fifth overtime. Minnesota outscored the Boilermakers 8-5 in the sixth and final overtime period to claim a 59-56 victory. After a last-second win over the Badgers in Madison on the 21st of February, Minnesota could claim the conference title with wins over Iowa and Wisconsin at Williams Arena.

With their title hopes on the line, the Gophers faced off against their rivals for the crown in front of a record-breaking crowd. Williams Arena was packed beyond overflowing as 20,176 crammed in to watch the Hawkeyes

eke out a 72-70 win behind center Bill Logan's 25 points. Mencel and Garmaker combined for 35 points but it wasn't enough. Still with a chance to tie for the conference title, Minnesota faced Wisconsin in the final game of the season. This time a mere 14,249 fans watched as the Badgers stunned Minnesota, 78-72. With two consecutive home losses, the Gophers dropped into a second place tie with Illinois as the Hawkeyes claimed the Big Ten title outright. At the close of the season, Chuck Mencel was named the Big Ten MVP by the *Chicago Tribune*, was a first-team All-America selection and was voted

■ *George Kline (left), Jed Dommeyer (right).*

David Tucker and Coach Ozzie Cowles.

■ *Whitey Skoog.*

all-conference. Mencel also eclipsed Jim McIntyre's career scoring mark with 1,391 points. With a season average of 24.2 points per game, Dick Garmaker finished 17th in the nation in scoring and was an NCAA consensus first-team All-American.

Following the loss of Garmaker and Mencel, Minnesota stumbled to a 6-8 conference record in 1955-56. In 1956-57 the Gophers returned to the upper-echelon of the conference, as they posted a 9-5 conference mark, good enough for third place. Minnesota was led by forwards George Kline (18.1 points per game), Dave Tucker (11.5), and center Jed Dommeyer (16.4). Kline was named first-team All-Big Ten and he broke the single-game scoring mark of Maynard Johnson when he ripped the Hawkeyes for 40 points in the Gophers' 102-81 win over Iowa at Williams Arena.

The 1956-57 season saw the beginning of the Gopher basketball broadcast career of Ray Christensen on WLOL and, later, WCCO-AM. In Christensen's *Golden Memories*, written with Stew Thornley, Ray recalls his most memorable game from that inaugural year: "The game I remember the most in my first season doing the play-by-play was at home against Iowa near the end of February 1957, Minnesota won the game easily, by a score of 102-81, and George Kline set a new school record with 40 points. He almost didn't get the

■ *The Gophers wait for a Purdue player to shoot a free throw in a 1959 televised game (top), Gerald Butler goes up for a shot in that Purdue game, a 64-62 Minnesota win (left).*

■ Roger Johnson shoots over a Boilermaker defender (top). Williams Arena was sold out, as usual, for the Purdue game (right).

chance, though. Since the Gophers were so far out in front, Cowles substituted for all five starters with about three-and-a-half minutes left. Kline had 36 points as he left the game, two short of Maynard Johnson's total against Colorado. I was aware of the records but there was no way I could get word to Ozzie. Fortunately, Otis Dypwick, the University's sports information director, let Cowles know what was happening. Ozzie sent his big forward back onto the court with orders to shoot every time he touched the ball."

Although Kline returned in 1957-58, averaged 20.4 points per game, and was again an all-conference selection, Minnesota slipped to eighth place and finished with its first overall losing mark (9-12) since the 1944-45 team went 8-13 in Weston Mitchell's only season as coach. Kline was joined by junior guard Roger "Whitey" Johnson of Eau Claire, Wisconsin, and sophomore center Ron

Johnson from New Prague, who averaged 17.3 points per game. With 1958-59, the Gophers suffered their first back-to-back losing seasons since 1943-44 and 1944-45 as they slid to a ninth place finish in the Big Ten at 5-9. The tandem of Johnsons at guard and center was a hit, though, as Ron averaged 20.2 points per game and Whitey added 10.

After two consecutive losing seasons and no Big Ten titles in his 11-year tenure, Ozzie Cowles resigned after the 1958-59 season. Cowles finished his career at Minnesota with a 147-93 (.613) mark. The close of the Cowles era opened the door for a return of a former Gopher great and the first "M" man to lead Minnesota basketball.

■ *Ron Johnson.*

SECTION 4

Despite Ozzie Cowles' strong winning percentage during his tenure, Gopher fans were anxious for a Big Ten title, and for the end to the team's streak of losing seasons. Attendance and interest were down, and the Minnesota basketball program was beginning to fall into a malaise. The University decided the answer was right there in Minneapolis: John Kundla. Of course, Kundla had been a star on the 1936-37 Gopher squad that shared the Big Ten crown with Illinois, before going on to spend a year playing minor league professional basketball and then returning to the U as an assistant coach to Dave MacMillan. Next, Kundla was head coach at DeLaSalle High School in Minneapolis, spent two years in the Navy, and then went on to coach the University of St. Thomas in St. Paul.

Kundla really made a name for himself as a coach by leading the professional Minneapolis Lakers to six league championships in the 1940s and '50s with such greats as Hall-of-Famers George Mikan, Jim Pollard, and Vern Mikkelsen. That was when the National Basketball Association used a territorial draft system, which meant the Lakers had first dibs on local college players. Kundla and the Lakers used this system to their advantage, taking several Gophers, such as Don "Swede" Carl-

■ *Lou Hudson, whose retired No. 14 now hangs in the Williams Arena rafters, pulls down a rebound.*

son, Ken Exel, Tony Jaros, Warren Ajax, Bud Grant, Whitey Skoog, Ed Kalafat, Dick Garmaker, and Chuck Mencel. Kundla's regular-season record with the Lakers was 466-319, and his teams were 70-38 in the playoffs.

In 1959, Kundla left all that to return to his alma mater, even though the Gophers had finished ninth in the Big Ten the year before. With senior center Ron Johnson, sophomore forward Ray Cronk, and guard Paul Lehman returning, Kundla at least had a nucleus with which to build a winning program. "Ron Johnson was a great ballplayer, and Ray Cronk was one of my favorites," Kundla remembers. "He was all arms and legs, and he would just go and go."

Ron Johnson recalls his excitement and that of his teammates when they realized they would get to play for John Kundla. "John was just the nicest individual you could ever want to know. And he came in with a whole new concept of offense than we were used to, with a lot of ball movement and fast breaks. Ozzie Cowles was as much an expert on teaching shooting as there ever was, but he was conservative and he kept a tight rope around us. John was a breath of fresh air."

In the 1959-60 season opener, the Gophers fell to Southern Methodist 73-60, despite 20 points from Johnson and 11 from Cronk. They went on to race past Vanderbilt, 72-59, behind 25 points from Cronk, and they beat Nebraska and lost to Oklahoma. The 2-2 Gophers

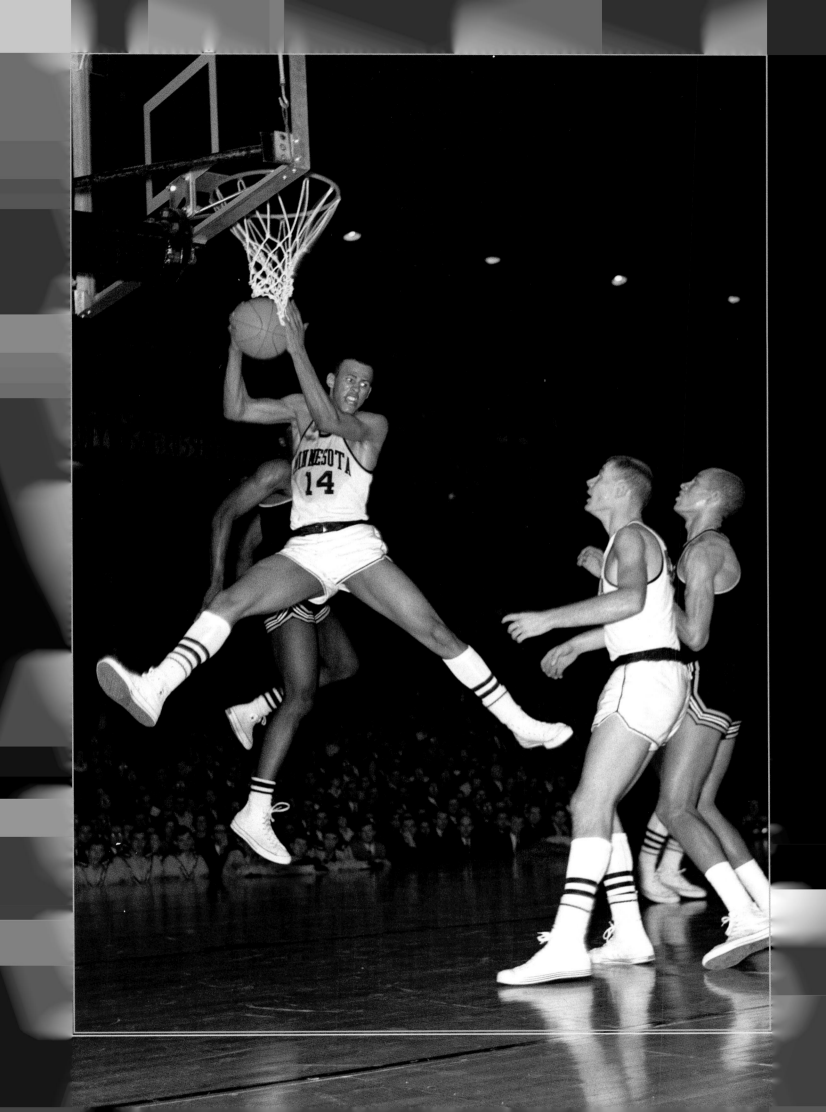

■ *Ron Johnson (above),*
Ray Cronk (below).

for a 73-72 victory. "That was not a good call," says Johnson, who still remembers that sequence vividly 36 years later. "That cost us the ballgame. It's just one of those things that stays with you forever." Minnesota went 1-3 the rest of its nonconference season, including three straight losses at the Dixie Classic in Raleigh, North Carolina, and entered the Big Ten season with a 4-6 record.

The Gophers were energized by the start of their conference schedule, though. They opened with a 70-61 win over Ohio State in front of 14,004 at the Barn, and at one point were second in the Big Ten at 4-2 after an 87-82 victory in Iowa City that included a team field-goal percentage of 72 percent which was, at the time, a conference record. But the Gophers slipped in the second half of their conference schedule and entered the season's final game against Ohio State with an 8-5 conference mark. The Buckeyes and their star, Jerry Lucas, were 12-1 and had already clinched the Big Ten title. More than 18,000 packed Williams Arena to cheer as the Gophers held Ohio State to a 39-38 lead at intermission. Minnesota led 42-41 early in the second half, but the Buckeyes pulled ahead for a 75-66 win. The Gophers' 8-6 record, though, was good enough for a third-place conference tie with Illinois and Northwestern, while Ohio State would go on to win the national championship.

In 1959-60, Ron Johnson averaged 21.1 points per game to total 1,335 points in his career as a Gopher (still 13th on the school's all-time list 36 years later). Johnson finished his collegiate career by being named first-team All-Big Ten and a UPI All-American honorable mention. He was invited to the U.S. Olympic team tryouts, and he was drafted by the NBA's Detroit Pistons in the second round. Johnson fondly remembers his time as the Gophers' star center, but often wonders what would have happened if he were playing in the current era, with the rules allowing freshmen to play. "We had to do everything in three years, and I think I came in as a freshman pretty ready to play. I wish I could have had that freshman year to play, but that was just not the case at the time."

Not only would John Kundla and the Gophers be without Ron Johnson in 1960-61, but they would not have Ray Cronk to help them either. Cronk was

returned home to face Missouri, an unbeaten national power. A disappointing crowd of 8,702 was at Williams Arena as Cronk and Johnson pounded the boards, outrebounding the entire Missouri team, and the Gophers defeated the Tigers, 80-62.

On December 22, 1959 John Wooden finally made it to Williams Arena as a coach—of the UCLA Bruins. Wooden's club opened a lead early and held it most of the game, even as Johnson scored 27 points and Cronk added 18. Their efforts appeared to pay off late in the game, and Minnesota closed the gap with Johnson tipping in a Wes Miller shot that would have made the score 69-68 in favor of UCLA. But Johnson was called for a foul on the way up and the officials disallowed the basket, leading many of the 9,370 fans to rain popcorn and pennies on to the court. After officials restored order, the Gophers rallied again, but UCLA managed to hold on

declared academically ineligible. John Kundla remembers being frustrated with the stringent scholastic requirements placed on athletes, especially compared to the more relaxed regulations in place today. "They had much tougher academic rules back then. If you didn't have a high enough GPA, they threw you out. And if you failed just one class, even if you got A's in everything else, you couldn't play. That hurt us a lot."

To have a successful 1960-61 season, Minnesota needed big years from sophomores Eric Magdanz of Minneapolis, Cal Sabatini of Hibbing, and Tom McGrann of Watertown, South Dakota, as well as veterans Dick Erickson, Bob Griggas, and Paul Lehman. The inexperience of the Gophers' squad showed immediately, as they dropped their first eight nonconference games before finally beating Michigan State in the Los Angeles Classic holiday tournament, as McGrann scored 22 points and grabbed 11 rebounds, and Griggas added 21 points. The conference season began just as badly as the exhibition campaign had, as Iowa pounded Minnesota, 71-46, while Bob McGrann was out sick. The conference home opener against Purdue drew a mere 5,845 to the Barn, and those few watched the Gophers fall, 65-64. Gopher football tackle Bobby Bell tried his hand at basketball in the next home game, against Northwestern, and helped Minnesota to a victory, but nothing could help the Gophers as they headed for Columbus and the defending national champions Ohio State. Jerry Lucas, John Havilcek, and the rest of the Buckeyes throttled Minnesota 75-56, to send the Gophers' conference mark to 1-3. But McGrann, Griggas, and Erickson picked up the pace to help the Gophers win five of their next six and eventually finish with an 8-6 conference record, earning them fourth place. "I had the misfortune of hitting Lucas and Havilcek for three years. They were almost unstoppable," says Kundla.

Ray Cronk was back in 1961-62, as were Tom McGrann and Eric Magdanz. While today's world of big-time college athletics fosters high—and sometimes unrealistic—expectations of high school sensations, Eric Magdanz proved decades ago that this is not a new phenomenon. Magdanz, a 6-foot-6 200-pounder, was a star at South High

School in Minneapolis, and Gopher fans expected much of him when he began his varsity career as a sophomore. But Magdanz averaged a mere 3.2 points per game in 1960-61, and he appeared shy and tentative on the floor. Sometime during the spring and summer of 1961, Magdanz figured out what his problem was, because he took the floor for the new season a different player.

"Magdanz came out of South High, and he didn't have a lot of experience," says Kundla. "He was a self-made player. Eric went out and worked all summer, and by hard work he became a great ballplayer."

Magdanz has similar memories. "I didn't do much my sophomore year. Offensively I was ready to play, but defensively I didn't have a clue, and I didn't get a lot of playing time as a result. I was a 6-foot-6 center in high school, and all of a sudden I was play-

■ *Eric Magdanz.*

ing 20 feet from the basket and facing the basket all the time. I spent a lot of time the summer before my junior year in the weight room, and then the rest of my game started falling into place."

The Gophers lost at home against DePaul to open the 1961-62 season, but Magdanz and McGrann each scored 16 points in the effort. Next, Magdanz scored 25 and Cronk added 23 as the Gophers beat Memphis State. Although Minnesota finished the preseason with a 4-6 record, Magdanz was well on his way to proving that he could live up to all those lofty expectations after all.

Magdanz kept that pace up as the conference season began. He scored 27 in the season-opening win at home against Purdue, then he and the entire Gophers squad attacked the basket against Indiana. They got past the Hoosiers, 104-100, in a game that set school records for both points scored and combined score. Magdanz and Cronk combined for 55 points, and five Gophers scored in double figures. Minnesota lost its next contest to Iowa, and then played host to top-ranked Ohio State. The Buckeyes were the dynasty of that era, and 17,208 fans of the Maroon and Gold saw Jerry Lucas come away with 32 points and 18 rebounds, John Havilcek score 25, and a senior bench-warmer named Bobby Knight add four points, as the Gophers were throttled, 90-76. The Buckeyes would go on to win their third straight Big Ten title and lose in the NCAA championship game for the second year in a row. Those two games against Iowa and Ohio State were the beginning of a seven-game losing streak that soured Gopher fans and dimmed any hopes of a first-division Big Ten finish. They finally beat Northwestern 73-64 to end the streak, but lost again to Purdue to drop their conference mark to 3-8. The remaining three games became a drive for respect, which the Gophers earned by sweeping all three to finish at 6-8 in the conference, as Tom McGrann set a new Gopher season rebounding mark, averaging nearly 12 per game.

The player that deserved respect the most got his share in the final 102-80 drubbing of Michigan, though only 4,975 Gopher fans turned out to see it. Eric Magdanz grabbed 18 rebounds, hit 16 of 25 from the field, and was 10 of 10 from the free throw line for a total of 42 points, a Gopher single-game record

that still stood in 1995. He set the new team conference scoring record of 352 points, or 25.1 per game. "I guess I felt tonight like I really belonged out on the floor," Magdanz said to the *Minneapolis Tribune's* Bill McGrane after the game. "I haven't always felt that way, but tonight I had the confidence. When I'd shoot I'd figure it was going in—I didn't wonder if it might go in."

Looking back, Magdanz now thinks it was just one of those nights. "It was a lot like any other game, but I got hot in the second half. There were some days where everything goes in. That was one of those days."

Minnesota had a brighter outlook for the 1962-63 season: Magdanz, McGrann, and Bob Bateman provided a solid foundation of seniors, and team observers were excited about the prospects for sophomore center Mel Northway of Minneapolis Patrick Henry High School and sophomore guard Terry Kunze of Duluth Central. The club lived up to that promise early by winning its first three nonconference games, but it fell flat after that, losing six in a row. Among the defeats was a 78-70 loss to Memphis State, in spite of 30 points from Eric Magdanz. Magdanz finally was able to spark a victory on New Year's Eve by scoring 28 to pull the Gophers ahead of Houston. When the conference season began, Minnesota split its first two contests, then beat Michigan behind Terry Kunze, who was 14 of 15 from the floor for 28 points, and Magdanz, who scored 20. The Gophers then pushed their conference record to 3-1 by beating Purdue 82-73, but they only went 2-6 the rest of the way to falter to a 5-7 conference record and a fourth-place finish. Despite the lack of team success, Eric Magdanz proved himself to be an outstanding basketball player after a disastrous sophomore season. He averaged 19.1 points his senior year and, incredibly, finished with more than 1,000 points for his career even after scoring only 72 as a sophomore.

The 1963-64 season was pivotal for the Golden Gophers. It was the year that the national issue of civil rights came to the University of Minnesota basketball program, however the U seemed to fare better than much of the rest of society. For all its history, Gopher players had come mostly from

■ *Ray Cronk goes up for a rebound against Memphis State in 1961.*

Minnesota, Wisconsin, and the Dakotas, and they all were white. But in 1963, John Kundla extended his recruiting arm beyond the midwest and brought the school's first three African-American basketball players. Lou Hudson, Archie Clark, and Don Yates came from North Carolina, Michigan, and Pennsylvania, respectively, and their impact on the Gopher basketball program was profound, both in terms of basketball and for the legacy they provided future African-American basketball players.

Lou Hudson was a three-sport star in Greensboro, North Carolina, and the hometown Wake Forest Demon Deacons desperately wanted to recruit the talented local hero to play there. But

coach Glen Reed to Greensboro, and Reed convinced Hudson to come north.

"It was a big-time transition for me," Hudson remembers. "I went from segregation to integration overnight. In fact, the Gophers used to make a trip down south every year to tournaments like the Dixie Classic, but they had to change their schedule because they weren't allowed to play at any of those schools with black players."

Archie Clark, one of 11 children from Ecorse, Michigan, was also a three-sport star who graduated from high school in 1959. But his chances for a college scholarship then appeared dim, so Clark spent three years in the Army. While serving in a Maryland unit, Clark played basketball for former Gopher

■ *Lou Hudson (left), Archie Clark (right).*

this was the segregated South, and there would be no black players at a predominantly white southern college for a long time to come. So Wake Forest Coach Bones McKinney got in touch with his old friend John Kundla and told him about Hudson, hoping the young athlete could get an opportunity to play outside the south. Kundla sent assistant

Buzz Bennett, who recommended him to Minnesota. Don Yates was a high school All-American in Uniontown, Pennsylvania, who gained the attention of Gopher coaches as well. Together, these three would give Minnesota its most exciting Big Ten title chance in a decade. "Those three really startled the crowd with their athletic ability. They ran the fast break like no one had ever seen before, and they had great shooting ability," Kundla remembers. "They were the first black basketball players at the U, and they were treated pretty well here, but on the road they were treated badly, especially in nonconference games. But compared to North Carolina where Lou came from, it was pretty darn nice. Archie Clark was mature. He had been in the service, and he was a very capable leader."

The Gophers won their first game of the season, 76-66, at Kansas State; Mel Northway had 18 points and 14 rebounds, Kunze and Hudson each scored 13, and Yates and Clark put in 10 apiece. The U beat Houston on the road 60-58, behind Hudson's 22 points. At home, Minnesota beat Iowa State and throttled South Dakota 107-62. Minnesota dropped two of its next three before heading to New York for the Holiday Invitational Tournament. Hudson

■ *Mel Northway and Coach John Kundla.*

and crew beat Cornell and St. Joseph's in preparation for the championship game against Villanova. In that game, Northway had 15 points and 15 rebounds, and Hudson added 26 points and 12 boards. It was not enough, though; the Wildcats pulled out a 77-73 victory.

Lou Hudson's performance in the 7-3 preseason was outstanding; his play during the Big Ten season was even better. This sophomore was well on his way to becoming a Gopher legend, and he was leading one of the best Minnesota squads in years. Only 6,641 fans made it to Williams Arena for the conference opener against Purdue, but thousands more watched the regionally televised game at home. They saw Hudson dominate with 36 points, and the Gophers come away with a 97-93 victory. Hudson had to spend part of the second half in the locker room getting stitches after he hit his head on the bottom of the backboard while leaping to block a Boilermaker shot. But still, he scored 24 of his 36 points in the second half.

The Gophers split their next two conference games; they lost to Ohio State, then beat Michigan State, 103-82, when Northway scored 20 points and grabbed an amazing 20 rebounds. Minnesota lost to Northwestern, then went on a tear with four straight wins, including a decisive 111-92 win over Wisconsin in front of a crowd of 12,175 that showed fan interest in the team was increasing again with the prospect of supporting a winner. Hudson scored 25 in that game, and five Gophers scored at least 14 points. For the fourth game in the winning streak, Minnesota played host to the conference-leading and second-ranked Michigan Wolverines before a frenzied crowd of 17,019. Six Gophers scored in double figures, including 19 each from Kunze and Hudson, as Minnesota came out on top, 89-75. That put the Gophers at 7-3, just one game behind Michigan and Ohio State, now the Big Ten co-leaders. But Illinois picked the next game against Minnesota to snap its five-game losing streak, ending the U's title hopes. The Gophers finished the season by beating Iowa at home and Wisconsin and Indiana on the road; in the Hoosier game, Minnesota came from behind in the second half and won, 90-89, on Archie Clark's 20-foot jumper with three seconds remaining. That final spurt put the

■ *Wes Martins comes down on an opposing player's back while Paul Presthus looks on in 1965.*

Gophers at 17-7 overall and 10-4 in the Big Ten, good enough for third place in the conference. Minnesota probably would have qualified for the National Invitational Tournament in 1963-64, but University rules prohibited the athletes from missing any more classes.

Lou Hudson was the engine that drove the Gophers to their new resurgence in 1963-64, but the third-place Big Ten finish would not have been possible without such a balanced team. Six players finished the year with double-figure scoring averages; Sweet Lou led the club with 18.1 points per game and Mel Northway was second with 14.3.

All six of those top players—Hudson, Northway, Davis, Clark, Kunze, and Yates—returned for the 1964-65 season, along with newcomers Paul Presthus, Wes Martins, and Dennis Dvoracek. For the first time in a long time, the Golden Gophers were a legitimate favorite to take the Big Ten crown. Minnesota lived

up to expectations early with seven straight nonconference wins. Terry Kunze was ruled academically intelligible after the fourth game, so Dvoracek, a 6-foot-6 junior forward from Eau Claire, Wisconsin, stepped up as a starter. Losing Kunze hurt the Gophers, Kundla remembers. "Terry was an excellent ball-handler, and a great ballplayer." But in the 88-69 win over Utah State, Dvoracek added 14 points to Hudson's 33. In its first six games, Minnesota didn't have very many tough tests, beginning with South Dakota State (a 101-55 win in the season opener), but that changed as the team traveled west in December for the Los Angeles Classic. The Gophers squeezed by Washington 77-76, only to run headlong into John Wooden and his defending national champion UCLA Bruins. Minnesota trailed 40-37 at halftime, but the Bruin dynasty was too deep for the Gophers, and UCLA's full-court press overpowered them, result-

> ...THERE WERE A COUPLE OF CALLS BY THE OFFICIALS THAT I'LL NEVER FORGET. THERE WAS ONE WHERE ARCHIE CLARK HAD ONE FOOT OVER THE CENTER LINE AND HE WAS CALLED FOR OVER-AND-BACK, BUT HE WAS SUPPOSED TO HAVE TWO FEET OVER THE LINE. I'M SURE THE OFFICIAL MADE A MISTAKE ON THAT ONE. THAT WAS A TOUGH LOSS TO TAKE.

ing in a 93-77 Gopher loss. The following night, Iowa topped a tired Minnesota team 76-74, and the Gophers finished the preseason at home by beating Detroit for an 8-2 preseason record.

The Gophers opened the Big Ten season by racing past Wisconsin 81-57 and losing to Illinois by three. The Illinois loss appeared to be an exception, though; Minnesota snapped off seven straight wins after that. Among them a 20-point victory over defending conference co-champion Ohio State, and a 15-point piece of revenge against Illinois, when Hudson, Northway, and Yates all broke the 20-point barrier. Hudson had back-to-back games of more than 30 points against Wisconsin and Northwestern during the streak, and the Gophers were primed for a Williams Arena showdown with Michigan, which was 9-0 in the Big Ten.

The Barn was shaking with the energy of 17,600 Gopher fans, but even that force could not overcome the strength of Wolverine stars Cazzie Russell (27 points), George Pomey (20 points), Bill Buntin, and Oliver Darden. The Gophers held Michigan to a 39-39 halftime tie, but Michigan pulled away for a 91-78 victory, sending Minnesota's record to 8-2, tied with Illinois for second in the conference. The Gophers rebounded quickly, beating Indiana at home and Iowa in Iowa City, then they headed to Ann Arbor for their much-anticipated rematch with the Wolverines. Facing a national power and a frantic sellout crowd, the Gophers played Michigan tight all night. Lou Hudson poured in 31, and Don Yates and Archie Clark combined for 36. Hudson tipped in a Clark miss with two minutes left to put the Gophers behind by only one, but Michigan held on the rest of the way for an 88-85 victory and the Big Ten championship.

Kundla remembers that game as his most difficult loss in his more than 30 years in organized basketball. "That was a good game, no question about it, but there were a couple of calls by the officials that I'll never forget. There was one where Archie Clark had one foot over the center line and he was called for over-and-back, but he was supposed to have two feet over the line. I'm sure the official made a mistake on that one. That was a tough loss to take."

Minnesota ended the season with an overtime win at home against Iowa; the Gophers finished 19-5 overall and 11-3 in the conference, by themselves in second place. Michigan went on to win the national championship, and the Gophers finished seventh in the final Associated Press poll. Hudson broke Eric Magdanz's single-season scoring record, averaging 23.3 points per game, and senior Mel Northway set a new team rebounding record, averaging 13.4 per game on the season. He was still fifth on the all-time Gopher rebounding list 30 years later. After the season, both Northway and Kunze were drafted by the NBA's St. Louis Hawks.

Even with the loss of Northway and Kunze, prospects once again looked bright for the Gophers in 1965-66. Most of the team would be returning, and Tom Kondla entered the starting lineup at center to replace Mel Northway. But what once looked promising quickly turned sour for the U: Don Yates had academic problems and left school to take a full-time job, and Lou Hudson spent much of the season hobbled by injuries. The Gophers breezed through their first three games, beating North Dakota, Iowa State, and Drake without much trouble. But the fourth game of the season—a home victory against Creighton—was nothing to cheer about for Minnesota. On the way to scoring 32 points and grabbing 12 rebounds, Hudson was undercut on a layup and broke his right wrist. He spent the rest of the season with a cast on his hand, but he still played in 17 of the 24 games and, incredibly, averaged 14 points per game. Fortunately, senior Archie Clark went a long way toward filling the void left by Hudson's impaired scoring and rebounding ability, averaging 24.5 points per game for the year; Paul Presthus, Tom Kondla, Dennis Dvoracek, and Wes Martins also averaged in double figures for the year. Minnesota's depth allowed it to start with a 5-2 conference record, but the thinned-out lineup could not keep up that intensity. The Gophers' final record for 1965-66 was 14-10 overall and 7-7 in the Big Ten, good enough for fifth place. Archie Clark was named first-team All-Big Ten and Hudson, cast and all, was second-team All-Big Ten. Sweet Lou fell just six points short of the school career scoring record then held by Ron Johnson, but he and Clark were

■ Dennis Dvoracek goes for a rebound against Wisconsin in 1966 (left), and Dvoracek and Bill Moore try to grab another board against the Badgers (below).

still 14th and 18th, respectively, on the Gophers' all-time list in 1995. Archie Clark was drafted by the Los Angeles Lakers and Don Yates was taken by the St. Louis Hawks. The Hawks also took Lou Hudson with the fourth pick of the first round. Sweet Lou had a stellar NBA career, scoring nearly 18,000 points and being named to the NBA All-Star team six times in his 11-year career.

The NBA's gain was a profound loss for the 1966-67 Golden Gophers. Without Hudson and Clark, Minnesota's backcourt was too inexperienced to lead the team in the competitive Big

Paul Presthus was the only player to graduate in 1967, so Gopher watchers had considerably higher hopes for a team with another year of experience under its belt for 1967-68. But the preseason did not bode well for the Gophers, as they stumbled to a 3-7 record. Among the defeats was a 95-55 drubbing by UCLA at the Los Angeles Classic. Tom Kondla scored 18 and had 12 rebounds in that game, but UCLA's Lew Alcindor came up with 28 points and 15 rebounds. It was that kind of year throughout, as Minnesota finished with a 7-17 overall record, a 4-10 Big Ten mark, and a second straight ninth-place

■ *Tom Kondla (left), Al Nuness.*

Ten, so John Kundla turned to junior center Tom Kondla and senior forward Paul Presthus. Kondla led the Gophers to a season-opening upset over Kansas State, 60-59, by scoring 33 points and pulling in 23 rebounds. Eight times Kondla scored at least 30 points, averaging 24.9 points per game. But that was not enough to carry the young Gophers, who finished with a 9-15 overall record and a 5-9 conference mark, to place them ninth in the conference.

finish. All that was despite 21 points per game from Kondla, a 14.4 average from junior guard Al Nuness, and 12 from junior forward LeRoy Gardner, a St. Paul Central High School graduate. Kondla was a second-team All-Big Ten selection, and he broke Ron Johnson's school-career scoring record and Lou Hudson's school-conference scoring mark.

That ninth season was enough for John Kundla. He retired after the 1967-68 season with an overall record of 110-105

(.512) at his alma mater, which included two third- and one second-place finishes. For his efforts as a player and coach for the Gophers, and his stellar leadership of the professional Minneapolis Lakers, Kundla was elected to the Naismith Basketball Hall of Fame in 1995.

"I wasn't a very good recruiter, and that was becoming more important," Kundla says. "For the first couple of years, everybody came because I had pro experience and they all wanted to play pro ball. I suppose I might have become complacent. I had a great stretch as a coach at Minnesota, but I

ing Green in Ohio, but that year he managed to guide the Falcons to the Mid-American Conference championship and a berth in the NCAA tournament. The Gophers were hoping for the same kind of success from Fitch when they hired him away.

Minnesota immediately showed improvement, raising its overall record in 1968-69 to an even 12-12 and showing a 6-8 conference record, good enough for fifth place. The Gophers hoped to continue their improving ways in 1969-70 with co-captains Larry Overskei and Larry Mikan, junior guard Eric Hill, and New York City junior college transfer

■ *Bill Fitch gives direction to his team during his brief tenure as Minnesota coach, 1968-70.*

suppose my biggest disappointment is that we never won a Big Ten championship. That's something I really wanted to do."

Kundla's departure meant the end of an era at the University of Minnesota. College basketball was no longer dependent on players from a school's own region; the days when the Gophers could expect to have the likes of Whitey Skoog or Tony Jaros attend the U because they grew up in the area were gone. National recruiting was beginning to take over at the nation's colleges and universities, and the Minnesota athletic department was determined to take advantage of that trend. To that end, Bill Fitch made his way to the U of M. Fitch had coached only one season at Bowl-

Ollie Shannon. Minnesota lost to Notre Dame at home and beat North Dakota on the road, then prepared once again to meet the preeminent power in college basketball, UCLA. John Wooden still brought with him a potent basketball team—the three-time defending national champions—but Lew Alcindor had graduated and moved on to NBA greatness. Also, this game was being played at Williams Arena. A boisterous crowd of 17,658 helped the Gophers to muddle through a first half of poor shooting to hold a 30-27 lead. Minnesota controlled the pace of the game, slowing UCLA with a zone defense and using the fast break frequently on offense; the U led by 55-48 at one point in the second half. With just over one minute remaining, the

■ *Ollie Shannon dribbles past a UCLA defender (left), and shoots over a Loyola player (right).*

■ *Larry Mikan in action during the 1969-70 season (left and right below).*

Bruins tied the game at 66, Ollie Shannon hit a shot to give Minnesota a two-point lead, then UCLA's Sidney Wicks tipped in a shot at the buzzer to send the game into overtime. Minnesota led 71-70 as the third period came to a close, but Henry Bibby hit a 30-foot jumper as time was running out to seal UCLA's 72-71 vic-

tory. Shannon hit 29 points and Mikan, Hill, and Overskei all scored in double figures, but it was not enough. In the next day's *Minneapolis Tribune*, Bill Fitch said: "We were only one rebound, or one pass, or one basket away. But I don't want to say anything to discredit our kids. What they did was by guts, desire,

■ *George Hanson, who coached the Gophers for only one season after a lengthy tenure as an assistant for John Kundla and Bill Fitch.*

and determination." Wooden could only say, "We were lucky."

Minnesota finished the 1969-70 nonconference season with a respectable 5-4 record, including winning its last three straight. Ollie Shannon proved a great pickup for Fitch, dominating the scoring column, while Mikan and Overskei proved to be outstanding rebounders. When the Big Ten contests began, the Gophers lost on the road to Ohio State, beat Indiana at home, and lost to Wisconsin in Madison. But then the U went on a tear, winning five of its next six conference games, as well as one nonconference contest, to boost its

Big Ten record to 6-3 and fuel hopes of a title run. But the Gophers folded down the stretch, winning only one of their final five conference games. They finished 13-11 overall, 7-7 in the conference, and in fifth place again. Eric Hill and Ollie Shannon both finished with 18.9 points per game, and Mikan averaged 17.2 points and 14.5 rebounds per game, including 28 rebounds in a home victory against Michigan. Mikan's season and single-game rebounding records still stood in 1995; like his father, hall-of-famer George Mikan, Larry Mikan was drafted by the Lakers when the season ended.

■ *Eric Hill shoots against Loyola during the 1969-70 season.*

But Larry Mikan was not the only loss for the Gophers in 1970. Just as he was beginning to rebuild the Gopher program with strong national recruiting and aggressive play, Bill Fitch answered the call of the NBA. The expansion Cleveland Cavaliers hired Fitch to be their head coach and director of player personnel, beginning a long and successful pro coaching career. "I think Minnesota is losing the best college basketball coach in America," Athletic Director Marsh Ryman said at the time. "We were delighted to have him for two years."

Fitch's departure caused serious rumblings in the Gopher program, especially among upperclassmen Eric Hill and Ollie Shannon, and newcomers Jim Brewer and Marvin "Corky" Taylor, who had been recruited by the former coach. Partly because of the sensitivity of that situation, Minnesota passed up the chance to hire Army coach and Ohio State alumnus Bobby Knight. Rather, the administration wanted somebody the players already knew and were comfortable with, so the U hired George Hanson as its head coach. In addition to playing for the

Gophers in the 1950s, Hanson had been a Gopher assistant since 1965, first under John Kundla and then under Fitch, so he was familiar not only with the program, but with the players as well.

But Corky Taylor was one of many who were still not happy with the Gophers' coaching situation. "George Hanson was a great guy, but he was not competitive enough for the modern era," he says. "When he recruited me, Bill Fitch told me his goal was to win a Big Ten title in my four years there. I'm from Detroit, and I chose Minnesota over Michigan because I liked Fitch better than Johnny Orr, who was coaching at Michigan. When he left Minnesota, I was very dejected. What followed was a very long year. It was hard to play in a half-empty building, and it was just a bad year for us as a team and for me personally. I remember feeling that collectively as a team we were better than this.

"The worst moment was getting blown out against Indiana (99-73), and the only suspense was whether they were going to score 100 points on us. Some of the Indiana players were taunt-ing us after the game. That was really hard to take."

Jim Brewer established himself early in his sophomore year as a dominating player; he finished the 1970-71 season averaging 16.6 points per game and 13.8 rebounds per game, and was named second-team All-Big Ten. Ollie Shannon averaged 20.3 points and Eric Hill added 16.8, but none of that was enough to stop the Gophers' slide back into mediocrity. George Hanson's team was 11-13 overall and 5-9 in the Big Ten, placing it in fifth place for the third straight year. Attendance, which had been slipping steadily for four years, hit a new low of 6,500 per game. The program was lethargic—on the court, off the court, and in the stands, the energy that had once characterized a successful program had disappeared. George Hanson was asked to step down after just one season, and the search began for a vibrant head coach who could revive a program on the verge of a coma.

SECTION

The University of Minnesota men's basketball program was in dire need of a major turnaround in 1971. What once was a national basketball power had become an also-ran in the Big Ten, with four fifth- and two ninth-place finishes in the previous six years. The University had a new athletic director, U football legend Paul Giel, and the basketball search committee was looking for a similar infusion of energy on the raised floor of Williams Arena. The committee thought it had its man in Cal Luther, the head coach at Murray State University. Luther accepted the job, then abruptly changed his mind and turned it down, leaving the search committee to start over. The result of that second round of hiring was a 30-year-old coach from small Ashland College in Ohio named Bill Musselman.

Musselman had become head coach at Ashland when he was only 24 years old, and in six seasons his teams built a remarkable record of 128-31. Musselman was fiery, intense, and driven, and the search committee was impressed with his overarching commitment to winning immediately. "I don't believe in rebuilding years," Musselman told the committee in his interview. Thinking back now, Musselman remembers that this was a calculated statement, and not bluster. "I already had a lot of confidence in myself based on my record at Ashland College, and we

■ *Dave Winfield leaps for a loose ball before his baseball superstar days.*

already had a great center there in Jim Brewer, who was good enough to be All-Big Ten. We had the ability to get the job done with discipline and good defense, and I believe you can teach anybody to be a good defensive player."

The team Musselman fielded for the 1971-72 season reflected this view: It was a combination of returning upperclassmen and a collection of junior college transfers Musselman rounded up to rescue a program clearly in need of a rebuilding year.

The club was anchored by junior center Jim Brewer from Chicago and junior forward Marvin "Corky" Taylor from Detroit, as well as returning guards Bob Murphy of Brooklyn, New York, and Keith Young of Columbus, Ohio. Musselman added three junior college transfers: Ron Behagen, a New York City native who had been playing at Southern Idaho Junior College in Twin Falls, where he averaged 24 points and 13 rebounds per game; Clyde Turner, who had averaged 28 points and 14 rebounds for Robert Morris Junior College in Carthage, Illinois; and Bob Nix, who had scored 16 points per game at Henderson County Junior College in Athens, Texas. Aside from assembling a talented team, Musselman had managed to put together a tall one. Brewer and Turner were 6-foot-8, Behagen and Taylor were 6-foot-9, and Nix was 6-foot-3. When all five of them were on the court at once, it

■ *Bill Musselman works the Williams Arena bench during his first season, 1971-72.*

was one of the tallest lineups in the nation, a perfect compliment to Musselman's physical, banging style of play.

Some people wondered whether Musselman should be turning to junior college transfers to turn the Gophers around, but in retrospect, the coach is unapologetic. "Those three transfer players helped a lot. The Gophers had averaged 6,500 fans the year before, and to get interest and to improve the team, we had to take advantage of Jim Brewer by giving him some help. The key was that we had the best center in the league, and a point guard and a center mean everything in every level of basketball. I had to try to win it all when Brewer was there."

And if those weren't enough tall players, Musselman invited a Gopher baseball star, 6-foot-6 Dave Winfield, to practice with the team. Winfield had played only one season of high school basketball, but he was an outstanding natural athlete with uncanny rebounding skill. In his book *Winfield: A Player's Life*, Winfield remembers his introduction to Gopher basketball:

"Playing for the Gophers that year were a half-dozen NBA prospects—Jim Brewer, Ron Behagen, Clyde Turner, Keith Young, Bob Murphy, and Corky Taylor. When I showed up, they didn't exactly put out the welcome mat. Each of these guys had serious hopes of playing pro ball, and they needed to start to attract pro scouts. So there I was, not even officially on the team, of all places, practicing with them, often outhustling them in scrimmages, threatening to take someone's job. From the beginning, no one much liked seeing me run into the

■ *Jim Brewer goes up for a shot against Marquette (left), and slams home a breakaway dunk during the 1971-72 season (above).*

■ *Clyde Turner lays the ball in at Williams Arena.*

arena from the underground tunnel that connected it to the gym where I took baseball practice, but one guy, Ron Behagen, Wild Bee, was downright hostile. A few days before the first game of the season, Mussleman calls me aside to tell me how much he likes my intensity, likes the way I pull down rebounds against guys a half-foot taller than I, how much he wants me to play for him. I'd made the team! And once that's finally established, the team accepts me and many of the guys became my friends."

The 1971-72 Gopher team was loaded with talent and potential. Rarely was a coach's first season filled with such high expectations, but that was all right with Musselman; he brought those expectations upon himself and his team. Now the task was to come through on those lofty promises. Musselman had

put together, he remembers, "the best rebounding team I have ever seen in college basketball, bar none. When we played Marquette, those were the best rebounding games I've ever seen. I thought it was two pro teams playing."

In the season opener, Clyde Turner scored 28 points to lead the Gophers past North Dakota, 69-49, in front of a crowd of 10,980 at Williams Arena. But for Bill Musselman, this 20-point victory was not enough. As he told the *Minneapolis Tribune* then: "We coasted. That's not the way to be a champion. We didn't have the killer instinct. When we lose to a great team but play our best, I'll be the first to hug each of these guys. But when we win by 20 and play poorly, I'm going to tell these guys, too."

The Gophers split their next two on the road, beating Iowa State and losing to Bradley in overtime. They returned home to beat Butler easily by 21 points, as five Gophers scored in double figures. They had two weeks off for final exams before they returned to their toughest contest yet—and possibly of the entire season—against undefeated Marquette, which was then ranked second in the nation. Bob Lackey riddled the Gopher defense for 23 points, and Marquette's defense stopped the Gophers cold; Marquette walked out of the Milwaukee Arena with a 55-40 victory. The U beat Drake at home and flew to Hawaii for the Honolulu Classic. It fell to Temple by three points, then beat the Hawaii Marines service squad, 86-71, in a tough game that would be a precursor of future conflicts as Ron Behagen was involved in several verbal and physical scrapes. Minnesota beat Texas Christian in the Classic's consolation final, then whipped Loyola of Chicago at home, 84-59; Behagen scored 25 and Turner added 21. The Gophers finished their nonconference schedule at 6-3 behind tough defense, aggressive rebounding, and the valuable college transfers, Behagen, Turner, and Nix.

The result of this energetic play was a dramatic decrease in empty seats at Williams Arena, and a corresponding increase in fan intensity at home games. Musselman and his players gave the crowds their money's worth. Besides 40 minutes of basketball, Gopher fans were treated to a pregame show reminiscent of the Harlem Globetrotters: the players entered to a darkened arena, ran through a giant, spotlit Gopher cutout; they formed a circle and flipped the ball back and forth with dazzling behind-the-back passes, through-the-leg dribbles, and finger-spinning demonstrations to the tune of "Sweet Georgia Brown." It was a display that often angered opposing coaches, who saw the pregame demonstration as showy and crass, but the fans loved it and the Gopher players felt it pumped them up and increased their intensity level.

"I was very detail-oriented in practice, and we ran lots of drills," Musselman remembers. "The pregame warmup was designed, first of all, to generate interest and get people into the arena, but it was also to help players with their coordination, and to reduce turnovers. We worked a lot on fundamentals. I don't think anybody worked harder on fundamentals than we did."

Corky Taylor agrees with that. "Musselman was a very tough coach. Sometimes the practices were harder than the games. It was certainly a different level of intensity from the previous year," he remembers. "Sometimes he had us hold a 20-pound medicine ball over our heads, put on a 20-pound weight belt, and we had to continuously jump over a three-foot bench until he blew the whistle for us to stop. It seemed like forever. But when you took the belt off, you felt like you could jump 10 feet." As for the pregame warmup, Taylor agrees with Musselman that it got the crowd fired up and helped the team with its ball-handling skills. "But to be honest, as the season wore on, it got a little tiring."

Musselman was also very intense before games, Taylor recalls. "We used to have a pregame meal, and Musselman wanted us to be quiet and reflective, and he wanted it to be a very serious time. But being boisterous was very relaxing for us. So trainer Snapper Stein came to the meal late one day, and the waiter was wearing an apron

■ *Corky Taylor goes up for a shot against Marquette.*

■ Bill Musselman's Gophers were known almost as much for their pregame show as for their play.

■ Some opponents thought Minnesota was showing off, but the coach and players said the drills helped their skills.

that said, 'Go Gophers.' Snapper looked at his food and said, 'After this, I might have to go.' We all exploded with laughter. Musselman was really mad, but we went out and played a great game."

The second-largest crowd in school history—19,121—packed Williams Arena for the Big Ten opener against fifth-ranked Indiana and its new coach, Bobby Knight. Turner, Behagen, Nix, and Young all scored in double figures, accounting for almost all of Minnesota's scoring, and with 17 seconds left to play the Gophers trailed by only one point. Indiana's John Ritter fouled Bob Nix, who cooly sank both free throws to give Minnesota a one-point lead. Jim Brewer blocked Rick Ford's last-second shot, and the Gophers came away with a 52-51 upset as wild Minnesota fans clamored onto the raised court.

The Gophers coasted past Northwestern at home and beat Wisconsin and Michigan State on the road—with Keith Young scoring 27 in Madison and Clyde Turner pouring in 31 in East Lansing—leading up to the much-anticipated showdown of the 4-0 Gophers and the 3-0 Ohio State Buckeyes at Williams Arena. The atmosphere in the Barn was charged; 17,775 fans were excited at the prospect of watching the game that could well decide the Big Ten championship, and the Gopher and Buckeye players were equally fired up for their biggest game of the year to that point. It was a matchup that would have been worthy of the cover of *Sports Illustrated* under any circumstance, but what happened that night put the Minnesota Golden Gophers in the national spotlight in the worst possible way—one that would threaten to overshadow the best Gopher season in at least 35 years.

It was a battle between two large and physical teams, and the result was a tough, tenacious game, with plenty of banging under the basket and pushing and shoving around the perimeter. At the close of the first half, Ohio State's seven-foot center Luke Witte appeared to elbow Bob Nix in the head, but no foul was called, much to the disgust of the vocal Gopher crowd. Minnesota went into the locker room with a one-point lead, but Ohio State managed to turn the momentum and take a 40-32 lead with five minutes remaining. Minnesota put together a small run, and

Nix hit a jump shot from the right corner to shave the Buckeye margin to 50-44 with 47 seconds left. The game would never get more than 11 seconds closer to its conclusion.

After Nix's basket, Luke Witte headed downcourt, looking for a pass. Teammate Alan Hornyak threw it to Witte, but Clyde Turner reached Witte at the same time as the ball, and the resulting collision sent Witte to the floor. Turner was called for a flagrant foul and ejected. Corky Taylor extended a hand to help Witte up. Taylor maintains that Witte spit at him. Witte said he did not. Taylor kneed Witte in the groin, and while the giant center lay on the ground in pain, Ron Behagen stomped on Witte's head. Both benches immediately cleared and several Gopher fans leaped onto the raised court. In the ensuing havoc Buckeye players Mark Wagar and Mark Minor also sustained injuries that required them to be taken to the University Hospital along with Witte.

Paul Giel, who had only been Minnesota's athletic director for a few months, decided after consulting with the game officials to end the game and declare Ohio State the winner. Fairly or not, the melee gave Minnesota the worst possible publicity. *Sports Illustrated* devoted two pages to the incident. Ohio State officials said Musselman incited the fight with his competitive attitude and the flashy pregame warmups. The governor of Ohio even suggested publicly that Corky Taylor and Ron Behagen be thrown in jail for their actions. In reality, the University and the Big Ten both suspended the two for the rest of the season, and no further action was taken.

"The fight was wrong. It was something that got way out of hand," says Musselman, looking back. "But I think our kids got a bum rap for that. The officiating in that game was pathetic, the worst I've ever seen in my life, and the referees just lost control of the game. I felt it was unfair because the players that were involved were good people."

"I definitely got a bad rap," remembers Taylor. "I sacrificed a lot of myself for the benefit of Gopher basketball. My style of play was not necessarily Bill Musselman's style of play. And what a lot of people don't realize is that Luke Witte and I are pretty good friends. He has invited me to his house. We first

> ## "THE FIGHT WAS WRONG. IT WAS SOMETHING THAT GOT WAY OUT OF HAND," SAYS MUSSELMAN, LOOKING BACK. "BUT I THINK OUR KIDS GOT A BUM RAP FOR THAT.... I FELT IT WAS UNFAIR BECAUSE THE PLAYERS THAT WERE INVOLVED WERE GOOD PEOPLE.

■ **Opposite** *Ron Behagen (left) and Clyde Turner leap for a rebound against Iowa.*

talked in 1975 or '76, and we both understand that the aftermath of the whole situation was not where we were as two individuals. The politics of what happened and the media were a whole different dimension.

"Being labelled as the total villain was the hardest part for me. I was the bad guy. It was very hard to deal with."

The Gophers still had a season to play, and they had to do it without two of their top players. They were left with a starting lineup of Jim Brewer, Clyde Turner, Bob Nix, Keith Young, and their resident baseball player, Dave Winfield. The "Iron Five," as they would become known, had to carry the weight of the rest of the Big Ten season by themselves. "I thought that, provided we stayed out of foul trouble, we could still win it all," remembers Musselman. "If we started fouling out, then we'd be in trouble."

Minnesota traveled to Iowa City for the first game after the brawl—this was always a tough rivalry, but the Gophers had the extra wild card of not knowing how the crowds, opposing players, or officials would react following their newfound fame. At one point during the game, Winfield accidentally knocked a Hawkeye player to the ground, drawing blood, and the crowd began a thunderous round of booing and foot-stomping. The Iowa crowd subsided, though, as did the Hawkeyes, and the Gophers extended their Big Ten record to 5-1. "That game was like walking on eggs, very tense," says Musselman. "The players just didn't know what to expect, but really the crowd treated us pretty well."

The Hawkeyes traveled to Williams Arena for a rematch the next game, and the Gophers won again, 53-52. Bobby Knight's Indiana Hoosiers blew out Minnesota in Indiana by a score of 61-42. But the Gophers rebounded, winning two straight over Northwestern and Wisconsin, to set the stage for a showdown with second-place Michigan in Ann Arbor. The Gophers took a 31-23 lead to the locker room at halftime, but Michigan rallied to win 64-52 and leap into first place in the Big Ten with three games remaining. But the Iron Five, though tired, was not finished yet. They beat Purdue and Illinois before thunderous sellout crowds at Williams Arena to clinch a tie for the conference title—the school's first in 35 years—and earn the

16th spot in the Associated Press coaches' poll. The Gophers moved on to West Lafayette, Indiana, for the year's final regular-season game against Purdue. Jim Brewer and Clyde Turner each scored 12 points, as the Gophers withstood a late rally by the Boilermakers to win, 49-48, and go to 11-3 in the conference, earning their first outright Big Ten title since 1919.

That display of determination by a team that had earlier in the season been vilified and left for dead also earned Minnesota its first postseason tournament bid. The Gophers played their first NCAA Mideast Regional game in Dayton, Ohio, against the Florida State Seminoles. Florida State easily handled the Gophers, 70-56, and Minnesota finished its season with a 77-72 consolation round victory over Marquette. Jim Brewer was named Big Ten MVP, and the Gophers finished the season ranked 10th in the nation. True to his promise, Bill Musselman really did not believe in rebuilding years, and he made his first season one of the most memorable in Gopher history, for reasons both bitter and sweet.

"The Ohio State incident overshadows the true accomplishments of that particular team," remembers Taylor. "This was a once-in-a-decade team, like the University of Houston team with Hakeem Olajawan and Clyde Drexler. The only comparable U team that I can remember is the team with Mychal Thompson, Kevin McHale, and Ray Williams."

The best news for Minnesota was that the entire Iron Five, along with the suspended Corky Taylor and Ron Behagen, returned for the 1972-73 season. The Gophers were a consensus pick to repeat as conference champions, and they promised to be a national power as well. Behagen made an impressive return, scoring 27 in the season-opening win over California-Irvine. It was the first of nine straight nonconference wins, many of them routs, including a 111-66 trouncing of Western Illinois and a 78-38 dismantling of San Francisco State. Behagen, Turner, Winfield, and Brewer all averaged in double figures for the nonconference season.

The 9-0 Gophers believed people when they said the team would be unstoppable, and they entered the Big Ten season to a rude awakening. They lost the conference opener in Iowa City

"

THIS WAS A ONCE-IN-A-DECADE TEAM, LIKE THE UNIVERSITY OF HOUSTON TEAM WITH HAKEEM OLAJAWAN AND CLYDE DREXLER. THE ONLY COMPARABLE U TEAM THAT I CAN REMEMBER IS THE TEAM WITH MYCHAL THOMPSON, KEVIN MCHALE, AND RAY WILLIAMS.

"

65-62, behind Hawkeyes center Kevin Kunnert, his 26 points and 15 rebounds. Minnesota came back to win easily at home against Wisconsin, then renewed its rivalry against second-ranked Marquette at the Barn. Nearly 18,000 fans crammed into the arena, and another 4,000 bought tickets to watch the game on closed-circuit television next door in the hockey arena. The Gophers led the entire way and rode the thundering crowd noise to a 64-53 win and an 11-1 record.

But Indiana coach Bobby Knight pumped his players up when the Gophers came to town for the next game, and the Hoosiers handed Minnesota an 83-71 defeat and a 1-2 conference record. It was a splash of water in the face of a team that needed a reminder that it was overconfident; the Gophers may have had one of the most talented teams in the country, but they still needed to show up and play every game. They learned their lesson after the losses to Indiana and Iowa; Minnesota reeled off a phenomenal nine straight Big Ten wins, against Michigan State, Wisconsin, Purdue, Ohio State, Indiana, Illinois, Michigan, Northwestern, and Purdue. The Gophers were 10-2 in the Big Ten, and a second straight conference championship was in sight when Iowa came to Williams Arena for the second-to-last game of the regular season.

■ *The Gophers in action against Michigan in 1973.*

■ *Phil Saunders launches a jumper against Michigan.*

The Gophers retired Jim Brewer's number 52 in a pregame ceremony before a sellout crowd of 17,857. At half-time, Minnesota led ninth-place Iowa 46-33. But the Hawkeyes, led by 7-foot center Kevin Kunnert, rallied to take the lead late in the second half. The Gophers managed to retake the lead 77-76 with less than one minute to play, but Kunnert hit a layup and was fouled. He made the free throw, and the 79-77 defeat sent the Gophers into a first-place tie with Indiana as the Gophers headed to Evanston to take on Northwestern. Behagen, Turner, Brewer, and Young all scored in double figures, but the Wildcats still came out on top, 79-74. Minnesota had followed up its Big Ten

championship of the year before with a second-place finish and its first bid to the National Invitational Tournament at Madison Square Garden in New York City.

Ron Behagen had 18 points in the Gophers' first NIT contest to lead the team over Rutgers, 68-59, and send Minnesota to the semifinals against Alabama. Clyde Turner took his turn as the Gophers' scoring threat with 21 points, and Minnesota led most of the way. But similar to their late-game collapses against Iowa and Northwestern, the Gophers let the Crimson Tide tie the score at 59. Alabama then went on an 8-0 run and wound up with a 69-65 win to end the Gophers' season. But Minnesota finished with its first-ever 20-win season (21-5), and its 10-4 Big Ten record was good enough for second place.

"It seems to me now that we all felt—including me—that with everybody back, including Behagen and Taylor, that we could win anytime we wanted to," says Musselman. "We got a little complacent. I think it was harder to share playing time for the five guys who had won everything a year before. When you know you've got more talent than the year before, it's always in the back of your mind.

"But I don't think that team ever gets enough credit. Those guys worked hard in practice, harder than anybody realized. I would like to see any other team in University of Minnesota history that worked harder in practice. We had three-hour practice sessions, and that team never once dogged it in practice."

A record five Gopher players were selected in the NBA draft: Jim Brewer was the draft's second selection by the Cleveland Cavaliers, Ron Behagen was picked seventh overall by the Kansas City Kings, Clyde Turner was taken by the Milwaukee Bucks, and Corky Taylor went to the Boston Celtics. And Dave Winfield achieved a feat that is still unmatched in sports history: He was chosen by the Atlanta Hawks of the NBA, the Utah Stars of the ABA, the San Diego Padres of Major League Baseball, and the Minnesota Vikings of the NFL, before choosing baseball.

"By recruiting junior college players and already having Corky Taylor and Jim Brewer and Dave Winfield in the same class, we had all our best players in one class. I don't think any team in the country lost as many senior starters in one year as we did," says Musselman.

Corky Taylor never caught on with the Celtics—the Ohio State publicity followed him even then, forcing General Manager Red Auerbach and Coach Tommy Heinson to send him to Europe, where he played for one season—but he has no regrets about playing at the University of Minnesota, even after everything that happened there. "The team I was on was important in terms of building up basketball in the state— players like Kevin McHale have said they wanted to become Gophers after watching that team. Former players like Mel Northaway and Archie Clark helped me a lot. And in return, I spent a lot of time with the players that came

after me, like Mychal Thompson. That's important. It's a special thing to be an M man, and I was proud to carry that on."

Those five players formed the core of Minnesota's great teams of the previous two years, and Bill Musselman wasn't left with much. He recruited junior college transfer Dennis Shaffer from Mason City, Iowa, and freshman Philip "Flip" Saunders, who would start right away, along with juniors Phil Filer and Pete Gilcud, both junior college transfers from the year before. The Gophers jumped out to a 6-2 nonconference record behind double-figure scoring from Shaffer and Filer, before running into 12th-ranked New Mexico. That first true test showed that this was not a particularly deep or experienced club, and New Mexico walked away with a 102-68 win. Minnesota ran through the rest of its relatively easy nonconference schedule to finish at 6-4, but the Big Ten would not be that simple. The Gophers lost

■ *Saunders goes up with the ball against Northwestern.*

■ *Mark Olberding goes to the hoop against Michigan State.*

their first four conference games, though the home losses to Michigan and Michigan State were each by one point, and they fell to Ohio State in Columbus by only four. They came back to win five of their next six to even their conference mark at 5-5. But reality set in during the final three conference games; Minnesota lost all of them, finishing with a 6-8 conference record in sixth place. Dennis Shaffer led the team in scoring with 17.3 points per game.

"I felt that team overachieved," Musselman remembers. "It was proba-

bly as overachieving a team as I've ever coached. I felt some of my Ashland College teams had more talent. Our center was 6-foot-6, we didn't have any size, and we weren't a quick team. But we beat Wisconsin twice with their seven-footer. How we ever beat people with seven-footers is beyond me."

The Gophers' prospects looked a little better for 1974-75. Bill Musselman had veterans Dennis Shaffer, Flip Saunders, Charles Sims, Pete Gilcud, and Phil Filer returning from the previous season, and he recruited junior college transfers Mark Landsberger and Mark Olberding, and freshmen Mychal Thompson and Osborne Lockhart. Once again, the Gophers opened fast during their nonconference schedule. They entered the Big Ten season with a 7-1 record, and with Landsberger, Shaffer, Olberding, and Saunders all averaging in double figures, and Thompson averaging 9.6 points per game. Olberding was the star of the Big Ten opener at Wisconsin, scoring 20 points and pulling in eight rebounds as Minnesota took away a 61-46 victory. The Gophers beat Purdue, 54-51, and trounced Illinois, 75-47 at home to push their conference record to 3-0, fueling hopes of another Big Ten title.

But once again, the Gophers were in for a reality check as they moved further into the conference season. They traveled to Columbus to take on an Ohio State team that was not as strong as in years past, but the Buckeyes snapped a losing streak, beating the Gophers 76-67. Minnesota then lost to Indiana on the road by 20 points to fall to 3-2 in the conference. But they reeled off five victories in their next six games, and were 8-3 and tied for second place when they headed home to take on Indiana. The Hoosiers, though, were on their way to a 31-1 season and the Big Ten title, and they easily dispatched the Gophers 69-54 before a sellout crowd in the Barn. Minnesota split its final six games, finishing at 11-6 and a respectable third place in the Big Ten, and 18-8 overall.

But things quickly began to turn bad for Bill Musselman and the Golden Gophers. Mark Landsberger, who finished the 1974-75 season second in scoring for the Gophers, transferred to Arizona State; he was one of 11 players who transferred from the Gophers during the four-year tenure of the intense

■ *The Gophers play for a sold-out Williams Arena crowd.*

and demanding Musselman. To make matters worse, the University and the NCAA were investigating Musselman's program for alleged rules violations. Many of the transgressions Musselman was accused of were minor, such as his allowing Gopher players to stay overnight at his summer basketball camp at Gustavus Adolphus College in St. Peter, Minnesota, after they played basketball there well into the night. But there were also allegations of cash payments from boosters to players, players scalping their complimentary tickets, and recruiting violations, and the NCAA took the violations very seriously. It was another stressful distraction in what had been a controversial tenure almost since the day Musselman took the Gopher job in 1971.

"When I looked at my situation in 1975, the University did not pay me a lot of money, and the pressure of that job, with the football program being down, was tremendous. I was told I had to fill the arena because the program needed money, and we not only filled the arena, but we also filled the hockey arena. If it wasn't for the basketball camp I ran during the summer, I would hardly have made any money. I love the University of Minnesota, it's a great school, and I have great memories there. But for the pressure that I was under, I just couldn't do it forever."

Musselman says now that he had already turned down one American Basketball Association coaching job after his first season at Minnesota— a guaranteed contract from the league's Memphis franchise that was several times the annual salary of $20,000 the University paid Musselman when he was first hired. With the aggravation the Minnesota job brought with it, Musselman often wondered to himself why he turned that first job down. So when another opportunity came up to coach in the ABA, he snatched it up, signing with the San Diego Sails on July 28, 1975. Musselman brought further controversy on himself by convincing Mark Olberding to leave the University with him before his eligibility was used up and sign a seven-figure contract with the Sails.

Bill Musselman left the University of Minnesota with a 69-32 record, the best winning percentage ever for a Gopher head coach. He also made good on his promise to bring a Big Ten champi-

onship to Minnesota, and he fulfilled the athletic department's mandate that he fill Williams Arena for every game. But the NCAA ultimately decided the Gophers had committed 128 rule violations during his time there, banned the school from national television appearances and postseason play for two years, and reduced the number of available scholarships to three from six for those same two years.

The University of Minnesota men's basketball program was ready for some smooth sailing. As the search committee geared up to select its fifth coach in eight years, its task was to find somebody who could win and draw fans on a regular basis, and who could keep the program above reproach and in the good graces of the community.

■ **Opposite** *Mychal Thompson pulls down a rebound with Mark Olberding helping out.*

■ *Musselman had some advice for Olberding as he prepares to enter the game.*

SECTION 6

After four seasons with Bill Musselman as head coach, the next leader of the Minnesota Gophers would have to be brave. Not only would that coach have to face the defection of several Gopher players—Mark Olberding and Mark Landsberger chief among them—but he would have the specter of an NCAA investigation from indiscretions that had happened during the Musselman era hanging over his head.

Jim Dutcher took the challenge. After serving as head coach at Eastern Michigan and then as Johnny Orr's chief assistant at Michigan for three years, Dutcher felt he was ready for a Big Ten head coaching job, and he was willing to take on a seeming basket case of a program to get it. Actually, though, Dutcher didn't even know he was a candidate until he was 4,000 miles away.

"I didn't even know the job was open," Dutcher remembers. "We were playing some exhibitions in Egypt, and I was walking through the lobby of the Cairo Hilton when some guy I'd never met before walked up to me and said he'd heard I was a finalist for the job at Minnesota. I thought I'd better find out more about it."

Once he took the job, Dutcher's first step was to fly to Arizona and meet with Mark Landsberger. Landsberger had not yet attended his first class at Arizona—which would have made his

■ *Trent Tucker celebrates the Gophers' 1982 Big Ten championship by cutting down the Williams Arena net.*

transfer irreversible—and Dutcher wanted to pursuade him to come back to Minnesota. He failed, but Dutcher still had more flying to do. He headed to Miami, where he met in the airport with Mychal Thompson and Osborne Lockhart to try and convince the two Bahamian sophomores (principally the budding superstar Thompson) to stay. This time, he succeeded. "There was a question about everybody, since the program was in such disarray," Dutcher says. "I met with Ray Williams and Flip Saunders, I met with everybody. Once I was finished I had six scholarship players and six walk-ons."

The Gophers opened the season with some relatively easy tests; they cruised over South Dakota State, 96-74, with Mychal Thompson scoring 31 points and pulling down 15 rebounds and Flip Saunders adding 22 points; they whipped North Dakota, 74-60, behind 27 points from Thompson; and they dumped Loyola of Chicago, 68-55.

Then the Gophers, picked to finish in the Big Ten's second division, took the Williams Arena floor against the Marquette Warriors, who were ranked second in the nation. Thompson had 29 points and 16 rebounds, Lockhart had 16 points, and Ray Williams had 17. Minnesota shot nearly 58 percent from the floor, 77 percent from the line, and outre-

bounded the physical Warriors 32-26. And the Gophers won, 77-73.

Minnesota ran its nonconference record to a perfect 8-0 with victories over Montana State and Stanford on the road, and Penn State and Creighton at home to take the Pillsbury Classic, before opening Jim Dutcher's first Big Ten season against Purdue at Williams Arena. The Gophers thoroughly outplayed the Boilermakers in the first half and walked into the locker room holding a 14-point lead. But that lead evaporated in the second half as the Gophers, who often used only six players a game during the 1975-76 season, had to turn frequently to their bench because of foul trouble. The game was tied at 83 at the end of regulation. Then Mychal Thompson fouled out with 33 points and 12 rebounds, and Gary Korkowski and Dave Winey fouled out as well. Gus Johnson hit 11 points for the Gophers in two overtimes, and Osborne Lockhart added six of his 20 in the extra periods, but it wasn't enough to hold off the Boilermakers, who came out on top, 111-110.

The Gophers then went to Jim Dutcher's former home at Crisler Arena, and were throttled by Michigan, 95-72. They returned to Williams Arena and earned their first Big Ten victory for Dutcher, 77-68 over Illinois, led by Ray Williams. The 6-foot-2 guard played most of the game at forward and came through, scoring 26 points, grabbing 12 rebounds, and handing out five assists. But when Iowa came to the Barn, the Gophers could not keep up with the Hawkeyes, losing 71-68.

The Gophers played the next game, at Northwestern, without Mychal Thompson. He was in St. Louis to testify before the NCAA Council after admitting he sold his complimentary game tickets, a violation of NCAA rules. Thompson had been declared ineligible, but he was trying to have that eligibility restored. The distraction was enough to make Minnesota plod to a 49-31 halftime deficit, and even a valiant comeback effort wasn't enough; the Gophers lost, 85-77.

Thompson was not successful in convincing the NCAA to restore his eligibility, so he and his attorneys tried a different tack: They sought and received a court order, allowing Thompson to play until the issue was finally resolved. So he hopped a plane to Madison to be

a part of a truly bizarre 96-84 victory over the Badgers. In a game with five technical fouls, including two against Dutcher, Badger Coach John Powless spent the final 10 seconds of the game

■ *Ray Williams goes up for two points in the 1977 Pillsbury Classic at Met Center in Bloomington.*

■ *Mychal Thompson runs into an Illinois player as he goes in for a layup.*

leading the Wisconsin pep band and 5,566 fans in a rendition of "Three Blind Mice." He was upset because while Thompson had drawn four personal fouls in the first half, the officials didn't call the fifth foul that would remove him from the game until there were four minutes left and the Gophers were comfortably ahead. In the meantime, Thompson scored 29 points and had 17 rebounds; Osborne Lockhart added 28 points, Ray Williams 26, and Phil Saunders 14.

Back at Williams Arena, the Gophers lost 85-76 to Indiana in a game in which both teams shot better than 61 percent from the floor. They came back, though, to intimidate Ohio State, win-ning 82-69. The chief intimidator was Mychal Thompson; besides scoring 34 points and grabbing 12 rebounds, the 6-foot-10 center also blocked 12 Buckeye shots. Dave Winey had his best game of the year to that point, scoring 12 and hauling in 9 rebounds. The tables were turned on the Gophers a few days later in East Lansing, as Michigan State dom-inated them from the opening tip, win-ning 75-63.

With a conference record of 3-6, the Gophers were playing for respect as February rolled around. They earned some in their next game, traveling to Champaign and handling the Illini, 72-62. Thompson had 30 points, and four of the five starters, including Winey,

Williams, and Saunders, all scored in double figures. It was back to reality in Iowa City, where the Hawkeyes shut down the Gophers and held them to their lowest point total of the season as they won, 65-58. Things got worse from there. A relatively weak Northwestern club came to Williams Arena and embarrassed the sloppy Gophers, 75-69.

As bad as the Gophers were against the Wildcats, they were that good in the next home game against the Wisconsin Badgers. Thompson had 33 points and 17 rebounds; Williams had 17 points, 11 assists, and nine rebounds; Lockhart had 17 points; Winey added 10 points and 10 boards; and every Gopher in uniform got in the game. The end result was a 98-74 victory for a team whose pride had taken a severe beating during the previous eight losses in 12 conference games.

But pride can take a team only so far, and not as far as a win over the talented Indiana Hoosiers. The Gophers traveled to Bloomington to take on the top-ranked team in the nation, with hopes of snapping Indiana's 54-game regular-season winning streak. Indiana was just too much, winning 85-76. The Gophers bounced back in Columbus, beating Ohio State, 89-73, and they came back home in a nationally televised game to beat Michigan State, 71-61.

Then came 13th-ranked Michigan, the Gophers' final home game of the season, and a major test of the team's pride. Pride won out—with the help of 32 points and 10 rebounds from Thompson, 13 points and 13 boards from Winey, and 25 points from Williams — and the Gophers stunned the Wolverines, 81-79. The Gophers lost their final game on the road to Purdue to finish at 16-10 on the season, 8-10 and in sixth place in the conference. Thompson was second in the conference in scoring with 26.4 points per game, Williams was fourth at 22.1, and Thompson led the Big Ten in rebounding by more than a full board per game at 12.3.

If 1975-76 was a rebuilding year, the Gophers of 1976-77 considered themselves fully rebuilt. Not only were Mychal Thompson, Ray Williams, Osborne Lockhart, Phil Saunders, and Dave Winey returning from the previous year, but Jim Dutcher also brought in a new recruit from Hibbing High School, a 6-foot-11 freshman named Kevin McHale. Because of the NCAA probation as a lingering reminder of the Bill Musselman era, the Gophers could not appear on television, they could not go to a postseason tournament, and they would not be ranked in the prestigious Associated Press poll, though they could be included in other polls.

"We had a great blend of players that year, with McHale coming in—that was an important factor, bringing in a big guy who could score," Dutcher says.

After a close, 86-82, exhibition win over Athletes in Action, the Gophers opened their nonconference season against North Dakota State and began a series of victories—many of them routs —that would take Minnesota all the way into the Big Ten season. North Dakota State fell, 101-68, as Osborne Lockhart had 29 points. Detroit came next, and Mychal Thompson scored 31 points on 15 of 17 shooting, despite sitting out more than 15 minutes of the game with foul trouble. Four other Gophers scored in double figures, and the Gophers won easily, 104-80. Northern Michigan was next to topple at the Barn, going down 96-50 behind a balanced Gophers scoring attack that saw Williams with 21, Thompson and McHale with 16 each (Thompson also had 11 rebounds and McHale 12), and Lockhart with 15. Nebraska did a better job at controlling the tempo of the game and actually led at halftime, but the Cornhuskers still lost, 66-58.

After a break for final exams, the Gophers welcomed Vermont to Williams Arena for Minnesota's fifth straight easy win, 96-61. Then they traveled to Milwaukee for their first true test of the season, against second-ranked Marquette. The Gophers, determined to show they were among the nation's elite despite their 18th ranking at the time, led by 19 at the half, and by as many as 24 early in the second half. But Marquette, which would go on to win the National Championship, cut that lead to two with less than three minutes remaining. Behind 23 points and 16 rebounds from Thompson, and determined leadership by Williams, Minnesota held on to beat the Warriors, 66-59.

Minnesota slipped past Kansas State, 62-60, and ripped Cornell, 84-54, and Montana, 102-81, to move its record to 9-0 before starting the Big Ten season. They opened against Iowa before 17,508 fans at Williams Arena, and going in the

■ *Osborne Lockhart dishes out an assist against Indiana.*

third straight meeting the two teams headed to overtime, this time tied at 55. But Ray Williams had fouled out in the middle of the second half, and the Gophers missed his leadership as they fell, 66-64, to end their 11-game winning streak and move their conference record to 2-1.

But a team with that much talent and determination was not going to let a conference loss set it back; the Gophers promptly went on a five-game tear, beginning with an 82-64 rout of Wisconsin before 16,892 at Williams Arena. Ray Williams dominated the game, with 28 points, 13 rebounds, and four assists including a dazzling behind-the-back blind pass and a full-court bomb to Osborne Lockhart. Michigan State came next, losing to the Gophers, 75-70, at Williams Arena. Then the Gophers headed to Bloomington to take on Indiana—always a herculean assignment. The team's Bahamian contingent—Thompson and Lockhart—were the only Gophers in double figures, but they scored 59 points between them and led Minnesota to a stunning 79-60 victory over the Hoosiers. The next game, against Ohio State, was switched from Columbus to Williams Arena at the last minute because of an energy shortage in Ohio due to a coal strike, and 16,192 still turned out to cheer on a tired and sluggish Gophers team to a 77-67 victory over the Buckeyes. The Gophers followed that with another home victory, this one 79-53 over Northwestern.

The fifth-ranked and conference-leading Michigan Wolverines came to the Barn next, for a much-anticipated showdown between the two conference powers. Thompson and Williams scored 20 points each, McHale added 18, but the Gophers' defense collapsed under the weight of the Wolverines' running game, and Michigan won, 86-80.

Dutcher remembers that as a game the Gophers could have won, if only the officials had payed better attention. "We were tied 80-80, and a Michigan player put up a shot that hit one of the guide wires running above the court. Phil Hubbard caught it and put it in, and they won the game. We were all waiting for a whistle that never came, since those wires were out of play, and Michigan scored on a dead ball."

The Gophers had another challenge coming up: Don't let that crushing

Gophers appeared to be the better team. But much of that better team—Williams, Winey, and McHale—fouled out, and Thompson played with four fouls for much of the second half. Minnesota almost blew a 22-point lead with seven minutes to play, but Osborne Lockhart came through with 21 points, and the Gophers pulled out a tough 78-68 win.

Illinois was an easier test. The ninth-ranked Gophers, especially foul-magnet Mychal Thompson, held their fouls to a minimum, and they coasted, 83-69. The Gophers headed to West Lafayette to take on Purdue, and for the loss lead to a letdown against Ohio State. But Minnesota came to Columbus and did just the opposite, whipping the Buckeyes 91-65, led by Kevin McHale's best game to that point, 23 points, 15 rebounds, and four assists.

Minnesota raised its record to 19-2 overall, 10-2 in the Big Ten with a 65-61 win over Indiana at the Barn, then headed to East Lansing to try for its seventh road win in eight tries. The end result was a 99-77 thumping of Michigan State. Then came the showdown in Ann Arbor, as Michigan and Minnesota met to determine who would control

Williams. Minnesota escaped a tenacious Illinois team, 72-70, at home, then they barely beat Wisconsin on the road, 64-61, when Dave Winey made a last-minute layup to put them ahead for good. The season wrapped up on a positive note, as five Gophers scored in double figures and they walloped Northwestern, 105-82.

The Gophers' final 1976-77 record was 24-3 overall and 15-3 in the Big Ten, an amazing record for a second-place team. They beat three NCAA Tournament teams (Marquette, the ultimate champion, Kansas State, and

their own destiny for the Big Ten title. But it was never really a contest. Michigan outplayed the Gophers from beginning to end, outrebounding, outshooting, outdefending, and eventually outscoring Minnesota, 89-70.

While the Gophers' Big Ten title hopes were foundering, they still had four games left in which to preserve the school's best record since 1919. And for the fourth time in as many tries, they had to play an overtime game against Purdue. This time it was at Williams Arena and this time, finally, the Gophers won, 84-78, thanks to 29 points, 16 rebounds, and seven assists from Ray

Detroit). Mychal Thompson and Ray Williams became Minnesota's first All-Americans since Ron Behagen and Jim Brewer in 1973. Thompson averaged 22.0 points and 8.9 rebounds per game, and Williams had 18.0 points, 7.5 rebounds, and 6.1 assists per game. And nobody really cared that Thompson eventually lost his court case, was ruled retroactively ineligible for the entire season, and the Gophers were forced to officially forfeit all those games for a record-book tally of 0-27, 0-18 in the conference. What everybody knew was that in terms of record and talent, this was possibly the best bas-

■ *Coach Jim Dutcher shouts instructions to his team at Williams Arena during its 81-79 win over Michigan in 1976.*

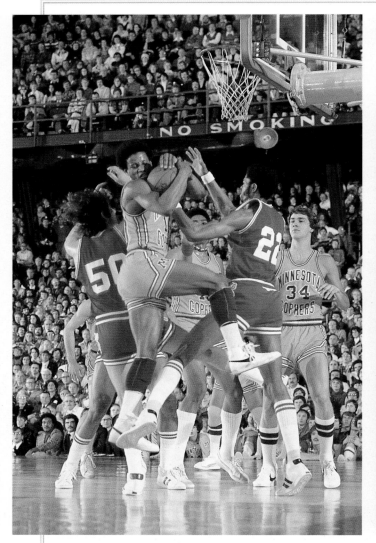

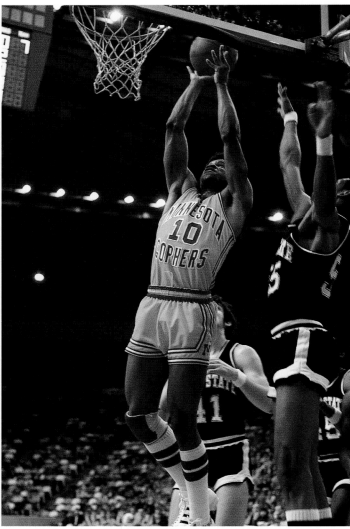

■ *Ray Williams pulls down a tough rebound at Williams Arena (left) during the Gophers' trememdous 24-3 season in 1976-77. At right, Williams goes up for two points in the 1977 Pillsbury Classic at Met Center in Bloomington.*

ketball team in the University of Minnesota's history.

"I didn't even really know they had done that," McHale says of the official forfeits. "It didn't really matter, though. We had played the games, and we had won the games because we were the better basketball team, and we and everybody else knew it."

"It was incredible that we were 15-3 in the conference and wound up in second place," Dutcher says. "From a talent standpoint, we had a team that would have been able to compete for a national championship."

The Gophers had to live with the loss of Ray Williams to the NBA in 1977-78, but they still had Mychal Thompson (who turned down a million-dollar pro contract to return for his senior year), Kevin McHale, Dave Winey, and captain Osborne Lockhart, and they still hoped for something close to their superb season of the year before. But what happened in November and December quashed that optimism pretty quickly, as Thompson had to sit out a

seven-game NCAA suspension, Winey a three-game suspension, and McHale and likely starter Ricky Wallace started the year with injuries. The suddenly-inexperienced Gophers suffered through a miserable nonconference season.

"I injured my achilles tendon right away, and it bothered me a great deal," McHale remembers. "Then I tried to come back too quickly and I injured my foot. It was very frustrating."

After a home exhibition victory over the tired and overmatched Cuban national team, the Gophers lost on the road to South Carolina, 62-55, as sophomore guard James Jackson, a transfer from Boston College, led Minnesota with only 12 points. They edged lowly Eastern Kentucky, 61-59, behind sophomore Steve Lingenfelter's 15 points and 16 rebounds—despite the fact that Lingenfelter lost one of his front teeth early in the game. The Gophers traveled to Chicago and lost to Loyola, 70-66, and returned to Williams Arena to try for a third straight upset over Marquette, the defending national champions. But the Warriors were not about to let that happen again, and they stomped on the Gophers, 61-44. Minnesota continued its anemic offensive performance against Nebraska; only Jackson scored in double figures (11 points) in a 63-49 loss.

Mychal Thompson returned from his suspension in time for the Pillsbury Classic opener against Air Force, and with a front line of Thompson, McHale, and Winey averaging over 6-foot-10, Minnesota won, 66-50. They won again in the Classic final, this time against 17th-ranked Florida State, 88-74, to bring their nonconference record to a paltry 4-5 and prove Thompson's importance to this basketball team.

The Gophers started the Big Ten season in difficult fashion, against Michigan State and its vaunted freshman, Earvin "Magic" Johnson. He proved why he had the nickname, too, scoring 31 points in his first conference game, outpacing even Mychal Thompson's 27 points in an 87-83 Spartan victory. The Gophers kept waiting for things to get better, but they stayed bad. Michigan, a team the Gophers should have beaten, did the beating instead, 69-65.

After going 0-2 on the road in its first two Big Ten games, the Gophers could not afford to lose at home. They didn't, beating Indiana for the third straight time, 75-62, behind Mychal Thompson's 21 points and 12 rebounds. Minnesota hit its stride against Ohio State, crushing the Buckeyes, 72-47. The Gophers beat Illinois, 70-66, as Thompson scored 27 points and grabbed 12 rebounds. Then they headed to Madison, overcame a 13-point deficit and beat Wisconsin, 61-51. But Purdue and center Joe Barry Carroll stopped the Gophers cold in West Lafayette, 72-64, wasting Kevin McHale's best game to that point, with 18 points and 10 rebounds.

Minnesota was tired, sluggish, and the team shot poorly in its next road game against Northwestern. Fortunately the Wildcats were worse, and the Gophers escaped with a 69-58 win. They returned home inspired by the news that Michigan had upset Michigan State, and the Gophers were then only one and a half games out of first place in the conference with 10 games left to play. They used that inspiration to shoot 64 percent from the field and bury Iowa, 82-71. Then the Gophers beat North-

western again, 80-69, as the Bahamian duo dominated; Osborne Lockhart had 25 points and Mychal Thompson added 23. Thompson had 24 points and 14 rebounds as the Gophers won yet again, this time 64-55 against Wisconsin at Williams Arena. Thompson was on a roll. He kept on rolling through Iowa City, scoring 34 and adding 16 rebounds to bury the Hawkeyes, 78-65. Then it was on to Champaign to face Illinois. Minnesota scored its sixth straight win and its 10th in its last 11 games, 75-69. Best of all, that victory put the Gophers at 10-3 in the Big Ten, good enough for a share of first place.

Williams Arena was packed with 17,477 screaming fans as Purdue took the raised floor as the last team that had beaten the Gophers. Minnesota had been criticized by some for its lack of intensity, but nobody was saying that after the Gophers played a white-hot game, shooting 58 percent from the floor and outmuscling the Boilermakers inside. The final score was 79-72 Minnesota, and the Gophers were poised to walk away from the 1977-78 season with

■ *Mychal Thompson puts in a breakaway finger-roll against Indiana.*

the conference crown. The very next day nationally-ranked Louisville came to the Barn for a nationally-televised game against the exhausted Gophers. But they were also the pumped up Gophers, and they came through again, behind 21 points from McHale, 20 from Thompson, and 14 from Lockhart, to win, 72-71.

Minnesota went on to Columbus to face lightly-regarded Ohio State, but perhaps they were looking past the Buckeyes to the season-ending showdowns with Indiana, Michigan, and Michigan State. The Buckeyes forced overtime, then outplayed the Gophers in the third period to win, 94-87, and snap Minnesota's eight-game winning streak and knock the Gophers out of a share of first place. They followed that with a dismal road performance against Indiana, getting shellacked, 68-47. The Gophers finally got their act together again against Michigan at Williams Arena, winning 84-78 on the strength of dominating performances from Kevin McHale (25 points and 11 rebounds) and James Jackson (22 points). But Michigan State also won that day, clinching the conference championship, but not dampening the intensity that would charge the meeting of the two teams at Williams Arena for the season finale.

In their last game as Gophers, Lockhart scored 17, Winey two, and Thompson 20. Those 20 added to Thompson's all-time Minnesota record and set the all-time Big Ten Conference scoring record. At halftime, Athletic Director Paul Giel retired Thompson's number 43. All that, and the Gophers lost, 71-70. But their 12-6 conference record was good enough for a tie for second in the conference, and even after their atrocious start, Minnesota finished with a respectable 17-11 overall record. Thompson was named All-American for the second straight year, this time as a consensus pick, again led the conference with a 22.7 scoring average, and he was second in rebounds with 11.6.

"We had another good year in '77-'78, but we missed not having Flip Saunders and Ray Williams," McHale says. "And as for Mychal, all the distractions finally got to him."

As November 1978 rolled around, Mychal Thompson was in Oregon starring for the Portland Trailblazers after walking out of Williams Arena with the school scoring and rebounding records.

Osborne Lockhart was on his way to the Harlem Globetrotters, for whom he would still be playing nearly two decades later. Dave Winey had graduated as well. It was left for junior Kevin McHale, Hibbing's favorite son, to lead a talented, but young, squad to follow up two successful seasons without the nucleus responsible for that success. McHale could turn to only one veteran among the regulars, James Jackson. He had to rely on several freshman, including a promising forward named Trent Tucker, in addition to forward Leo Rautins, guard Darryl Mitchell, forward Brian Pederson, and guard Mark Hall.

"It was a rebuilding year," says Tucker, reflecting on his decision to come from Michigan to attend the U. "We had five freshmen and one junior, Kevin McHale, and it gave me an opportunity as a freshman to play right away."

With that lineup, the Gophers opened their season against Idaho in front of 16,553 hopeful fans at Williams Arena. The veterans led the team, with Jackson scoring 21 and McHale adding 19 points and 12 rebounds, as the Gophers coasted to a 72-57 win. Unfortunately, that would be a high point of the 1978-79 season.

Nebraska won the Gophers' next contest, in Lincoln, 58-48, as McHale led an anemic Minnesota offence with only 14, and Tucker was the only other Gopher in double figures with 10. Leo Rautins scored 31 points to lead Minnesota to a grueling, double-overtime home win over Loyola. But the Gophers deflated again on the road, falling to Kansas State, 72-62, mostly because the Gophers made only 43 percent of their field goals. Two weeks off for winter finals didn't help the Gophers much. They fell to Marquette in Milwaukee, 72-55, again shooting less than 45 percent from the floor. The Gophers returned home to face the South Florida Brahman Bulls with Trent Tucker out with a hyperextended knee, Kevin McHale missing most of the game with a sprained ankle, and Leo Rautins playing despite suffering from a draining viral infection. Still, the Gophers managed to hold off the weak Bulls, 69-54.

That game was a momentary spell of good shooting for a Gophers club that had tremendous trouble putting the ball in the hole. Minnesota entertained South Carolina at Williams Arena,

■ **Opposite** *Kevin McHale goes up for a dunk as two Purdue defenders watch helplessly.*

played good defense, and walked away the losers, 57-53, on 35 percent field goal shooting. The Gamecocks didn't even have to substitute; their five starters played the entire game against the poor-shooting Gophers. That led Minnesota to the start of the annual Pillsbury Classic, and the overmatched Houston Cougars. McHale had 20 points and 17 rebounds, Mitchell added 15 points and 13 rebounds, and freshman Gary Holmes had 13 boards on the way to an 80-67 win. In the championship game, only Kevin McHale hit double figures for Minnesota (22 points and 14 rebounds), but it was enough, as the Gophers slipped past Georgia Tech, 57-56, for their fifth straight Pillsbury Classic title.

After a lackluster, 5-4 nonconference schedule, the Gophers were hoping for better luck—and better shooting—against their Big Ten foes. Indeed, they shot better against Michigan in the conference opener, as five Gophers scored in double figures, led by 18 apiece from Mark Hall and Trent Tucker. But the outcome was more of the same: an 88-75 defeat. The Gophers then had to face the nation's top-ranked team, Michigan State, on the road, and they nearly beat the Spartans. Minnesota shot 55 percent, led by 19 from McHale. Mark Hall held Magic Johnson to nine points on two-for-10 shooting, though Magic did dish out 12 assists. The Spartans barely escaped with a 69-62 win.

The Michigan State game, though a loss, was a good loss. It gave the Gophers confidence enough to head home and walk over Indiana, 80-63, behind 26 points from McHale, 19 from Hall, and 16 from Tucker. The Gophers almost got overconfident for the next home game against Northwestern. In the locker room, trailing by nine points, Dutcher launched into an ear-splitting diatribe that woke up his team, which rallied to win, 60-58. The Gophers hit the road, and they played well against 11th-ranked Ohio State, but not well enough. The Buckeyes overcame 25 points from Mark Hall and won, 83-80. Back at friendly Williams Arena, Kevin McHale scored 31 points to lead the Gophers past the Badgers, 82-72, on 67 percent shooting.

Purdue came to Williams Arena and very nearly lost to the Gophers, but the Boilermakers' superb shooting and physical play resulted in a 64-61 Min-

nesota loss. Iowa's fast break and hard-nosed play were too much for the young and tired Gophers in Iowa City, and the Hawkeyes powered to an 81-64 win. And the Gophers' shooting failed them again in the next game at Champaign. They shot a mere 32 percent from the field and were beaten 67-57. The Gophers had one more chance against Iowa, this time before a sellout crowd at Williams Arena, but the result was even worse. Minnesota shot 39 percent to Iowa's 62 percent, and seven Hawkeyes scored in double figures on the way to a 97-71 Iowa rout.

Three months into the season, the Gophers finally got their first road win, riding Kevin McHale's 32 points to a 74-72 win over Wisconsin. But they returned home and lost to Illinois, 59-57, as Trent Tucker's seemingly sure layup was blocked from behind as the clock wound down. The Gophers tried once more for an upset of Ohio State, and McHale did his part with 28 points and 13 rebounds. But the team that had come close so many other times that season did it again, putting together a strong run only to fall short, 74-68. It wasn't that close next time, on the road against Purdue. The Boilermakers blew out the Gophers from beginning to end, 80-56.

Jim Dutcher had lifted Trent Tucker from the starting lineup in favor of Bill Duffy in a desperate effort to build some momentum and win some games. But it was Tucker who came off the bench, pulled down the rebound of an errant Kevin McHale shot, and put in the follow-up with six seconds remaining to give the Gophers a 73-71 overtime win over Northwestern in Evanston. They moved on to Bloomington, and Indiana outscored the Gophers two-to-one in the second half and ran away with a 71-46 win. Minnesota was able to return home next, but they had to face Michigan State, which would clinch the Big Ten championship with a victory. The Spartans got their win, 76-63, to plunge Minnesota to 5-12 in the conference, and 10-16 overall, with just one game left to play.

It was a frustrated Gopher team that took the Williams Arena court against Michigan. And they took their frustrations out on the Wolverines; Darryl Mitchell hit 24 points, McHale had 16, and Tucker 13, on the way to a 78-69 win.

"It was a very difficult year, because we had a lot of young guys, and I was

> **WE WERE BACK TO FULL SCHOLARSHIP STRENGTH THAT YEAR, SO WE HAD SIX FRESHMEN," DUTCHER REMEMBERS. "THAT WAS A VERY FRUSTRATING YEAR ALL AROUND, BUT IT WAS ESPECIALLY FRUSTRATING FOR KEVIN, PLAYING WITH ALL THOSE FRESHMEN— THAT PROBABLY KEPT HIM FROM BREAKING MYCHAL'S ALL-TIME SCORING RECORD. BUT KEVIN WAS NEVER A PROBLEM. HE JUST LOVED THE GAME TOO MUCH.**

the only upperclassman on the team," McHale says. "Those guys really didn't understand how to play yet. I suppose I was the team leader, but I'm a firm believer that people lead themselves. But we didn't really have enough of a mix of older and younger players."

Their 6-12 conference record put them in eighth place, the Gophers' worst position since John Kundla's last season as coach in 1967-68. McHale was the only Minnesota player to average in double figures, with 17.9 points, and he added 9.6 rebounds per game.

"We were back to full scholarship strength that year, so we had six freshmen," Dutcher remembers. "That was a very frustrating year all around, but it was especially frustrating for Kevin, playing with all those freshmen—that probably kept him from breaking Mychal's all-time scoring record. But Kevin was never a problem. He just loved the game too much."

But Jim Dutcher could look forward to the return of Trent Tucker, Mark Hall, Darryl Mitchell, and Gary Holmes, all one year more mature. That was in addition to transfers Gary Copperud, Carl Dale, and Andy Thompson, and a crop of freshmen that included Ben Coleman from Minneapolis North High School, Zebedee Howell, Bruce Kaupa, and a 7-foot-2 center from Lake City, Minnesota, named Randy Breuer. They knew they could look back on 1978-79 as an official rebuilding year, and cause Gopher fans to look forward to better things.

But the Gophers were picked to finish near the bottom of the Big Ten in 1979-80, and they opened with a sloppy win, with McHale putting in 21 and Tucker adding 20 to pace a 77-56 win against Eastern Michigan, Dutcher's former team. Things got even easier against Fresno State, with McHale scoring 21 points and grabbing 13 rebounds to dominate the overmatched Bulldogs. The Gophers began to relax against North Dakota, but Dutcher chewed them out at halftime and the team responded with an 87-60 win behind 24 points from McHale, 16 from Mark Hall, and 10 points in 18 minutes from Zeb Howell. Against Nebraska at Williams Arena, Minnesota clung to a 58-52 lead with less than four minutes remaining. But the Gophers went on a 17-6 tear, behind a final total of 26 points and 11 rebounds from McHale and 23 points from Hall, and won, 78-58.

Those nonconference wins were wonderful, but they all came at home. Nobody knew how the Gophers would perform on the road, and when they traveled to Tennessee, the prognosis was not good. Hall scored 21 against the Volunteers, but he and his teammates threw the ball away far too much, and a 20-12 first-half lead eventually turned into a 71-64 defeat. Things got worse in Tallahassee as the Gophers took on Florida State. The game justified McHale's frustration about being the only grizzled veteran on a team that could win a lot of games if only it had more experience. McHale scored 32 points and had seven rebounds despite playing much of the second half with a sprained knee, but even that was not enough to stop the Seminoles from routing Minnesota, 112-91.

Undefeated Kansas State came to the Barn and ran into a 14-foot wall of Gophers that stopped them, 78-61. The 6-foot-11 Kevin McHale scored 23 points and had 11 rebounds, and the 7-foot-2 Breuer added 18 points. Rutgers came next for the first round of the Pillsbury Classic, and they were hopelessly outmanned by Minnesota, which had six players in double figures and won, 98-59. In the final against Texas A&M, McHale and Tucker each hit a pair of free throws in the final 20 seconds to give the Gophers their sixth straight Pillsbury Classic title, 69-63.

After its 7-2 nonconference schedule, Minnesota opened the Big Ten season with consecutive road games against Michigan and Michigan State. In Ann Arbor, Breuer led the Gophers with 17 points and 11 rebounds, and the Gophers outrebounded, outshot, and out-assisted the Wolverines. But Michigan went to the line 24 more times than the Gophers and held McHale to just 14 points; as a result, the home team came away a winner, 71-67. Things went a bit better in East Lansing, as the Gophers flew to a 40-15 halftime lead. The Spartans came back in the second half, but Minnesota had four players with at least 15 points—McHale and Tucker with 19 apiece, Mitchell with 16, and Hall with 15—and they won, 93-80.

Back at Williams Arena, Wisconsin held the more-talented Gophers at bay for most of the game, but 5-foot-11 guard Carl Dale sparked Minnesota with two late steals and with tough defense on Badgers star Wes Matthews, and the

Gophers finally pulled out an 82-76 win in overtime. Illinois came to town two days later, and the fatigued Gophers had a difficult time dragging themselves up and down the court. But Illinois helped by sending Minnesota to the free throw line 29 times (they made 27 of those tries), and captain McHale scored 25 points to lead his team to a 79-75 victory.

McHale was shooting 61 percent from the floor until the next game, at second-ranked Ohio State. But on this night he hit only five of 14 field goal attempts, including one of nine in the second half, and the Gophers couldn't overcome his lack of production, losing 75-70 in overtime. But Minnesota was not inclined to lose two games in a row, and they didn't ever want to lose at Williams Arena, so when No. 11 Purdue came to town, McHale and the entire team rose to the occasion. Tucker scored 19, Hall had 12, Breuer and McHale had 10 each, and McHale added seven rebounds and five blocks. Minnesota upset the Boilermakers, 67-61.

They were not so lucky in Iowa City, where the Hawkeyes beat the Gophers, 80-73, despite 23 points from McHale and 17 from Hall. But they traveled to Evanston and bounced back with a 74-64 win, behind 22 points and 12 rebounds from McHale. The win was especially important because it put the Gophers at the top of the Big Ten at 6-3—not bad for a team most people had predicted to finish eighth or ninth in the conference before the season began. But they had to play Iowa again, this time at Williams Arena. The result was no better than the month before; the Hawkeyes held McHale to four points on 2-for-11 shooting, and only Mitchell, Holmes, and Tucker scored in double figures with 18, 17, and 14 points respectively. The result was a 73-63 Iowa win.

The Gophers had a chance to redeem themselves in their next game at Purdue. But they shot an anemic 41 percent from the floor, led by 14 from Hall, and they made critical mental errors throughout the game to give Purdue a 58-56 win and a two game lead over the Gophers, who were then tied for fourth in the conference. They recovered and snapped their two-game losing streak with a 72-55 home win against Northwestern, thanks in large part to sophomore transfer Andy Thompson. Trying to walk in the shoes of

his older brother, Mychal, Thompson hit all four of his field goal attempts, both his free throws, grabbed four rebounds, had two assists, stole the ball twice, and didn't commit a turnover.

Ninth-ranked Ohio State came to the Barn to meet a Gopher team needing a win to jump back into a tie for the conference lead at 8-5. McHale scored 20 points and had 10 rebounds to lead his team to another victory for the Big Ten's sleeper team, 74-70. But the Gophers' next three games would be on the road, beginning with Indiana at the always-difficult Assembly Hall. Minnesota's share of the conference lead didn't last long there, as Indiana smothered the Gophers' offense and won,

■ *McHale puts up a shot against Mississippi.*

67-54. The Gophers traveled to Champaign to take on Illinois, and they played catch-up most of the game. They finally did catch up, sending the game into overtime; Illinois outscored Minnesota 4-2 in the extra period and won, 60-58. The road trip ended, mercifully, in Madison, but not before Wisconsin had its way with the Gophers. It was the Badgers' senior night, and their senior reserves started the game, played the entire first half, and whipped the Gophers' starters. The score at the half was 33-18 Badgers; only Mitchell scored in double figures with 19 points, and the Gophers lost easily, 70-55.

Minnesota had to snap its losing streak and regain some momentum if it had any hope of qualifying for postseason play, and the Gophers did just that against Michigan State. Captain McHale reenergized his game with 29 points, Mitchell added 21, and Tucker had 14 as the Gophers pasted the Spartans, 87-73, to go to 16-10 overall and 9-8 in the Big Ten with one regular-season game remaining. The finale was Senior Night for Minnesota's lone senior, and McHale basked in the glow of his great career as the clock ran out in the second half. He stood under the Michigan basket, holding the ball above his head in one hand, smiling broadly after his team pulled out a 68-67 victory, behind his 16 points and 12 rebounds, and 16 more points from Mitchell.

That 17-10 record was not good enough for the 48-team NCAA field, but it did net the Gophers an NIT bid, and they opened up at home against Bowling Green. The Falcons focused on McHale all night, and managed to hold him to only 10 points, but he grabbed 12 rebounds, and Mitchell picked up the slack with 19 points on the way to a 64-50 Gopher victory. Mississippi was Minnesota's second-round opponent in the Barn, and this time the Gophers barely pulled out a 58-56 win after Ole Miss failed to capitalize on several chances in the final 25 seconds. The Gophers pulled their third straight home NIT game, this time against Southwestern Louisiana. And this time it wasn't even close. Tucker and Breuer had 18 points apiece, Hall had 16, McHale 15, and Holmes 10, and Minnesota walked to the final four in Madison Square Garden by a score of 94-73.

The Gophers were in the NIT semifinals for the first time ever, but there they found something familiar: their opponent, Illinois. It would be the third meeting of the two teams that season, with each of them winning its home game. The Gophers outplayed the Illini for three-fourths of the game, but Breuer's tip-in with 10:54 was their last field goal of the game. If not for sinking 15 free throws in the last 10 minutes and Breuer scoring 24 points overall, Minnesota never would have escaped with the 65-63 victory they got. But it was still a win, and it sent them to the NIT finals against Virginia and its 7-foot-4 freshman center, Ralph Sampson.

The Gophers shot only 38 percent that night, and McHale finished his college career with an off night, scoring eight points. Mitchell led the Gophers with 18 points, and Breuer added 12, but they could never overcome the dominating Sampson, nor could they shake their offensive woes. Virginia won the NIT title by a score of 58-55.

"The NIT was a good experience for us," says Dutcher. "Illinois was tough in the semis, and the caliber of the NIT was just so much better back then."

"We weren't ready to play in the NCAAs yet, so the NIT was a great experience for us," Tucker remembers. "It was a good field, we got to play against guys like Andrew Toney and Jeff Lamp. It was good basketball. Against Virginia, it was a real nip-and-tuck game, and I thought we could have won. It was our first time seeing Ralph Sampson as a real big-time player. But it was a great experience going to the Garden and playing in the mecca of basketball."

For McHale, 1979-80 was bittersweet. "Randy Breuer and Trent Tucker came in that year, and they were the future of the team. I was just one of those guys who was not in a recruiting class with anybody. I was just there and I was the only person in my class; I had nobody I played four years with, who I could develop with.

"I hoped we would have gotten to the NCAAs that year, but we were just off probation, it was my only year eligible to go to a postseason tournament, and I was just happy to get into postseason play."

In a season in which they were picked to finish in the bottom three in the Big Ten, the Gophers finished with a 21-11 record. McHale, who averaged 17.4 points and 8.8 rebounds per game his senior year, was off to begin his spec-

■ *Tommy Davis pushes the ball up the floor in a game against Indiana.*

tacular career with the Boston Celtics, but the Gophers would be returning the entire rest of their roster the following season. And that gave Minnesota fans cause for boundless optimism.

Looking back on his career as a Gopher, McHale has only fond memories, despite a few frustrations. "When I look back on my experience of going to school, very little of it was basketball," he remembers. "The whole experience was much bigger. It was the most enjoyable time in my life. I played with great players, I played with guys who really enjoyed playing together. Coach Dutcher was a super, super man, a guy who gave you a lot of latitude to improve and to run your own life. He

gave you a lot of responsibility, and he was very professional. He said, here's what I expect, and here's what will happen in return. For a guy like me, that was perfect."

As the Gophers began the 1980-81 season, their roster looked like one of a Big Ten title contender. Guards Darryl Mitchell (the team captain) and Mark Hall; forwards Trent Tucker, Andy Thompson, and John Wiley; and centers Brian Pederson, from Prior Lake, and Gary Holmes were all seasoned juniors, though Pederson had sat out the last season because of a bad back. Sophomores included center Randy Breuer, from Lake City; forwards Ben Coleman and Zebedee Howell; and guard Bruce

■ *Trent Tucker gets an easy inside basket against Michigan State.*

Kaupa, from Woodbury. Forward Jim Peterson, from St. Louis Park, and guard Brian Hansen, from Duluth, were incoming freshmen. After the unexpected success of the previous year, the Gophers took the court for their first game as one of the favorites to win the conference crown.

The Gophers opened at home against North Dakota State, who were overmatched and allowed Tucker to score 22, Hall 17, and Mitchell 14, on the way to a 99-64 Minnesota win. Florida State came to the Barn next, and Coleman chose that game to establish himself as a scoring threat, pouring in 27 on the way to a 79-66 Minnesota win. The Gophers then headed for the road—

Chicago, to be more specific, to take on Loyola. Tucker scored 22, Hall put in 21, and Breuer dominated inside with 16 points and 10 rebounds, and Minnesota coasted, 100-83.

Marquette came to Williams Arena, and the Gophers opened up a 10-point lead midway through the second half. But Marquette rallied offensively, tightened its defense, and came away with a 92-84 win, despite 21 points from Breuer and 18 from Hall. From that loss, the Gophers had to bounce back on the road against Louisville, the defending national champions. They did just that, winning an ugly game, 62-56, as no Gopher scored more than 14 (only Breuer had that many).

Minnesota next hosted Yale in the opening round of the Pillsbury Classic, and it was no contest as Minnesota breezed to a 95-54 win. Texas Tech met the Gophers in the Classic finals, and Minnesota continued its streak of winning every a game in the seven-year history of the tournament. Led by 17 points from Hall, the Gophers won that game, 72-56. From there it was on to another tournament, this one the Winston Tire Classic in Los Angeles. The Gophers took on host Southern California in the opening round, and they overcame a flat start to defeat USC behind 17 points in 23 minutes from Holmes. In the final, they faced sixth-ranked North Carolina. Hall scored 23, Tucker added 14, and Holmes had 11 points and 12 rebounds as the Gophers upset the Tar Heels, 76-60.

The Gophers entered the Big Ten season having finished their nonconference schedule at 8-1. Their first game was at home against Wisconsin, and Hall scored 25 and Tucker added 17 to lead the Gophers past the Badgers, 76-60. Michigan came to the Barn and beat the Gophers in a double-overtime heartbreaker, 68-67, despite 18 points from Coleman, 17 from Mitchell, and 16 from Hall. Minnesota, now ranked 20th in the nation, traveled to East Lansing next to take on Michigan State, and Hall had 21 points, Holmes had 18, Breuer added 15, and Tucker put in 14 to lead the Gophers to an easy 86-77 win over the Spartans.

The Gophers moved on to Champaign to play Illinois, but they didn't seem to really show up until the second half. The players wearing maroon and gold in the first half were buried by the Illini by 15 points, but Tucker, with 20 points on several long-range bombs, almost singlehandedly led his team back in the second 20 minutes. Still, Illinois held on to win, 80-76. The Gophers made it into a losing streak when they hosted Ohio State at Williams Arena. The Buckeyes shot 72 percent from the floor and outrebounded the Gophers by 10, and the inevitable result of those statistics was a 76-63 Ohio State win.

The Gophers were 2-3 in the Big Ten, and they realized they needed to play better basketball the rest of the way if they had a hope of contending for the conference championship. That started in Iowa City, when they shot 64 percent behind Breuer's 17 points, held the

ninth-ranked Hawkeyes to 39 percent from the field, and won, 60-48. But the great play didn't last, and they lost at the Barn again. This time the culprit was Indiana, and it came in spite of a 12-point Gopher lead early in the second half. But the Hoosiers came back in a game where the box score read more like a game from the 1940s. The teams were tied at 43 at the end of regulation, and they both came alive in the five-minute overtime, with Indiana getting the better of Minnesota, 56-53.

Minnesota had to show it could win again; the season was getting to the point at which the Gophers were no longer looking at winning the conference and were more concerned about qualifying for postseason play. Fortunately, they were able to come together and even their Big Ten record at 4-4 by moving past Northwestern, 74-63, behind 19 points from Tucker. The Gophers hit the road to play Purdue, and they overcame a nine-point deficit to trail by only two with two minutes remaining. But they collapsed like a bad souffle after that, with four missed field goals and seven turnovers to help the

■ *Jim Dutcher shouts instructions to his players in 1983. Assistant Jimmy Williams is standing behind him.*

Boilermakers to a 13-0 run and a 74-59 win. The Gophers almost gave away another road game in the final minutes, this time to lowly Northwestern. But thanks to 23 points from Hall and 21 from Breuer, they withstood a late Wildcats rally and won, 68-62.

The Gophers had eight games remaining in their regular season, and they would be on the same emotional see-saw their first 10 conference games had been. They lost 60-58 in overtime to Iowa at the Barn. They beat Ohio State, 82-76, on the road, thanks to 26 points from Breuer and 20 from Hall. They lost 74-63 at Indiana on 40 percent shooting. They finally pulled it all together for a convincing 76-59 home win against Illinois, behind 22 points from Tucker, 21 from Breuer, and 12 rebounds from Howell.

The Gophers finally managed to string together a winning streak, and it was an improbable one for them—it came at home, and it was in double overtime, the team's first extra-period triumph in four tries that year—as they beat Michigan State, 92-89. In that game, Breuer continued his dominating play with 25 points and nine rebounds. But the good times couldn't last. The Gophers traveled to Ann Arbor and were run through a shredder by Michigan, 83-67. So they closed their regular season in a familiar fashion: with an overtime loss, this time in Madison as Wisconsin won, 60-58. The loss put the Gophers' record at 17-10 overall, and in fifth place in the Big Ten at 9-9. An NCAA bid was once again out of the question. It was back to the NIT.

The smallest crowd in a decade—7,097—showed up at Williams Arena to watch the Gophers pick apart Drake, 90-77, to open the NIT behind 21 points each from Holmes and Breuer. The second-round game was against Connecticut in Hartford, and it was Trent Tucker night. The junior guard hit 14 of his 17 shots, almost all of them from beyond 20 feet, and all seven of his free throws to total 35 points and key an 84-66 Gophers rout of the Huskies. But Minnesota's season ended three days later at Williams Arena, as the Gophers were thrashed in their own building for the sixth time in 1980-81, this time by West Virginia, 80-69.

That final loss put Minnesota at 19-11 for the season, respectable numbers at first blush, but disappointing ones considering the talent the Go-

phers put on the floor and the expectations put on the team by the fans, the media, and the players themselves before the season. Breuer finished the season averaging 15.2 points per game, Tucker averaged 14.8, and Hall had 14.5. The best news for Minnesota was that there was not one senior on the entire team, so virtually the entire cohesive unit would be back the next season, ready as a group to try again to meet those lofty expectations.

"We had a very talented team my junior year, but it was a very disappointing year," Tucker says. "We should have put ourselves in position to win the national championship, but we didn't do it. We never gelled together as a group. We lost that early game to Michigan, and our season was a see-saw after that. We probably had more talent than in 1981-82, since we had Mark Hall all season and Ben Coleman. When we lost to Michigan, we lost our swagger. Something went wrong after that. People got hurt and didn't play, we lost our togetherness.

"Now the pressure was really on us for the next season. The expectations were really high. The Class of '82 were seniors, and it was a question of whether you had matured enough. That was the time for us to show what was expected of us. Our minds were different, and we approached the game differently. We understood it was not about us individually, but us as a team. We had no more excuses."

But the Gophers, ranked 10th in the nation in preseason polls, did not open the 1981-82 season on a good note, even though they got a win. They beat San Francisco State, 88-69, but the Gophers were down at halftime. They came back in the second half and Breuer finished with 20 points and Holmes with 18, but they would have to play better if they were to live up to their own expectations, let alone everybody else's. They did just that when Dayton came to the Barn. Breuer dominated with 31 points, and the Gophers coasted, 90-74.

The next game was in Chicago against Loyola, and while John Wiley made only two baskets all night, one of them was huge. He tipped in a shot with two seconds left to give the Gophers a 61-60 win as Breuer again lit up the scoreboard with 28 points. Less than six months after topping Drake in the NIT, the now-eighth-ranked Gophers again

THE EXPECTATIONS WERE REALLY HIGH. THE CLASS OF '82 WERE SENIORS, AND IT WAS A QUESTION OF WHETHER YOU HAD MATURED ENOUGH. THAT WAS THE TIME FOR US TO SHOW WHAT WAS EXPECTED OF US.

faced the Bulldogs at the Barn and again beat them easily. Five Gophers scored in double figures, including 20 from Mitchell and 17 points and 10 rebounds from Breuer, as the Gophers coasted, 80-55. Even that win was frustrating for the Gophers, though, as they heard boos among the 14,713 people in attendance who though Minnesota's lead wasn't big enough as the game wore on.

The Gophers traveled to Milwaukee to take on Marquette, and they expected a tough game. They didn't get it, and cruised by the Warriors, 76-54. Their next road game was against Kansas State, and that was a very tough one. Too tough. The Wildcats smothered Breuer and held him to 12 points, and the rest of the team could not make up the difference; Minnesota lost, 62-52.

The Pillsbury Classic was next, and the Gophers had never lost a game in the tournament they hosted. That wouldn't change against Army, which didn't have a player taller than 6-foot-7 and was hopelessly outmanned. Every Gopher except freshman walk-on Kelly Scott played at least 17 minutes, and every player scored as the Gophers barely broke a sweat in their 79-37 victory. Arizona promised to be a tougher test, but Minnesota won that game, 91-62, behind 21 points each from Mitchell and Tucker. The Gophers ended their non-conference schedule at 8-1 with a 75-67 win over Long Beach State, with 25 points from Breuer and 22 from Tucker.

Minnesota, which had moved to the No. 6 ranking nationally, opened its Big Ten season in a confident mood as the team traveled to take on Ohio State. That confidence was quickly shattered, as the Buckeyes frustrated the Gophers into 37 percent shooting and a 49-47 loss. Michigan State in East Lansing was next, and the Gophers desperately needed to beat the Spartans and earn a split of their first road trip. They took a 40-23 lead with 13 minutes to play, but the Spartans erased that lead before the Gophers, led by 17 points from Tucker, took control again and won, 64-58.

The Gophers had dropped to 11th in the polls as the No. 5 team, Iowa, came to the Barn. Seniors Tucker, Mitchell, and Holmes had never beaten the Hawkeyes at Williams Arena, but 22 points from Breuer helped change that with a 61-56 Minnesota win. The woeful Michigan Wolverines came to Williams Arena next, and the Gophers did not

play nearly as well. But they did play well enough to win, 67-58, with 21 points from Tucker, 18 from Breuer, and 15 from Mitchell.

The Gophers were ranked fifth in the nation as they took on Wisconsin in Madison, and Mitchell scored 18 points to lead his team to a 78-57 drubbing of the Badgers to move their Big Ten record to 4-1 and keep them in a tie for the conference lead. That evaporated with the next game, though, as Illinois came to the Barn and dispatched the Gophers, 64-57. But Minnesota came back against Northwestern in Evanston, behind Tucker's 18 points and the team's sinking of 21 of 24 free throws, winning 61-53 to run its conference record to 5-2 and remain one game behind Iowa in the standings.

The Gophers headed to Assembly Hall to take on Indiana, and the result was dictated by the fact that all five Minnesota starters scored in double figures and the Gophers went 19-for-20 at the line to win, 69-62. Back home at Williams Arena, Purdue never had a chance. Tucker scored 21, and Breuer and freshman Tommy Davis had 11 apiece as the Gophers stomped the Boilermakers, 73-50. But Indiana came to the Barn and returned the favor Minnesota had paid in Bloomington. Freshman center Uwe Blab stuffed Breuer and held him to nine points, and the Hoosiers won, 58-55. The Gophers, at 7-3, were still in second place, but they had fallen two games behind league-leading Iowa.

"Bobby Knight said after that game that this would end our chances in the Big Ten, and that fired everybody up," Dutcher says.

The Gophers hosted Wisconsin, the last place team in the league, and did not play very well. But they didn't have to play all that well to beat the Badgers, and behind 20 points from Tucker and 19 from Breuer, they managed to win by a 71-60 count. On the road against Purdue, Minnesota found itself down by one point with one second remaining after a lackluster game against the Boilermakers. Mitchell, who led the Gophers with 18 points, calmly sank his only two free throw attempts of the game to give his team a 53-52 win. It turned out to be a big one for the Gophers, since Iowa lost that day as well, and they finally managed to trim their deficit in the standings to one game with six left to play.

■ *Following pages* Darryl Mitchell puts up an outside jumper against Michigan.

Northwestern was next at home, and Minnesota dispatched the Wildcats, 76-66, as Mitchell again led the team with 18 points and Breuer added 17. The eighth-ranked Gophers traveled to Champaign hoping to avenge their earlier loss to Illinois, but the Illini continued to be a pain the Gophers just couldn't shake. Minnesota simply did not play as well as Illinois, and the Illini's 77-65 victory showed that. But the Gophers did catch one break—both first-place Iowa and third-place Indiana lost as well, so Minnesota remained one game back in the Big Ten race.

Three days after that game, senior Mark Hall issued a statement that he was quitting the Gopher basketball team. Earlier in the season, Hall had been declared ineligible to play because of academic problems, but he had been reinstated under a temporary restraining order from U.S. District Judge Miles Lord. In the meantime, though, Hall had been accused of misusing University telephones for long-distance calls and for not paying his apartment phone bill. The ensuing publicity had become a drain on the team, and Dutcher had long thought the controversy was keeping the media from focusing on the significant accomplishments of the rest of his team. If Hall had not quit, he would have been asked to leave the team.

Minnesota picked up the pieces and traveled to Ann Arbor, where the Gophers hadn't won for 19 years. Mitchell had taken an elbow to his face and Breuer had twisted his ankle in a particularly brutal practice the day before. But they still managed to come out as 61-50 winners, and they still remained one game back in the title hunt.

The showdown was yet to come. It was against Iowa on its home court, in front of 13,365 basketball-mad Iowans in a battle with the potential of deciding the Big Ten crown. "Iowa was an easy game for us to get up for," Tucker says. "We knew right away what had to be done, it was a game where if they won, they were two games up and in the drivers' seat, we had no fans there, and it was the last game in their field house."

The Gophers and the Hawkeyes played to a 53-53 tie after regulation. Each team scored in the first 30 seconds of the first overtime, but neither could put down a basket for the remaining four minutes, 30 seconds. The same was true of the second overtime, which was totally scoreless. And they went another five minutes without anybody scoring a point until Mitchell was fouled as he went up for a shot as time ran out in the third overtime. Mitchell, who led the Gophers with 21 points for the game, calmly sank both free throws for a 57-55 triple-overtime victory and a tie for first place in the Big Ten between Minnesota and Iowa. "It was very gratifying to go into a very hostile environment against all odds," remembers Tucker. "It was a great relief when I could look at my teammates and say, I've got guys on my team with a lot of guts and big-time character. If you want to be a champion, you've got to win in a hostile environment."

Back at Williams Arena, Michigan State did everything it could to play spoiler. Iowa had lost that day, and a Minnesota win would guarantee the Gophers at least a share of the Big Ten crown. But the Spartans held the Gophers to 36 percent shooting, and it took a pair of free throws from Gary Holmes with 11 seconds remaining to seal a 54-51 Minnesota victory and win at least a tie for first in the conference. "Michigan State was the toughest game we played all year," Tucker remembers. "They came in with nothing to lose, and we had to get back in the race. All the pressure was on us to win, and we didn't play as free and loose as we should have. But some guys made key plays down the stretch when we had to."

Ohio State came to the Barn on Senior Night to face 17,378 wild, screaming fans and a Minnesota team ranked seventh in the nation and determined to win this game and gain the Big Ten title all for itself. Breuer responded with a career-high 32 points and 12 rebounds and Tucker added 23 points. The Gophers shot 68 percent from the floor, outrebounded the Buckeyes 38-25, and came out on top, 87-75. "We played about as well in that game as we played all year," Dutcher remembers. When the final buzzer sounded, the team stayed on the floor, basking in the glory and acknowledging the cheers of the fans who were finally behind this team, the first Minnesota club in a decade to claim the Big Ten championship. The Gophers finished the regular season at

■ *Randy Breuer goes up for one of his 228 career blocks at Williams Arena.*

22-5, and 14-4 in the conference—ironically, one game worse than their 15-3 finish in 1976-77, when they finished second in the Big Ten.

The Gophers flew to Indianapolis to play Tennessee-Chattanooga in the Mideast Regional. They played an ugly game, but got some lucky bounces along with 20 points from Tucker, 17 from Breuer, and 16 from Mitchell, on the way to a 62-61 victory. Then it was on to Birmingham, Alabama, to take on Louisville. Once again, the Gophers didn't play a crisp game, and the Cardinals were not as forgiving; despite 22 points apiece from Breuer and Tucker, the Gophers fell, 67-61. They ended their season at 23-6 overall. It might not have been the best Minnesota team in history—debate usually centers around the 1971-72 Big Ten championship team and the 1976-77 team that went 24-3—but it was a team that played together and won when it had to, including some difficult road games won under tremendous pressure. "The ability to win on the road was the key to our success that year," Dutcher says. "And what people forget was that there were only 32 teams in the NCAA Tournament back then. People don't recognize us as a Sweet 16 team, but that's what we were."

Breuer and Mitchell were both named first-team All-Big Ten. Breuer again led the team in scoring, with a 16.6 average, and he added 7.2 rebounds and 2.6 blocks. Tucker, who in 1982 was named Minnesota's only All-American of the 1980s, scored 14.4 points per game, Mitchell had 13.4, and Holmes scored 8.7 per contest. The latter three were all seniors and would not be back the following season, but the Gophers would try to keep the momentum of their championship season going behind the leadership of Breuer and the talents of returnees Tommy Davis, Zebedee Howell, and Jim Shasky, as well as newcomers Marc Wilson, John Shasky, Barry Wohler, Alonzo Skanes, and Roland Brooks.

The Gophers opened the 1982-83 season at Williams Arena against North Dakota State, and Brooks, a 24-year-old transfer from College of the Sequoias, made the most of his 19 minutes, scoring 14 points, to go with 19 points and 13 rebounds from Breuer and 18 points from Davis, on the way to an 83-61 victory. The Gophers headed to Ames, Iowa, to take on Iowa State. Despite 28 points and 11 rebounds from Breuer, the Gophers couldn't hold their 11-point halftime lead, or a six-point lead with 40 seconds to go, and they wound up losing 80-78 in overtime. It was on to Des Moines and Drake, and another overtime game. But this time it was the Gophers who came back to force overtime. Davis, who finished with 25 points, hit two clutch baskets in the final minute, and Wilson, who scored 14, hit six of those points in the extra period to lead Minnesota to a 70-65 win.

U.S. International, a small San Diego school, came to the Barn for a sloppy game that the Gophers won, 87-72, behind 27 points from Breuer. Minnesota hit the road to play Dayton, and Breuer hit 22, Wilson scored 15, Davis had 12, and Howell muscled his way inside for eight rebounds and tough defense as the Gophers won, 71-65. Marquette, including All-American Glenn "Doc" Rivers, was next at Williams Arena for a nationally-televised game. The Gophers walked all over the Warriors, holding Rivers to six points and the entire Marquette team to 37 percent shooting while five Gophers scored in double figures—Breuer with 23, Wilson with 16 and seven assists, Petersen and Davis with 14 apiece, and Howell with 10—on the way to a 100-66 rout.

Minnesota flew to Florida to take on Jacksonville, and the impressive freshman Marc Wilson took control of the game, scoring 21 on the way to a 62-48 Gophers win. They came back to the Barn to host Indiana State and the entire team had a chance to pad its statistics in a 120-82 shellacking of the Sycamores. Seven Gophers scored in double figures, three had at least 20 points—Skanes with 22, Breuer with 21, and Howell with 20—and Breuer and Peterson had 11 rebounds apiece, with Howell adding nine to lead an assault on the boards. Breuer had 23 points and 10 rebounds in the nonconference finale at home against Montana State to lead a 62-45 victory, as the Gophers prepared to defend their Big Ten title with an 8-1 record in hand.

Illinois was the only team that had beaten the Gophers twice during the championship season, and Minnesota was out for revenge when the Illini came to Williams Arena. They got it, 75-49, behind 19 points each from Breuer and Davis. The Gophers next managed to outlast Purdue at the Barn, 54-48, as Wilson stepped up for 17 points and Davis added 15. But the Gophers had to travel to Michigan's Crisler Arena next, and they continued their pattern of frustration there, falling 63-58, despite 20 points from Breuer and 12 rebounds from Peterson.

In East Lansing, Breuer scored 25 points against Michigan State, but the real hero was reserve Barry Wohler, whose only shot of the night was a 15-foot jumper with four seconds remaining that fell to give the Gophers a 69-67 win over the Spartans. Wilson pulled his hamstring in that game, an injury that would hamper him for the rest of his college career. Tenth-ranked Iowa was next at the Barn, and while the Gophers were ranked 16th in the nation at that point, they didn't play like it. Wilson was out with a strained hamstring, and the only fireworks the Gophers could produce were 16 points apiece from Breuer and Davis on the way to a 68-52 loss. Their next home game was against Northwestern, and this was a considerably easier game, as Breuer scored 19 and the Gophers won, 68-53.

In Madison, Breuer had 20 points and 11 rebounds and Brooks added 11 in a 63-58 victory, but once again Wohler shined in his brief playing time, canning a three-pointer on his only attempt late in the game to put the Gophers in the lead to stay. The win put the Gophers at 5-2 in the conference and in a tie for the Big Ten lead. They came through again in Columbus, as Ohio State took the Gophers to two overtimes, only to see Minnesota pull away to an 89-80 win. The score was tied at 62 at the end of regulation, and the Buckeyes were up 72-70 with no time remaining on the clock when the officials sent Davis to the line on a controversial foul call. Davis—who hadn't taken a shot in the game's first 30 minutes but still scored 22 points on the night—calmly sank both free throws to send the game into the second overtime. Breuer also scored 26 points and had 12 rebounds for the Gophers.

But the euphoria was short-lived. In Bloomington, sixth-ranked Indiana dismantled the Gophers, 76-51, sending Minnesota, which shot only 31 percent from the field, into second place in the Big Ten. The conference scheduler must have been feeling particularly nasty when he made up that year's calendar, because the next game was between the same two teams, only at Williams Arena. The results were not any better for the Gophers. They wasted 28 points and 14 rebounds and an excellent defensive effort from Breuer by shooting 42 percent from the floor and a horrible 30 percent from the free throw line—including four straight misses in the closing two minutes with the Hoosiers leading by only two. The result was a frustrating 63-59 defeat.

The Gophers continued the slide on their home court as Ohio State came to town. Breuer scored 22, Davis had 19, and Brooks added 14, but the Gophers played a flat, uninspired game and lost, 74-69, to send their conference record to 6-5 and drop them into a tie for third place. The Gophers expected an easier test when Cincinnati came to town for a nonconference game, but even that was an adventure. Wilson scored 14 and Brooks had 12, but Breuer was held to a career-low four points and Minnesota barely escaped with a 49-46 win. Breuer managed to find his shot as Wisconsin took the Williams Arena floor. He dominated the Badgers with 31 points and 16 rebounds as Minnesota moved past the last-place team, 78-71.

The Gophers traveled next to take on Northwestern, and they might have taken the Wildcats too lightly. Whether it was that or something else, Northwest-

ern plastered Minnesota, 83-66, to all but eliminate the Gophers from contention in the Big Ten at 7-6. Tommy Davis was the hero who got the Gophers back on track in Iowa City, as he hit a 25-foot three-pointer with five seconds to play to give his team a 71-69 win over Iowa. That shot went with his 12 rebounds, and 24 points and 13 rebounds from Breuer. But there would be no winning streak this time; Michigan State came to the Barn and beat the Gophers easily, 79-67, to send the Gophers to 17-8 overall and put them on the bubble for the NCAA tournament.

The Gophers hosted Michigan for Senior Night, the last home game of their careers for Breuer and Howell. Both came through with strong games—17 points, 10 rebounds, and an incredible nine blocked shots for Breuer, and 13

■ *Jim Petersen goes up for a rebound as Randy Breuer gets knocked to the deck. Petersen developed, in Jim Dutcher's words, "From a below-average freshman to a much-better-than-average senior."*

points for Howell—to go with 22 points for Davis and 14 for Brooks on the way to an 88-75 Gophers win. On the road at Purdue, the Gophers could not match that intensity. They shot 40 percent for the night, losing 68-62. Any NCAA hopes that remained were dashed after two overtimes in Champaign, when Illinois won, 70-67.

It was on to the NIT, where the Gophers took on DePaul on the road in the first round. After going 8-3 in postseason play the previous three years, the Gophers felt good about their chances with the Blue Demons, but despite 26 points from Breuer and 17 from Wilson, they fell, 76-73.

The Gophers ended their season at 19-11 overall; they finished in fifth place in the Big Ten at 9-9. They said goodbye to Breuer, who averaged 20.4 points and 8.9 rebounds per game in 1982-83, when he was again a first-team All-Big Ten selection. More importantly, Breuer finished second at the time on the Gophers' all-time scoring list with 1,755 points and third in all-time rebounds with 716. Often, college players are remembered for greatness based on their professional careers, and Breuer was not spectacular as a pro. But he was as a Gopher, and while he is not often mentioned in the same breath as players like Kevin McHale, Mychal Thompson, and Willie Burton, he was clearly one of the best ever to play at Minnesota.

For 1983-84, Dutcher was faced with a rebuilding year, though he had several lettermen returning. Seniors Jim Petersen and Roland Brooks would start at forward, junior Tommy Davis and sophomore Marc Wilson would start at guard, and sophomore John Shasky would start at center. Off the bench, he was relying on sophomores Dave Dahlke and Alonzo Skanes, junior Barry Wohler, and senior Bruce Kaupa, as well as incoming freshmen Mike Carpenter, a 7-foot-2 center; Gerald Jackson, a 6-foot-4 guard; Kevin Smith, a 6-foot-7 forward; and Paul Van Den Einde, a 7-foot center from Willmar.

The Gophers opened at home against South Dakota State and several players had big nights in their 93-77 victory. Davis had 29 points and 10 rebounds, Wilson scored 18, Brooks put in 13, and Shasky and Petersen each scored 11 and pulled down 11 and 10 rebounds, respectively. They went on to an easy 96-70 win over Indiana State,

with 21 points from Davis, 16 from Wilson, and 15 points and 12 rebounds from Petersen. But in Milwaukee, Marquette won, 77-60, and the score was deceptive. The Warriors should have won by more, as only Wilson hit double figures with 22 points.

The rest of the nonconference schedule was a blur of wins for the Gophers, though not all of them were easy. Davis scored 16 to lead a 65-49 home win over Oregon. He added 23 in the next game at the Barn, a 52-50 win over Jacksonville. North Dakota came to Williams Arena and also put a scare into the Gophers, but they managed to pull out a 78-73 victory. The Gophers traveled to take on Detroit, and Petersen led them to a 60-56 win with 26 points. Wilson scored 17 and Davis added 14 to help Minnesota past Montana State, 55-52, in Bozeman. And Shasky had 18 points and seven rebounds to pace a 66-64 home win over Iowa State to end the Gophers' nonconference schedule at 8-1.

But the Big Ten promised to be a different story for this young team, and Illinois started the education with an 80-53 pasting of the Gophers in Champaign, as Dahlke led Minnesota with only 10 points. They traveled next to Purdue, where Wilson scored 22, Davis had 18, and the Gophers couldn't stay with the Boilermakers, losing 72-69. Michigan came to the Barn and helped continue the Gophers' losing streak, winning 66-62 despite 18 points from Brooks.

The Gophers finally got their first Big Ten win when Michigan State came to Williams Arena. They almost blew a 13-point lead with nine minutes left, but Wilson hit four clutch points in the final two minutes on his way to 22 points for a 69-61 win. They stretched their streak to two in a row in Iowa City with a 56-49 upset over Iowa, led by 18 points from Davis, 15 from Brooks, and eight points and 10 rebounds from Shasky. But it was too good to last: They played Northwestern in Evanston and shot 39 percent against the Wildcats, losing 52-50 in overtime.

Madison came to the Barn with Jimmy Williams filling in as head coach for Dutcher, who was attending his father's funeral. Shasky helped give Williams a perfect coaching record with 18 points and 16 rebounds on the way to a 75-62 Minnesota win. Indiana came to town next, and the Hoosiers were clearly the superior team; they took the

Gophers to school, 67-54, shooting 62 percent from the floor to the Gophers' 44 percent. Ohio State hit Williams Arena and was run over by the Gophers, 83-61, led by 22 points from Petersen, 19 from Brooks, 16 from Davis, and 14 from Wilson. But the venue for the next game was the Buckeyes' home court, and they returned the favor with a 73-62 win as they forced 22 Minnesota turnovers.

In Bloomington, the Gophers were down by 15 points in the second half, but they fought back to close the gap, shooting 71 percent from the floor on the night, and Davis scored 33 points on 15-for-16 from the field. In short, they did everything right except win; Indiana did that, 74-72. The next game was in Madison, and Brooks hit an 18-foot off-balance jumper with two seconds left to seal a 68-67 come-from-behind

Gophers win and move their record to 13-8 overall and 5-7 in the Big Ten. Minnesota took a break from the Big Ten, taking on Cincinnati on the road, and Petersen had 15 points and Brooks added 14 to pace a 65-61 win over the Bearcats.

Northwestern came to the Barn and found itself down 30-13 at halftime. But the Wildcats scored 44 in the second half and almost overcame the Gophers, who hung on to win, 63-57. Iowa was next at Williams Arena, and this time the Gophers trailed from beginning to end, falling 62-50. It was time for the annual Michigan State-Michigan road trip, and the Spartans were first in East Lansing. The only bright spot for Minnesota was 25 points for Davis on the way to an 83-62 Michigan State rout. The Gophers did a much better job

■ *John Shasky goes up for a jumper against the Wolverines during the Gophers' 1986 home victory over Michigan. Just two games later, nearly half the Gopher team was suspended, and senior Shasky had to take a critical leadership role the rest of the year.*

against Michigan, holding the Wolverines to 39 percent shooting, but they still came up short, 51-50.

The Gophers ran their losing streak to four with an anemic 53-41 home loss against league-leading Illinois; only Davis scored in double figures with 18. Minnesota closed its season at home against Purdue and lost its fifth straight, 63-62. At least the Gophers could draw hope by their comeback from a 14-point deficit to come within a hair of beating the Boilermakers, who shared the Big Ten title with Illinois. Minnesota ended the season at 15-13 overall, and they tied for seventh in the Big Ten with a 6-12 record. Davis led the Gophers with a 16.0 points per game average, while Wilson averaged 11.3, Petersen 11.2, and Brooks 10.7.

The 1984-85 Gophers would be even more youthful than the year before, with senior guard Tommy Davis and four juniors: guard Marc Wilson, Alonzo Skanes, transfer Tyrone Thomas, and center John Shasky to provide leadership. Dutcher would also have sophomore guard Gerald Jackson, sophomore forward Kevin Smith, sophomore center Paul Van Den Einde, and redshirt freshman center Dave Holmgren from Prior Lake, another 7-footer. Incoming freshmen included guards Todd Alexander and Tim Hanson, also from Prior Lake, and forwards Mitchell Lee and George Williams.

Davis scored 25 and Wilson had 20 points to open the season at home against Wisconsin-Green Bay, and it was just enough for a 75-71 Minnesota win. Shasky hit a basket with 15 seconds remaining to give the Gophers a heartstopping 61-60 victory over Connecticut at the Barn. Minnesota finally had a relatively easy win, 85-71 over Montana State, behind 20 points from Smith. But it was back to close games when Princeton came to town and the Gophers barely escaped with a 46-44 win.

After three close calls in their first four home wins, the Gophers were destined for trouble when they left the Twin Cities. They found it in Terra Haute, where Indiana State beat them, 94-86, despite a huge game from Shasky (27 points and 19 rebounds), 25 points from Davis, and 18 from Wilson. The Gophers were back home for Oregon, and Davis scored 28 to lead the Gophers 57-53 over the Ducks. They next headed to Tucson to play unbeaten Arizona. The Gophers

shocked their opponents by coming away with an 88-79 win, thanks to 23 points from Davis, 16 from Alexander, and 15 from Shasky. But they moved on to Arkansas' home court, and the Razorbacks won easily, 56-46, as the Gophers shot 34 percent from the floor. The Gophers lost their first game at home when Detroit came to town and won, 77-67. But they ended their noncoference season on a positive note—and with a 7-3 record—with a 70-61 victory over Marquette at the Barn as five Gophers scored in double figures.

It was a rocky 10 games for Minnesota, so folks were skeptical when sixth-ranked Illinois came to town to play the Gophers. But Davis scored 19 points, including a breakaway layup with three seconds remaining, and Shasky had 16 points and Alexander 11 to lead the Gophers to a stunning 60-58 upset over the Illini. Purdue was next at Williams Arena, but the Gophers could not match the intensity of their previous game and fell, 74-65. Minnesota's third straight conference home game produced its second upset. This time the victim was No. 19 Iowa, and Davis again was the leader, scoring 18 points as Minnesota won, 65-57.

In Ann Arbor, though, Michigan would have none of that. The Wolverines continued their Crisler Arena mastery over the Gophers with a convincing 97-56 rout. Against Michigan State two days later, the Gophers came back and rescued their pride with an 81-75 win over the Spartans. Wisconsin came to the Barn and the Gophers had a rare easy game there, blowing past the Badgers, 72-62, as Davis scored 21 and Shasky had 12 points and 15 rebounds.

The Gophers were 11-5 overall and 4-2 in the conference as they played host to 0-6 Northwestern, but the players had other things on their minds. Freshman forward Mitchell Lee had been arrested the night before and charged with criminal sexual conduct. He was held out of the lineup for that game, as he would be for the rest of the season. The news hit the Gophers hard, and they played like a team distracted, losing to the Wildcats, 56-51. The team's legal problems continued the following week, as Todd Alexander was arrested and charged with misdemeanor theft. Alexander stayed in the lineup pending resolution of his case, but the team was again distracted and showed it in a 76-62 road loss to Ohio State.

"It was kind of all around," Wilson says of the legal problems of Lee and Alexander. "Those were distractions that affected the team, because we were trying to focus on the game, and there were these external issues that were more upsetting because that was what everybody was talking about."

Some questioned Dutcher's decision to allow Alexander to play while his legal questions were sorted out, and they wondered why he failed to categorically condemn Lee after the sexual assault charge. But Wilson says that those were Dutcher's strengths, not weaknesses. "That's the part of Coach Dutcher that people just can't understand. He wants to deal with a problem instead of throwing away a problem. He's willing to take the risk, to be a father figure, to offer direction and show leadership."

The Gophers stayed on the road to take on Indiana, and they still had not gotten their heads in the game. They lost this time, 89-66. The Gophers played a much stronger game in Iowa City, trying to retain their pride even though they knew their hopes for postseason play were all but gone, and Davis scored 28 and Shasky added 19 in an encouraging 70-65 loss to 12th-ranked Iowa. Michigan State came to the Barn next, and freshmen Alexander and Williams stepped up to lead their team to a much-needed victory. Alexander scored 23 and Williams had 16 as the Gophers won, 73-64. They again played a good game, this time at home against No. 3 Michigan, but came up just short, 66-64. Van Den Einde only played nine minutes in that game, but he scored two of his four points on two free throws in the final minute to tie the game. Nevertheless, the Wolverines managed to sink the last shot to win.

In Evanston, Minnesota sought revenge for Northwestern's win earlier in the season, and they got it in the form of a 74-48 rout in which Williams and Shasky each scored 17, Wilson had 14, and Davis added 10 points and 10 rebounds. But Wisconsin poked a hole in the Gophers celebratory mood with a 65-61 win in Madison that put the Gophers at 13-11 and dashed any Minnesota hopes for postseason play. And things got even worse from there. Dutcher suspended Alexander from the

team after a second misdemeanor theft allegation, and the Gophers fell to Indiana, 79-68, at home. They rallied at the Barn against Ohio State behind 21 points from Davis, 20 from Wilson, and 18 from Shasky, but fell short, 78-77. Purdue added to the Gophers' woes with a 79-67 Boilermakers win in West Lafayette, and Illinois avenged its earlier shock and ended Minnesota's season with an 82-56 rout in Champaign.

The Gophers finished with a 13-15 overall record, and they were eighth in the Big Ten at 6-12—a conference finish identical to the previous season. Davis was named first-team All-Big Ten as he led the team with 19.1 points per game, while Shasky had 13.6 and Wilson added 10.4. Wilson, Shasky, Hanson, Holmgren, Lee, Williams, Kevin Smith, and Alexander would be back the following season, and the Gophers were hoping to get lifts from newcomers Kelvin Smith, Mark Anderson, Ray Gaffney, and Terence Woods. "We thought in 1985-86 we had a good chance," Dutcher says.

■ *Guard Terence Woods brings the ball upcourt at Williams Arena in 1985.*

The Gophers started the 1985-86 season in Hawaii at the National Airlines Tournament. They walked past tiny West Virginia State, 120-106, behind 29 points from Woods, 28 points and 14 rebounds from Shasky, and 20 points from Wilson. They lost to Middle Tennessee State, 92-79, in the second round despite having five Gophers scoring in double figures, led by Lee with 21 points and 10 rebounds. And they topped BYU-

■ *Marc Wilson directs his team at the Barn. Wilson was a critical senior member of the Gophers' Iron Five team of 1985-86.*

Hawaii, 87-80, as Shasky scored 33 points and had 12 boards and Wilson added 29 points. The Gophers' home opener was a pleasant 95-63 rout of San Francisco State behind Wilson's 16 points. Minnesota beat Division II South Dakota, 66-57, at home, but Dutcher was so disappointed with his team's performance in that game that he called a practice for 7:00 the next morning. The practice worked, as the Gophers ripped their next opponent, Eastern Illinois, 87-69, at the Barn.

Detroit came to Williams Arena and ran into 20 points from Wilson, 16 from

Alexander, and 14 from Shasky as the Gophers won, 83-71. They then played host to undefeated Arkansas, and made them once-defeated Arkansas. Wilson had 21, Alexander added 17, and Kevin Smith had 15 points in a 71-64 victory. Minnesota could only manage to shoot 43 percent against Colorado State, but they hung on for a 62-59 win. Marquette hosted Minnesota in Milwaukee and snapped the Gophers' seven-game winning streak, 74-63, as no Minnesota player scored more than 12 and no one had more than six rebounds. They took on Connecticut in Hartford and lost by a point, 70-69. But they came back at the Barn to walk over Oklahoma State, 71-59. The Gophers finished their nonconference season with an easy win against Alcorn State, 110-72, in which six Gophers scored in double figures, led by Shasky's 21. That put the Gophers at 10-3 as they prepared to head to Champaign to open the Big Ten season against Illinois.

Minnesota came out flat, and the Illini capitalized on that, shutting down the Gophers, 76-57. The next road game was against Purdue, and the Gophers put themselves into an 0-2 conference hole with a 68-61 defeat. Then it was 0-3. This time Iowa took it to the Gophers, 75-62, at Carver-Hawkeye Arena, in Minnesota's first game without Mark Anderson, who was ruled academically ineligible for the winter quarter, and Lee, who was back in Minneapolis waiting for his sexual assault trial to begin.

Finally, it was back to the Barn, against No. 2 Michigan. But senior Wilson led his team with 24 points and Alexander added 16, as the Gophers won a convincing victory over the stunned Wolverines, 73-63. Then the Gophers overcame 45 points from Michigan State's Scott Skiles on the strength of 27 points and 11 rebounds from Shasky and 18 points from Alexander to post a 76-71 win.

Next Minnesota traveled to Madison to take on the Badgers. They won, 67-65, on an Alexander jumper at the buzzer. But during the celebration that followed in Madison that night, three Gophers—Mitchell Lee, Kevin Smith, and George Williams—allegedly brought a local woman back to their hotel room and sexually assaulted her. Lee had just been acquitted that month of his last rape charge, and these new charges devastated not only the Gophers team, but the entire University and the state of Minnesota as well.

"Coming into my senior year, we had a pretty good team, and we were ready to challenge for the upper echelon of the Big Ten," Wilson remembers. "We got off to a bad start in the Big Ten season, but we put things together and we were rolling. We won at Wisconsin at the buzzer, we were ready to roll, then Boom! The next morning we took three steps backwards.

"We got on the plane in Madison at 8 a.m., and they took us off the plane at 10, and started questioning us one-by-one."

As the three players prepared to face arraignment in Madison, University President Kenneth Keller was back in Minneapolis, announcing that the school would forfeit its next game against Northwestern, and he even raised the possibility of eliminating basketball at Minnesota altogether. That was enough for Dutcher. He felt Keller was out of line, and he decided he couldn't coach with that kind of lack of support from the administration, no matter what some of his players had done. He resigned, effective immediately, and assistant Jimmy Williams was left to coach what had become a shell of a team.

"The whole thing was more devastating to the University than anything else," Wilson says. "Some decisions were made that needed more time, and in retrospect, I'm sure some of the people involved would have made different decisions."

Dutcher defends his decision to resign, and he defends the way he handled his players. Indeed, one consistent comment of those who played for Jim Dutcher is that he clearly laid out what was expected of his team members, allowed them to either follow the rules or disobey them, and made them live with the consequences. "Guys that can understand that and grow turn out to be pretty good individuals," Dutcher says. "Guys that can't have problems. Mitch Lee was one of those guys, and Mark Hall was, too.

"You just can't abandon people in those situations. At the first sign of trouble you just can't cut them lose. And when all this happened, I was very upset at how it was handled. I thought that forfeiting the Northwestern game was punishing the wrong people."

Besides the three players who had been charged with sexual assault—and who were kicked off the team for violating team rules during the incident, even though they were later acquitted of the charges—Terence Woods and Todd Alexander were also suspended for the rest of the season after the ensuing investigation, also for violating team rules. That left Marc Wilson, John Shasky, Kelvin Smith, Ray Gaffney, Tim Hanson, and Dave Holmgren as the only scholarship players left on the roster. Williams picked up football players Roselle Richardson, Pete Holson, Ray Armstrong, Jon Retzlaff, and Tim Juneau to sit on the bench in case of an emergency, but Wilson, Shasky, Smith, Gaffney, and Hanson would become the second "Iron Five" in Minnesota history.

That five took the floor against Ohio State in the unenviable position of competing in the toughest conference in the country with only half a team. "At the tip, Brad Sellers said to me, 'Oh, it's going to be a long night for you guys,' " Wilson remembers. "I said, 'Don't be surprised.' " The Iron Five sat out a total of two minutes between them, each scored in double figures, and pulled off one of the great emotional victories in school history. All 13,443 fans in the Barn were on their feet cheering as Minnesota left the floor with a 70-65 victory.

"That was probably the biggest victory I ever had at the University," Wilson says. "No matter what I do, I don't think I can ever get that feeling again, that one game was so special.

"At the time, we probably came together as a team, though you can't say how good you are based solely on wins. I always thought we were a great team then in the sense that we talked to each other, hung out together, came together. We shared a lot and we played well. The intensity was there, and the younger guys were willing to accept leadership."

But the rest of the season would be a long, tiring journey. Indiana used its depth to overcome an 11-point deficit at Williams Arena and win, 62-54. The Gophers then shocked Iowa, 65-60, behind 22 points for Wilson and 18 for Shasky. In Ann Arbor, Michigan never gave the exhausted Gophers a chance in its 92-56 rout. The next game, at Michigan State, was closer, but the Spartans still won, 76-66. Northwestern came to the Barn and gave Minnesota its third straight defeat, 65-60. The Iron Five just plain ran out of gas at home against Wisconsin, as the Badgers ran the Gophers up and down the court and won, 70-64. No. 16 Indiana rarely loses at home, and there was no way they would lose against a Minnesota team as worn out as this one. Everyone on the Minnesota bench played at least two minutes, including Juneau who was in for 17, as Williams tried to give his Iron Five just a little rest. But the result was a 95-63 Hoosier win. Ohio State was the next team to beat the Gophers on the road, this time 68-55. The Gophers very nearly had another victory at home as they came from behind twice and beat Purdue before falling short, 64-63. And the season mercifully came to an end at the Barn as No. 19 Illinois came in and overcame 18 points from Wilson, 17 from Shasky, and 16 from Smith to win, 73-64.

Those final eight straight losses put the Gophers at 15-16 overall and 5-13 in the Big Ten for their third consecutive eighth-place finish. Wilson finished with a 16.2 points per game average, followed by Shasky with 15.0 points and 7.0 rebounds, Smith with 7.6 points, Gaffney with 6.4 points, and Hanson with 4.4 points. On the final statistics sheet for the 1985-86 season, after Holmgren, who was bothered all year by sore knees, and after all the football-player walk-ons, there is the "Other" category. Those "Others" averaged 44.4 points per game. But beyond that, they and their actions, and the response of the school and the community that followed, left a mark on the Minnesota basketball program that would have to be cleaned off by hard work—not only on the basketball court, but in the court of public opinion, which did not hold Golden Gopher basketball in the highest esteem just then.

It would be up to whomever accepted the challenge of being the next Minnesota head basketball coach to change all that.

SECTION 7

On April 1, 1986, the University of Minnesota men's basketball program was like a mess of broken pieces scattered across the Williams Arena floor. Less than four months earlier, the University president had called into question the very existence of the team and its participation in the Big Ten, three of its players stood accused of sexual assault, one other player had left the team, and its coach had resigned in anger over the lack of support he and his charges had received from the administration.

On April 2, the University took a major step towards picking up those pieces. Clem Haskins flew to Minneapolis from Bowling Green, Kentucky, where he had been head coach at Western Kentucky University for six seasons, and accepted the head coaching job at the University of Minnesota. The 42-year-old Haskins, a former college consensus All-American and NBA first-round draft pick, left a program he had rebuilt into a perennial 20-game winner. He took over a team that had won only five conference games the year before, and that would field six freshmen and a junior-college transfer and no one taller than 6-foot-7. He also was faced with the task of winning back the trust and support of fans, students, and faculty, who were tiring of losing seasons and off-the-court controversies and were staying away from Williams Arena in ever-increasing numbers.

■ *A sold-out Williams Arena crowd celebrates one of Voshon Lenard's three-pointers during Minnesota's stunning 106-56 upset of Indiana in 1994.*

Haskins knew what he was getting into, leaving an excellent program and walking straight into a swirl of uncertainty. "It wasn't a good job at the time," he says of the Minnesota job. "I felt like I should go where I'm needed. Minnesota needed me to give direction to the program, to get it headed in the right direction, to make a solid program. The community was divided over the program, and we needed to give people confidence in the Maroon and Gold again. Nobody was wearing Maroon and Gold. I was confident I could do that in due time."

Haskins managed to convince incoming freshman Willie Burton—one of the most highly sought players in the nation—to stay with his plans to attend the U. Haskins then signed center Richard Coffey, but he warned Gopher fans to prepare for the worst. Anything more than five wins in the team's 28-game schedule, he said, would be an achievement. "We were down to eight guys when we started," Haskins remembers. "The coaches had to work out with the players so we would have enough people. I knew on paper we wouldn't win very many basketball games. Everybody was 10 to 15 points better."

The Gophers began what promised to be a long season at home with a game against North Dakota State. Normally, NDSU would be a team Minnesota could handle easily, but this year Clem Haskins wiped a tear from his eye after the Gophers posted a 70-53 victory.

The Gophers followed that with an 86-72 road loss to Houston, but Kelvin Smith scored 20 points and Willie Burton came off the bench to add 13. Even though the Gophers lost, they played competitively against a strong team. Minnesota continued to play reasonably well, splitting its next two games, and they went into the contest against Austin Peay at the Barn with a 3-2 record.

The honeymoon stopped there. The Gophers lost 73-64 in a game in which Minnesota players didn't hustle, didn't execute, and didn't shoot well. Clem Haskins' postgame press conference went like this: "First of all, gentlemen, we're going to practice in about 30 minutes, so make it quick. I'm in no damn mood to come in here on a night when a group of guys plays like that." He spoke for about 30 seconds more and walked out of the room and back to his players. Haskins wanted to drive that point home,

■ *Ray Gaffney was one of the few veterans the Gophers had to start the difficult 1986-87 season.*

so he brought the team back into the deserted Williams Arena for a post-game practice that ended at 11:30 that night.

"I lost it," Haskins remembers. "I had never lost to Austin Peay in my life. It killed me personally. And I wanted to start building a foundation—we were not going to take a backseat to anybody at home."

The message came across. When the Gophers traveled to Michigan to take on Detroit, they were a different basketball team from the one that was embarrassed by Austin Peay. The result was a 76-68 win, and it propelled the Gophers to win their final three nonconference games and enter the Big Ten season with a 7-3 record. The Gophers continued to play above their heads as they plowed through their conference schedule. They opened at home against Wisconsin, and won 69-67 on Kim Zurcher's 15-foot jumper with three seconds remaining; Zurcher had 16 of his 18 points in the second half and Kelvin Smith scored 22 as Minnesota rallied from a 10-point second-half deficit. For the second time in the 1986-87 season, Clem Haskins shed tears after the game. Minnesota had to overcome another big second-half lead against Northwestern, as the Gophers won their sixth straight to go 2-0 in the Big Ten.

Reality, when it finally comes, can be an ugly thing. Minnesota fans and players were talking confidently about taking on Iowa, ranked second in the nation, in the sold-out Williams Arena. But the Hawkeyes bulldozed the Gophers, 78-57, in a game that was never close. The story did not get much better after that. Minnesota had to face two more top-10 teams in rapid succession, number six Purdue and number eight Illinois, and got pounded each time. The losses came one after another after that. Ohio State. Indiana. Michigan. Michigan State. Iowa. Illinois. Purdue. Indiana. Ohio State. Michigan. Michigan State. Wisconsin. Northwestern. In their final 16 games, the Gophers lost 16 times, to finish at 9-19 overall and 2-16 in the Big Ten, which left them in ninth place.

There was reason for optimism the following season. The six freshmen were now six sophomores, the team had shown improvement even as it lost its final 16 games, and the Gopher players had accepted Clem Haskins' hardnosed regimen of long practices and discipline in order to become a better team. But when Minnesota faced Drake in the 1987-88 season opener, it appeared that little had changed. The Gophers blew an 11-point second-half lead and lost their 17th straight game, 70-67. The losing streak ended two days later, when the Gophers took the Western Illinois Leathernecks, 84-52. But they lost their next two, against Toledo and Colorado State, and suddenly the Gophers were 1-3 against a nonconference schedule that did not promise to be overly intimidating. They recovered, though, behind Richard Coffey's dominating rebounding and the hot scoring hand of sophomore Melvin Newbern, who had sat out his freshman year for academic reasons. The Gophers won five of their last six and ended their non-conference schedule at 6-4.

Minnesota would quickly find out if it could compete in the Big Ten in 1987-88: the still-young team opened against Illinois, ranked 19th in the nation. They passed the test, even though they lost the game, 65-61 in overtime, with 20 points and 14 rebounds from sophomore Willie Burton. Minnesota had a chance to at least tie the game in overtime when Melvin Newbern intercepted a pass with 46 seconds left. He dribbled downcourt and fed freshman guard Kevin Lynch. Lynch passed up an easy eight-footer and tried to pass the ball to Burton. But Burton lost control of the ball, Illinois recovered, and Kendall Gill dunked at the other end with seven seconds remaining to give the Illini the win.

"To play those guys that close was a tremendous accomplishment," Haskins says. "We were not even in the same ballpark with them, but no one ever wanted to play us twice in the same day, because they knew they would be in for a dogfight. That game helped us develop self-confidence, and other teams developed respect for us."

Michigan's Glen Rice almost single-handedly destroyed the Gophers, scoring 40 points on 15-of-20 shooting as the Wolverines beat Minnesota, 103-71, for the 17th out of 18 games at Crisler Arena. The worst thing for a struggling team is to have to play three-straight top-20 teams, but the Gophers still had to face eighth-ranked Purdue; the Boilermakers won 82-74, even though Minnesota played them close in a game in which Purdue went to the line 32 more

times than did the Gophers. Minnesota had high hopes heading to Northwestern to take on a fellow struggling team (1-3 in the Big Ten), but even that was no help as the Wildcats walked away with a 65-61 victory. The Gophers' conference losing streak stretched to 21 games over two seasons when they lost at home to Ohio State, 85-76.

Finally, Clem Haskins was able to relax and celebrate a little after a game. Twenty-one conference games and one year and 18 days after his team's last Big Ten win, the non-smoker lit up a cigar to mark the end of the Big Ten's longest losing streak since 1946 with a 59-56 victory over Michigan State. That was also Minnesota's first Big Ten road win since January 23, 1986 in Madison—the game before the team was rocked by the sexual assault scandal. In the game

■ *Freshman Willie Burton puts in a layup against Illinois in 1987, part of Minnesota's infamous 21-game conference losing streak.*

■ *Melvin Newbern launches a layup against Illinois in 1988.*

■ **Opposite** *Richard Coffey, the Gophers' best rebounder since Kevin McHale, goes up for a board against Purdue in 1988.*

big to Illinois in Champaign, 86-50. The Gophers built a two-game home winning streak by beating Northwestern 82-67, led by Richard Coffey's 15 points and 16 rebounds, with 14 points from Kevin Lynch and 13 from Burton, who was battling a sore knee.

Michigan came to Williams Arena ranked 10th in the nation. At one point in the second half, the Wolverines led by 14 points, but the Gophers fought back and not only avoided a blowout, but had the ball with 19 seconds left, trailing by only two points. Guard Kim Zurcher brought the ball downcourt, looking either to shoot a three-pointer or to get the ball inside for a three-point play. He swung the ball to junior guard Ray Gaffney, who rimmed out a 12-foot jumper, and Michigan got the rebound, made two free throws at the other end, and avoided an upset, 82-78. As they left the court, the Gophers got a standing ovation from the crowd of 11,082.

Iowa, the No. 13 team in the nation, came to town three days later, and this time 16,406 turned out to see their team, which was playing better basketball than its record of 9-14 overall and 3-10 in the Big Ten would indicate. The Gophers played well and gave a strong effort, but they simply didn't have the talent to keep up with the quick and deep Hawkeyes. Iowa was up by only eight at the half, but they pulled away and went on to a 107-86 win, despite Tim Hanson's career-high 22 points for the Gophers. Minnesota's usual road woes continued, with losses at Wisconsin and Ohio State. Michigan State then visited Williams Arena to become the victim of the Gophers' fourth conference win. Willie Burton scored 20 points, and the Spartans' Kirk Manns missed the second half of a one-and-one with one second left, and Minnesota escaped, 62-61.

After losses to Indiana at home and Purdue on the road (bringing Minnesota's season road record to 2-12), the Gophers finished the season at 10-18 overall and 4-14 in the Big Ten. The record was slightly better than the season before, but still good enough only for ninth place. The Gophers then began the process of preparing for the following season, one that presumably would show the improvement that a now-veteran team ought to have.

But before that could happen, the team had to deal with yet another in a 17-year history of off-the-court hassles.

against the Spartans, Willie Burton scored the game's last nine points and led the Gophers with 20.

"I never thought that would happen," Haskins says of the losing streak. "There were times when I didn't know if we would win another one. But I had to get myself primed and ready to go the next day. I had to think of something different to say. I'd say something like, 'You still have all your limbs. Let's be thankful for that. Let's go.'

"It took a lot out of me. I aged about 10 years during that streak."

The celebration over that victory didn't last long, though, as the Gophers headed to Iowa City and were shellacked by the Hawkeyes, 76-51. They beat Wisconsin at home, 71-62, and lost

■ *Richard Coffey cele-*
brates a Gopher victory
during their 1988-89 Sweet
16 season.

This time it was another NCAA violation, for recruiting infractions that occurred during Jim Dutcher's tenure, and
the announcement a week before the
end of the season that the Gophers were
being placed on two years probation
and would only be allowed to have two,
rather than the usual three, coaches
engaging in off-campus recruiting for
the following year. The Gophers were
also banned from postseason play for
the 1987-88 season—not a crushing
penalty for a team that had just gone 10-
18 and had no hope of a postseason bid
anyway.

Clem Haskins began the 1988-89
season by promising little and trying to
keep hopes low. After two straight ninth-
place Big Ten finishes and a grand total
of six conference victories, Haskins
finally had a veteran nucleus and a
group of talented players, but he was
taking nothing for granted. "You win
with talent," he told the Minneapolis
Star Tribune before the season. "I'm not
running my players down, but I'm realistic. I think the average fan knows we
don't have the talent of other people, but
you can make up for that with hard
work, by staying together, and by playing your hearts out every night." Sixth or
seventh place, Haskins predicted.

Guard Ray Gaffney was a senior,
and Haskins was counting on him to
look for more shots and improve on his
previous season's scoring average of 9.4
points per game. Forwards Richard Coffey and Willie Burton, center Jim Shikenjanski, and guard Melvin Newbern
were juniors; all were coming off good
sophomore seasons and now needed
even bigger years. Guard Kevin Lynch
and forward Walter Bond were sophomores who had to prove themselves
coming off the bench. And the Gophers
had high hopes for the potential of 7-foot
freshman Bob Martin of Apple Valley.
The stage was set for at least a better
year than Haskins' first two as Minnesota head coach.

Things did not start well, though.
With Willie Burton sitting out the year's
first game for cutting class, the Gophers
blew a 15-point second-half lead and
lost to Ball State in overtime, 63-57. The
hurt didn't last long, as the Gophers
toyed with some lesser opponents, beating Youngstown State by 33, Maryland-
Eastern Shore by 44, and Florida
International by 24. But the Gophers'
first road game, against Drake, stopped
the team cold. Drake won, 66-52, as the
Gophers shot 32.2 percent from the floor
and only Willie Burton (19 points) scored

in double figures. Minnesota picked up its game for the rest of the nonconference schedule, whipping off wins against Marquette and Northern Illinois on the road and Detroit, Denver, and Kansas State at home to finish the nonconference schedule at 8-2.

Those games did little to help anybody predict how well the Gophers would play against Big Ten opponents. They played impressively against teams they should have beaten, but their performance against good teams was spotty. The conference opener against Wisconsin did not help clear the picture any; Minnesota played a lackluster game and fell to the Badgers, 75-67. They lost in Ann Arbor to seventh-ranked Michigan, then headed home to take on Iowa, which was ranked fifth in the nation. The Gophers left the raised floor of Williams Arena with an 80-78 victory on Shikenjanski's tip-in with time running out.

"The Iowa game was really the turnaround for us," Lynch says. "It gave us a lot of confidence. Melvin and Willie just did it all, and when we beat them we started to feel like we could beat anybody."

That was a significant win for Haskins, because they not only played a nationally-ranked opponent close, but they came through under pressure and won. "The time for moral victories was over," he remembers. "It was time to say, hey, if you're good enough to play people close, you should expect to win."

They beat Purdue, lost to Northwestern on the road, and came back to Minneapolis to face the nation's top-ranked team, Illinois. The Gophers shocked the Illini, 69-62, and began to turn heads around the nation as the new giant killers. But their conference record was still 3-3, and they were 11-5 overall. Not necessarily NCAA Tournament material; they still had a lot to prove. For the rest of the Big Ten season, Minnesota sometimes showed it belonged with the best teams in the nation, and sometimes it didn't. The seesaw season included a letdown loss at Michigan State, a home win over Ohio State, a road loss to Indiana, a last-second win over Wisconsin at Williams Arena, an upset victory over Michigan at home, a 38-point thrashing at the hands of Iowa in Iowa City, road losses at Purdue and Illinois, and a home loss to Indiana, before reeling off three straight wins against Northwestern, Michigan State, and Ohio State to finish the conference season in fifth place at 9-9, with a 17-11 overall record.

Lynch remembers that the Ohio State game was a key. "We felt like we had to win that game if we had any chance of going to the NCAAs. We played our butts off to win that game, because we figured, we didn't have much to lose, and we had a chance, so let's go for it."

It was those last three wins that showed Haskins that this team had both the will and the talent to compete with anybody. When they absolutely had to win their final three games to

■ *Clem Haskins watches his team during its 1989 NCAA Tournament appearance.*

Gopher Glory
128

...NO WAY DID I THINK WE'D GET INTO THE SWEET 16. IT WAS TOO FAR-FETCHED. THAT TEAM DID ONE WHALE OF A JOB.

have any chance to play in the NCAA Tournament, they did just that. "We won a lot of big games, but those last three were the most important. You could feel it in the air; we had finally turned it around."

The Gophers seemed assured of postseason play—at least a bid to the National Invitational Tournament—though they were on the bubble for the NCAA Tournament. But they got the bid Haskins felt they deserved, and headed to Greensboro, North Carolina, to play the same Kansas State team they had beaten by five points at Williams Arena two months before. This time the Gophers knew what to expect, they had the confidence of having knocked off several nationally-ranked teams, and they had a decidedly easier time the second time around, advancing to the second round with an 86-75 win. There the Gophers faced Siena, which had scored the biggest upset of the first round by beating Stanford. But this was the end of Siena's run; Minnesota played sloppy, uninspired basketball for most of the game and still came up with an 80-67 victory, advancing to the NCAA's Sweet 16 for the first time in school history.

"Once you get in postseason play, it's a whole new season," Haskins says, "but no way did I think we'd get into the Sweet 16. It was too far-fetched. That team did one whale of a job."

Hundreds of the Gopher faithful made the trip to East Rutherford, New Jersey, to watch the Gophers take on national powerhouse Duke. Remember, at the beginning of the season Clem Haskins was trying to keep expectations low by predicting a sixth- or seventh-place conference finish, and no one was predicting a run to the third round of the NCAA Tournament. Of course, everybody was predicting a Duke trip to the Final Four, and the Blue Devils made Minnesota little more than a stepping stone in that path with an 87-70 display that told Gopher fans just how far their program had to go to compete with the top schools in the nation. These fans were thrilled to be in the position to learn that lesson nonetheless. The Gophers had tasted success; now they had to prove they had the talent and the desire to taste it again.

"When we were getting ready to leave New Jersey, Bob Martin and I were

sitting around the airport," Lynch says. "All we could talk about was getting back to Minneapolis and starting to lift weights for next season."

The 1989-90 Gophers were a team with talent and experience and, for the first time in Clem Haskins' tenure at Minnesota, high expectations. After a summer tour of Australia and New Zealand where they went 7-0 against relatively easy teams, the Gophers settled down to practice, only to find they were ranked 20th in the nation in preseason polls—the team's first national ranking since it finished sixth in the final 1981-82 poll. It put added pressure on the team, especially since Willie Burton, who had led the team the previous year with 18.6 points per game, missed almost the entire preseason workout schedule because of ankle problems. Senior forward Richard Coffey was also coming off a serious knee injury, senior guard Melvin Newbern had had hernia surgery in the offseason, freshman center Ernest Nzigamasabo had had knee problems, and senior center Jim Shikenjanski began the year battling an infected foot blister.

There was a distraction on another front. Once again the NCAA was investigating the Gophers, who were already missing a scholarship for violations that occurred during Jim Dutcher's tenure, this time for alleged payments made to football and basketball players by former University administrator Luther Darville. Darville was convicted in November 1989 of misappropriating University funds.

The Gophers were confident when they travelled to Cincinnati to take on the Bearcats and their new coach, Bob Huggins. Three seasons later Cincinnati would go to the Final Four, but they were lightly regarded in 1989; Minnesota's opinion changed as the team headed back to Minneapolis with a 66-64 defeat. "That was a good loss for us," Haskins says. "We gave the game to them, and it woke everybody up."

The Gophers recovered their form quickly, rattling off nonconference wins against Chicago State, Toledo, Iowa State, Detroit, Kansas State, Washington, Northern Illinois, Youngstown State, and Rider, to move to 9-1. The win over Youngstown State was by 40 points, and they beat Rider by an incredible 68 points; this was a team entering the Big Ten season on a confident roll.

That confidence translated into a 91-74 whipping of Illinois to open the conference season. Melvin Newbern out-scored Illini star Kendall Gill 27-15, and Newbern's trash talking eventually led Gill to give the Gopher a forearm to the jaw, earning him an intentional foul. The Gophers, who had dropped out of the Top 20 after the loss to Cincinnati, jumped back up to No. 16 with the victory over Illinois.

The Gophers got a dose of reality, though, in the following two games. They travelled to Purdue and trailed the Boilermakers by 13 points at the half and by 18 with seven minutes to play.

ahead, 83-78. But the Gophers couldn't stay home forever, and they were forced to venture to Madison and another road loss.The Gophers were again down by a lot (21 points with 12 minutes left), and they again came back to lead with 50 seconds to play. But they lost, 77-75, on a last-second alley-oop dunk. They returned to Minneapolis to defeat Iowa, 84-72, as Burton had 21 points and 10 rebounds, Coffey 14 points and 13 rebounds, and Newbern 17 points and nine assists.

Then Indiana came to town to meet a newly confident Minnesota team and 16,636 fans. The Gopher seniors were try-

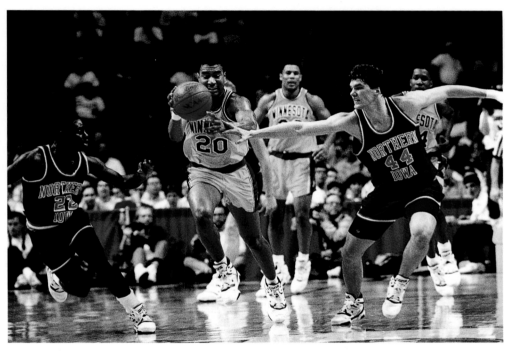

■ *Melvin Newbern slips past two Northern Illinois defenders during the Gophers' 1990 NCAA Tournament victory.*

Minnesota put up a furious rally and closed the gap to five points, led by Willie Burton's 22 points and 19 from Kevin Lynch. Purdue pulled away at the end, winning 86-78. Minnesota moved on to the arena of another top-ranked club—Michigan—and again played a solid game but came up short. The Gophers were down by 10 points with 1:35 remaining, but they cut the lead to one point with 34 seconds left. Despite Willie Burton's 20 points, Walter Bond's 19, and Kevin Lynch's 16, Michigan pulled away and won, 87-83.

Minnesota got a break in the following game at Williams Arena, running over Northwestern—which was living through the one-game suspensions of three of its five starters—by a score of 97-75. The Gophers followed that with another home game against a young team, this time Ohio State, coming out

ing to beat Indiana for the first time in their four years at Minnesota. In their effort, Willie Burton scored 22 points, while five other Gophers, Coffey, Shikenjanski, Lynch, Newbern, and Bond, all scored at least 14 points, and senior guard Connell Lewis added eight points. Minnesota shot 55.7 percent from the floor, hit 35 of 40 free throws, and committed only eight turnovers. The end result: a towering 108-89 Minnesota win that moved the Gophers to the 19th ranking in the Associated Press national poll.

Indeed, the Gophers were playing like a nationally-ranked team. They proved that beyond a doubt when they travelled to Michigan State and firmly shook off their road jinx, beating the Spartans, 79-74, to give Clem Haskins only his third conference road win in 31 tries, to move the Gophers up to the 17th ranking, and to put Minnesota in second

■ *Willie Burton puts up an outside jumper as the Gophers try to hold onto their thin lead against Syracuse in the 1990 NCAA Tournament.*

place in the conference at 6-3. But they had to travel to Illinois to face the Illini and Kendall Gill, who had not forgotten about the drubbing the Gophers had given them five weeks earlier, nor about how Melvin Newbern had rubbed it in. Gill exploded for 26 points and Illinois won, 99-72.

The Gophers would need a big run for the rest of the season to compete for the Big Ten title, but they seemed up to the task, eking out a 73-72 home win over Purdue. They lost their next Williams Arena contest to Michigan, 77-73, to end their 12-game home winning streak and fall to fourth place in the Big Ten at 7-5. They headed to Northwestern to break an unlikely hex: They had not beaten the lowly Wildcats in three previous tries. But the Gophers put a lethar-

■ *Jim Shikenjanski and Walter Bond try for a rebound against Syracuse in the 1990 NCAA Tournament.*

gic first half behind them to win, 90-72. Minnesota traveled to Iowa City and worked to put their label as road losers even further behind them; they won their third of four road games by a convincing 102-80 score.

Next was Bloomington, the home of the Indiana Hoosiers, one of the most feared venues in college basketball. But the Gophers were on a roll, and they rolled to victory number 20, only the fifth time a Gopher team had done so. This team that had won so many games was populated by five seniors — Richard Coffey, Willie Burton, Melvin Newbern, Jim Shikenjanski, and Connell Lewis — who had suffered as freshmen through the endless 9-19 season of 1986-87.

Those same seniors returned home to Williams Arena for their final time to take on Michigan State, but they lost an overtime heartbreaker, 75-73. Still, the five seniors received a long standing ovation from the sellout crowd as they took one final lap around the Barn's raised floor.

The 19th-ranked Gophers stayed at 20 wins through the regular season; they lost their final Big Ten game, 93-83, against Ohio State in Columbus, despite a career-high 31 points from Willie Burton. The Gophers finished at 20-8 overall, 11-7 in the Big Ten. Despite those final two losses, it was easily a season worthy of an NCAA bid, and it sent Minnesota to Richmond, Virginia, to take on the Texas-El Paso Miners in the Southeast Regional.

It was ugly. It was sloppy. UTEP turned the ball over 23 times and tried only 42 field goals in 45 minutes. Minnesota took a total of 86 shots from the field and the free throw line, and they missed 51, shooting 33 percent from the field. But Kevin Lynch kept the Gophers in the game by scoring 18 points, and they persevered in overtime, 64-61.

They were able to play again in Richmond, this time against Northern Iowa, who had upset Missouri in the first round. Willie Burton confirmed his role as the soul of a team that had come through tremendous adversity to play so well together; he scored a career-high 36 points and had 12 rebounds, and Melvin Newbern added nine assists to lead the Gophers to an 81-78 win over UNI and a berth in the Sweet 16 for the second year in a row.

The season before, Minnesota had been a team that was surprised to be in the third round of the NCAA Tournament, and it showed in a poor game against Duke. This time, the Gophers fully expected to get to where they were, and they were ready to meet Syracuse in New Orleans. The Gophers shot 79 percent from the field in the second half, and five Minnesota players finished in double figures, including 20 from Newbern, 18 from Kevin Lynch, and 10 from Bob Martin in 16 minutes. The result was an 82-75 victory, and the Gophers' first-ever appearance in the NCAA Final Eight.

The opponent would be Georgia Tech, with its deadly combination of Dennis Scott, Kenny Anderson, and Brian Oliver. But for nearly 40 minutes Minnesota was up to the task. Willie Burton scored 35 points and Jim Shikenjanski had 19. The Gophers dominated the Yellow Jackets inside and controlled the pace of the game, even though Georgia Tech wound up shooting an astounding 35 free throws to the Gophers' mere 11— a disparity that could well have meant the difference in the game. But Minnesota and its five seniors would not give up, and when down 93-88 with seven seconds left, Burton hit a three-pointer to cut the deficit to two. Kenny Anderson was fouled and missed the front end of a one-and-one. Coffey pulled down the board, threw to Mario Green, and Green found Lynch at midcourt. Lynch dribbled to the corner and launched a three-pointer over 6-foot-9 Johnny McNeil that would have sent the Gophers to the Final Four. The shot fell short as the buzzer sounded, and Minnesota's dream season was over with a 93-91 defeat.

"I kept thinking he was going to foul me, and when the shot didn't fall, I couldn't believe it," Lynch says. "I'm sad it didn't happen, but it was still a great year and we were very happy about it. Still, I sometimes think, 'What if ...' "

But it was still one of the best seasons in Gopher history. They finished 23-9 (11-7 and fourth place in the Big Ten), and advanced farther than any Gopher team since the 1919 national championship season. But the record and the achievements were made more remarkable by remembering what the program was like in 1986, when then-freshmen Willie Burton, Melvin Newbern, Jim Shikenjanski, Richard Coffey, and Connell Lewis, along with new coach Clem Haskins, stepped into a

I KEPT THINKING HE WAS GOING TO FOUL ME, AND WHEN THE SHOT DIDN'T FALL, I COULDN'T BELIEVE IT," LYNCH SAYS. "I'M SAD IT DIDN'T HAPPEN, BUT IT WAS STILL A GREAT YEAR AND WE WERE VERY HAPPY ABOUT IT. STILL, I SOMETIMES THINK, 'WHAT IF...'

Gopher Glory
134

Opposite page *Willie Burton goes in for a layup against Georgia Tech in the 1990 NCAA Tournament quarterfinal game. Walter Bond (left) drives to the hoop against Georgia Tech in the 1990 NCAA Tournament. Kevin Lynch (below) brings the ball up the court against Syracuse in the 1990 NCAA Tournament.*

dying program and in four years turned it from a doormat team that lost 21 straight conference games into one of the best-respected programs in the nation. They, along with juniors Kevin Lynch, Walter Bond, and the rest of the team, turned those four years into a Minnesota era, one that ended just a jump shot away from the Final Four.

"It felt really good to get to that point," Haskins remembers. "When you look at our program and where it started, I was just elated for those players.

"They showed tremendous class and character. They knew they had to overcome adversity, and they did because they were a group of young men who fed off each other. They wouldn't let one another get down. It's something that is tough to find in sports."

It was time for another rebuilding year in 1990-91. Willie Burton was playing for the Miami Heat, having been selected in the first round of the NBA draft. Richard Coffey, Jim Shikenjanski, and Melvin Newbern—the rest of the soul of the previous season—had all graduated as well. Kevin Lynch was back after averaging 13.4 points per game the year before, as was Walter Bond (10.5 points per game). But no other returning Gopher had averaged more than 3 points per game in 1989-90. No one was predicting the Final Eight for the Gophers this time.

Lynch remembers it was a difficult year for him. "There was a lot of frustration. I had grown up with the whole senior class from last year, and that was my era with those guys. It was just Walter Bond, Ray Metcalf, and me and a bunch of younger guys."

Minnesota opened its season at home against a strong Robert Morris College team, and won, 74-61, behind 19 points from Lynch and 12 from freshman Randy Carter. But Bond broke his foot during that game, and the Gophers could little afford to lose such a pivotal player in the season opener. The Gophers moved on to two overmatched opponents and ripped them both: Augusta College, 90-60, and Northern Illinois, 65-37. They took to the road and won there, too, 84-70 against Iowa State. Kevin Lynch continued to assert himself as the team leader, scoring 18 points and adding seven rebounds and four assists. Arriel McDonald had 17 points and seven assists, the front court of Carter, Ernest Nzigamasabo, and Dana Jackson

combined for 31 points and 20 rebounds, and Rob Metcalf replaced the injured Bond with 10 points and nine rebounds.

The Gophers continued their winning streak by defeating Santa Clara, 73-63. They did it by outrebounding the Broncos 42-29 and outscoring them from the bench 29-4, led by Dana Jackson's 15. Although they went 6-0 for the first time since 1976-77 by beating Oregon State, 64-53, Haskins very nearly brought the team back onto the floor for an Austin Peay-like practice because the Gophers had failed to put away the Beavers after leading 24-9 with seven minutes left in the first half.

The inexperienced Gophers had played well in running up their winning streak, but that record was deceptive. A superior Cincinnati team showed that with a convincing 72-64 win over the Gophers, who shot 38.2 percent for the game. Minnesota continued its journey with a trip to Seattle and a 72-61 defeat at the hands of the Washington Huskies. Then they faced 19th-ranked Virginia at Williams Arena, but were overmatched and fell, 79-72. Minnesota needed a confidence boost, and they got it in Ohio, where the Gophers took on Youngstown State and snapped their three-game losing streak with a 95-77 win. The Gophers broke out of their funk with 23 points from Lynch, 17 from Jackson, 15 from Carter, 12 points and 11 assists from McDonald, and, most importantly, 11 points from Walter Bond, playing in his first game since the season opener.

After a 7-3 nonconference season, it was time for the Gophers to find out how good they really were, and the beginning of their Big Ten schedule did not raise much optimism. Kevin Lynch scored 17 points in Madison, but it was not enough to help Minnesota, which fell 72-62 to Wisconsin. Three days later in Champaign, the Gophers outplayed Illinois, but they lost, 67-66, on a free throw with three seconds remaining.

The Gophers returned home demoralized from the Illinois loss, but they rebounded to overcome a 12-point halftime deficit against Iowa to win, 79-77, behind 26 points from Lynch, and 17 each from Bond and Rob Metcalf. They managed to string together a two-game winning streak with an ugly, sluggish 59-56 home win over Purdue in a game that was tied 20-20 at halftime. But strong defense will only carry a team so far when it is playing sloppy basketball

THEY SHOWED TREMENDOUS CLASS AND CHARACTER. THEY KNEW THEY HAD TO OVERCOME ADVERSITY, AND THEY DID BECAUSE THEY WERE A GROUP OF YOUNG MEN WHO FED OFF EACH OTHER. THEY WOULDN'T LET ONE ANOTHER GET DOWN. IT'S SOMETHING THAT IS TOUGH TO FIND IN SPORTS.

and shooting poorly. In East Lansing, the Gophers shot 40 percent from the field—the only bright spot was 25 points on 10-of-16 shooting with five three-pointers from freshman Arriel McDonald—and lost to defending Big Ten champions Michigan State, 73-64.

The Gophers, a team in need of victories either real or moral, came home to

In a season of games Minnesota predictably lost, the next game at Williams Arena against Michigan was particularly hard to take. That was a game the Gophers should have won, but they left the court carrying a 66-62 defeat. Then it was back to the games the Gophers were expected to lose. Indiana had replaced Ohio State as the

■ *Kevin Lynch was the leader of the young, inexperienced 1990-91 Gophers.*

host Ohio State, which was ranked fourth in the nation. Lynch pumped in 27 points and the Gophers turned in a furious rally to cut a 17-point Buckeye lead to only six with 38 seconds to play. Ohio State proved too strong, winning 80-70, but Haskins had a moral victory nonetheless. That spirit continued to Evanston, where the Gophers routed Northwestern, 85-68, behind Randy Carter's powerful 29 points and 15 rebounds.

fourth best team in the nation, and they came into Williams Arena, played a subpar game, and came out with a 77-66 win. Illinois was next at the Barn. Lynch scored 28 points, but the Gophers as a team made only one-third of their field goal attempts and fell, 94-74, for their fourth straight home loss.

The Gophers traveled next to Carver-Hawkeye Arena, and they lost again, 82-69. Clem Haskins decided at that point that it was time for a change; he kept seniors Lynch and Bond out of the starting lineup on the road against Purdue, replacing them with Bob Martin and Nate Tubbs. The seniors entered the game midway through the first half and Bond responded with 15 points, but it was not enough. The Boilermakers won, 89-82.

The Gophers played an outstanding game in Columbus against Ohio State, but even good execution and strong play from Randy Carter, with 17 points and nine rebounds, were not enough. Minnesota lost, 63-62, and Haskins lost his temper with the Big Ten officials, who had frustrated him all season. He received a technical foul during the game, and after the game he called the officials "jackasses," and said the Gophers had "big-time screws put to us." To make matters worse, Minnesota lost Walter Bond to another foot injury after he scored 13 first-half points on five-for-five shooting from the field.

Haskins settled down for the next game, at Williams Arena against Michigan State. Kevin Lynch also stepped up, scoring a career-high 29 points, but even that wasn't enough as the Gophers fell to the Spartans, 74-72, for their seventh straight loss and fifth straight at the Barn. The losing streak finally fell against Northwestern in a physical, uneven game. Lynch scored 22 points, Ernest Nzigamasabo had 21, Randy Carter scored 17, and mild-mannered Rob Metcalf was ejected after a flagrant foul with 11 minutes remaining; the end result of the battle for last place in the Big Ten was an 88-70 Gophers win.

Minnesota next lost on the road against Michigan, 68-60, then got clobbered, 75-59, by Indiana. The Gophers returned home for the season finale against Wisconsin in front of 16,622 fans. It was also the end of the college careers of Kevin Lynch, Walter Bond, Rob Metcalf, and Mario Green. Lynch scored 18 points and Metcalf and Green had 11 apiece; Bond missed his fifth straight game with a broken foot. It was a great ending to a frustrating season and a roller coaster four years for the seniors; Minnesota dominated the Badgers and came away with an 80-70 win. The Gophers finished the season 12-16 overall, and 5-13 in the Big Ten, worth a ninth-place finish.

After the season ended, the NCAA finally reached the end of a three-year investigation of the charges stemming from the Luther Darville case, taking away one basketball scholarship for one year in addition to placing penalties on the football and wrestling programs and placing Minnesota on probation for two years.

After a down year like the previous one, which was caused mainly by a lack of talent on the court, Clem Haskins and Gopher fans were looking forward to the 1991-92 season. It marked the freshman debuts of a recruiting class that had the potential to go as far as the Class of '90—that is, to within sight of the NCAA Final Four. Haskins brought in guard Voshon Lenard, from the same Detroit high school team that produced Michigan phenom Chris Webber; Ryan Wolf, a shooting guard from Martinsville, Indiana; Townsend Orr, another guard from Dolton, Illinois; forward Jayson Walton from Dallas; and forward-center Chad Kolander, the pride of Owatonna, Minnesota.

As promising as those five freshmen were, this was their first year in the Big Ten, and nobody was expecting them to run away with the conference championship just yet. So it seemed almost a little unfair when their first nonconference game in 1991-92 was against second-ranked Arkansas at the Maui Invitational in Hawaii. But the young team played well enough to make Haskins proud, living through the Razorbacks' game-long full-court press and losing, 92-83. They were led by sophomore Randy Carter, who had 19 points; sophomore Dana Jackson had 14 points, senior Bob Martin added 11, and Lenard and sophomore Arriel McDonald had 10 each. The next night, the Gophers controlled the tempo against Providence, and the result was an 89-82 Minnesota victory, in which Lenard scored 20 points, Martin had 15, and Orr had 12. Martin and Orr did not miss a field goal between them, going a combined 11-for-11. In the Maui Invitational consolation final, the Gophers showed they could play some defense as well. They were all over 25th-ranked Arizona State, forcing the Sun Devils into 27 percent shooting, and walking away with a stunning 69-37 victory.

The Gophers returned home to walk past overmatched Howard University, 95-54, behind a combined 24 points, 11 rebounds, and five blocks from centers

Martin and Nzigamasabo. They had a similarly easy challenge against Youngstown State, and they won that game, 98-59, with 11 points and 11 rebounds from Martin. Lenard scored 16 points in the next home rout, this one 86-59 against Akron.

The Gophers hit the road to take on Alabama-Birmingham. Randy Carter scored 20 points and had 10 rebounds and Lenard scored 18 points, all in the second half, but it wasn't enough; UAB won, 86-80. Back home, Martin scored 15 points and Lenard hit a jumper with two seconds remaining to give the Gophers a 68-66 win over Detroit Mercy. But their luck did not hold; Arriel McDonald missed a last-second three-pointer in Memphis and the Gophers fell to Memphis State, 65-62. But it was home again and back to easy opponents, as Minnesota quickly dispatched Weber State, 92-52, with 18 points and seven assists from McDonald.

The Gophers headed to Portland, Oregon, for the Far West Classic with Randy Carter in pain from an injured foot. A lot of questions remained unanswered after they had gone 7-3 against a schedule that sometimes did not test the team's abilities. They faced Oregon in the Classic's first game, and they easily won, 89-64, behind 18 points from Lenard, 16 from Jackson, and 14 from Orr. In the tournament's final game, they went against Oregon State, and did not fare nearly as well, losing 92-80. Returning home, Kolander scored 16 points against Iowa State, but the Gophers lost again, 76-73, to end their nonconference season at 8-5.

The Big Ten season began on the road at Indiana—not an appetizing prospect for a young, struggling team. The 10th-ranked Hoosiers proved that with a lopsided 96-50 defeat of the Gophers. But they learned lessons from that game. They walked into the Barn to take on No. 11 Michigan, and walked out with a convincing 73-64 upset of the Wolverines. Lenard paced his team with 25 points and 8 rebounds, and Minnesota's tenacious defense held Chris Webber to 4-for-14 shooting and Juwan Howard to 0-for-5. The Gophers came back from that game to eke out a messy 49-48 win over Wisconsin in Madison; Haskins was so wrapped up in the game that he dislocated his shoulder while making wild coaching gestures on the sidelines.

When Michigan State came to Williams Arena for the next game, the Spartans had supplanted Michigan with the 11th ranking nationally, but the result of the game was much the same. Riding Townsend Orr's 20 points in 18 minutes—including 5-for-5 from three-point range—and 10 points and six rebounds from Chad Kolander, Minnesota scored its second upset of the year, winning, 70-66. Next, the Gophers had to meet another nationally-ranked team, this time Ohio State, on the road, and while the outcome was not another upset, the team still played well. The Gophers got 19 points from Lenard and 16 from Orr, and they had a chance to win until the last 30 seconds, before coming up short, 72-69.

At home against Illinois, the Gophers shot 36 percent from the field and were outrebounded, 40-30, but they still took away a 54-53 victory on a last-second free throw by Dana Jackson. The Gophers, led by 17 points and seven rebounds from Martin and 14 points from Tubbs, walked past Northwestern, 92-50, at the Barn, but they were outplayed in Iowa City, as Iowa beat them, 87-70. Their next game was at Purdue, and they were frustrated there, 65-57. Minnesota then traveled to Evanston to take on Northwestern, the team they had beaten by a school-record 42 points 10 days earlier. This time, they found themselves tied with the Wildcats with 10 seconds remaining, and only a last-second jumper by McDonald saved them for a 57-55 victory.

Then it was time for the up-again, down-again Gophers to be up again as Indiana, ranked fourth in the nation, came to the Barn. Minnesota sought revenge for the 46-point thrashing they had taken in Bloomington earlier in the season, and they got it. A sellout crowd went crazy as they watched their team upset the Hoosiers, 71-67. But then it was down again. The Gophers went from that stunning victory to a stinging defeat in Champaign at the hands of Illinois, 74-58. In Ann Arbor, Michigan welcomed Minnesota to its home court to extract revenge for the upset earlier in the season. The result was a 95-70 Wolverines rout that sent the slumping Gophers to a 15-11 overall record, 7-6 in the Big Ten. They had five games remaining, four at home, and they most likely needed to win three of those games to earn an NCAA Tournament bid.

But Iowa came to Minneapolis and put a major crimp in the Gophers' hopes with a 79-64 win. The Gophers came back in the next game, riding McDonald's 22 points to a 76-57 home win over Wisconsin. Purdue came to the Barn and handed Minnesota a serious blow to its postseason hopes in the form of a 68-58 Boilermakers win. In order to have any chance for the NCAA field, Minnesota

After their late-season fold, the Gophers were happy to be playing any postseason game, even if it was an NIT game. McDonald scored 20 points, Lenard had 16, and Walton had 12 points and 12 rebounds. But it was a frustrating game for the Gophers—frustrating enough that Haskins was ejected for arguing with the officials with four minutes left in the first half—and Washington State held on for a 72-70 win to end Minnesota's season.

■ *The Gophers and their fans celebrate the 81-60 victory over Purdue in 1993.*

would have to win its final two games against national powers Michigan State on the road and Ohio State at home.

Michigan State outplayed Minnesota both offensively and defensively, and several Gopher mental errors led to a 66-57 Spartan win, essentially ending Minnesota's NCAA chances. Ohio State simply piled on the losses, routing the Gophers, 94-63, to send Minnesota's record over the final seven games to 1-6. Their overall record was 16-15, and their 8-10 Big Ten record earned them sixth place in the conference. It also earned them a National Invitational Tournament bid to play Washington State in Pullman, Washington, which the school accepted.

"We had a good year that year— we played about as well as we could expect," Haskins says, in response to those who felt the Gophers should have gone farther. "I think the expectations for that team were too great. Key players like Voshon and Jayson were freshmen. But we beat some good teams.

"It was a long year, and a rebuilding year. We did a good job, and I was very proud of those young men."

But the Gophers headed into the next year full of optimism. Only senior Bob Martin would not be back in 1992-93, and this team that had scored some stunning upsets along with suffering a share of crushing defeats was one year more mature. The Gophers hoped that extra dose of poise and experience would be enough to take this group to the next level.

Clem Haskins has taken a lot of grief over the years for packing his nonconference schedules with teams he once referred to as "cupcakes." The 1992-93 season opened no differently, but Haskins had no apologies; he felt the collection of low-level teams offered his players a chance to tune up and work on their skills in preparation for some more difficult nonconference opponents and the tough Big Ten schedule ahead —and it allowed the Gophers to build up their win-loss record to impress postseason selection committees. So it was no surprise when the Gophers rolled over exhibition opponents Athletes in Action, the Ukraine national team, and a Moscow club team. Then they ripped Division II Southern Illinois-Edwardsville, 108-64, and easily got past Middle Tennessee State, 88-65. Randy Carter had 16 points and nine rebounds in 21 minutes, but he left the game with a mild shoulder separation.

Minnesota was too strong and talented for Texas-San Antonio, which lost, 93-75. Bethune-Cookman was no match for the Gophers, falling 92-50, and Tennessee-Martin—led by Cal Luther, who had passed up the Minnesota coaching job that eventually went to Bill Musselman—suffered a similar fate, losing 92-63 in a game in which starting point guard Arriel McDonald left with a broken foot but Randy Carter returned to the lineup. The easy hyphen-row schedule ended with a road game against California-Santa Clara, which ended in an 87-63 victory. Minnesota entered the meat of its schedule with a 6-0 record— 9-0 counting exhibition games—but with not much of an idea of how good a team it had.

The Gophers traveled to Iowa State with McDonald and Carter in street clothes (Carter sprained his ankle in practice), and the Gophers paid the price for that and for poor shooting, suffering a stinging 99-65 defeat. Minnesota had to recover quickly from that loss to face Memphis and its superstar guard, Anfernee Hardaway. Senior reserve guard Nate Tubbs, filling in for McDonald, got the call to guard Hardaway and came through, holding the future NBA lottery pick to "only" 30

points in a strong 70-55 Gopher victory at the Barn. The Gophers wrapped up their nonconference schedule at 8-1 as they moved past another difficult opponent, Alabama-Birmingham, 74-59, behind 19 points and 10 rebounds from Jayson Walton, 15 points from Townsend Orr, and 11 from Ryan Wolf. Their parade of injuries continued, though, as McDonald and Lenard (groin strain) were out for the game, and Carter and Orr played with nagging injuries.

■ *Townsend Orr puts in a shot against Oklahoma in the 1993 NIT.*

The Big Ten season opened at home against Michigan State, and sophomore Chad Kolander chose that game to come into his own as an intimidating big man. Kolander had 13 points, but more importantly he held the Spartans' star center Mike Peplowski to only eight, and the Gophers won, 64-57. The good times continued against ninth-ranked Purdue. Nate Tubbs scored 16 points and senior

Dana Jackson held superstar Glenn Robinson scoreless for the final 14 minutes, as the Gophers cruised, 81-60.

The now-19th-ranked Gophers traveled to Iowa City, and there began a season of road frustration. Despite 20 second-half points from Lenard, Iowa came away with an 84-77 win. Wisconsin Fieldhouse was next, and the Badgers won, 79-70, despite being outplayed by the Gophers for most of the game. Minnesota next brought the funk to its own court, losing to Chris Webber and Michigan, 80-73. The Gophers shot better than 50 percent in both those games and still lost; they took the Williams Arena floor against Northwestern and clanged shots from all over the court but won anyway. Jayson Walton had 21 points and 10 rebounds, and Randy Carter scored 17 to overcome a 40 percent shooting night for Minnesota.

The Gophers hit the road again, only to run headlong into Indiana, one of the best teams in the nation. Minnesota led the Hoosiers from the opening buzzer until the final four minutes of the game. But in those final four minutes, the veteran Hoosiers were the team that executed, and they won, 61-57. But it was a game more famous for the actions of a politician than for anything that happened on the court. Minnesota Gov. Arne Carlson—an unabashed Gophers basketball fan—was so upset with the officiating in the Indiana game that he fired off a letter to Big Ten Assistant Commissioner Rich Falk complaining about it. "It had all the earmarks of a deliberate plan to simply take the game away from Minnesota," Carlson wrote on official gubernatorial stationery.

Penn State came to Williams Arena inexperienced, overmatched, and ready to fall. The Gophers played their role well, routing the Nittany Lions, 95-67, behind Carter's 16 points and 10 rebounds. But the Gophers were in for their worst road game yet. At Michigan State's Breslin Center, the Gophers could only manage 29.6 percent shooting on the way to a 75-63 defeat, which made the 18 points and 11 rebounds by Walton and 10 rebounds and five blocks by Nzigamasabo almost moot. Purdue was the next road game, and Glenn Robinson and Cuonzo Martin (54 points between them) made easy work of the Gophers, especially with Lenard and Walton combining for only 11 points.

Townsend Orr had 17 points and Ryan Wolf added 11 in 14 minutes, but it was not enough to prevent a 75-69 Boilermaker victory.

Voshon Lenard walked into the Barn to face 13th-ranked Iowa having missed 24 of his last 27 shots in the two previous Gopher losses. The slump ended there. Lenard hit 11 of 15 shots and scored a career-high 32 points, with Walton adding 15 more to lead the Gophers to a 91-85 upset over the Hawkeyes. Wisconsin was next at Williams Arena; Lenard poured in another 23 points, Arriel McDonald had 19 points and seven assists, and the Gophers buried the Badgers, 85-71, to even their Big Ten record at 6-6 and keep alive their hopes for an NCAA Tournament bid— although four of the Gophers' final six regular-season games were on the road.

Michigan and its Fab Five—one of the greatest recruiting classes in college history, then sophomores—ran over the Gophers at Crisler Arena. The Wolverines, led by Chris Webber's 26 points, were up 71-45 at one point before the Gophers put together a 20-4 run. Still, Michigan came out on top, 84-69. Fortunately for Minnesota, Northwestern was its next opponent away from home. The Gophers snapped their nine-game road losing streak, 79-60, behind 16 points each from McDonald and Carter, and 12 from Nate Tubbs. Lenard had 21 points, giving him 101 in the last four games, shooting 61.7 percent after going 3-for-27 in the two games before that. The win evened the Gophers' Big Ten record at 7-7, their overall record moved to 15-8, and Minnesota figured it could guarantee itself an NCAA invitation by at least splitting its final four games.

Indiana came to the Barn and was burned by Lenard's 22 points, but he had to be helped off the court with 1:14 remaining with a sprained ankle, and the Hoosiers pulled away for an 86-75 victory. Seniors Dana Jackson and Nate Tubbs said farewell with style, as the Gophers held off a furious Illinois run and overcame lousy free throw shooting to eke out a 67-65 win and put them firmly on the NCAA bubble. Minnesota traveled to Penn State and not only won there, but probably played its best game of the year, drubbing the Nittany Lions, 67-41. That guaranteed the Gophers at least a .500 record in the conference and, they thought, an NCAA berth. But they went to Columbus and fell to Ohio State, 69-58, in a game in which they played poorly, scoring only 18 points in the first half and shooting 37 percent over the entire game.

Still, the 17-10 Gophers hoped for the best. The school staged a reception for the televised tournament announcement, with the team members watching a big-screen TV, surrounded by the dance line, coaches, staff members, and a horde of media. So it was a shock when a silent room heard all 64 NCAA Tournament teams read, and nobody mentioned the Minnesota Golden Gophers. The team was finally paying for its weak nonconference schedule,

which ranked 247th out of 298 Division I teams, and for its 3-8 road record, with victories only at Northwestern, Penn State, and Santa Clara. But Haskins and his players argued that they finished 9-9 in a tough conference—the same as Purdue, which was invited to the tournament. Besides, the selection committee had said it would take injuries into account, and the Gophers had their five regulars—Voshon Lenard, Randy Carter, Chad Kolander, Jayson Walton, and Arriel McDonald—in the starting lineup only 10 of 27 games.

"It was a very bad feeling," Townsend Orr says of sitting in that room, with

■ *Arriel McDonald goes up with a shot in the Gophers NIT victory over USC at Met Center in Bloomington.*

■ *Randy Carter goes up for a short jump shot against Iowa.*

all those cameras recording the crushing blow. "We were hurt. We felt we had been rejected. We felt like we belonged in the NCAA." The team held a meeting after the selection announcement, and the players discussed their feelings. There was even talk—however brief—of turning down their invitation to the NIT tournament as a protest against the snub. "But we wanted to show everybody what kind of mistake had been made," Orr remembers. "We said, let's look at it from a positive point of view."

The Gophers accepted the bid to the second-echelon National Invitational Tournament and prepared to play Florida in their first-round game at Minneapolis' Target Center. However disappointed they were to have to settle for an NIT bid, the Gophers did not shrink. They played an intense, well-executed game against Florida before 11,944 fans. McDonald scored 17 points, and Minnesota played tenacious defense to top the Gators, 74-66.

The Gophers got to play at Target Center again for its second-round game against Oklahoma, and both the team and the fans were rejuvenated. A near-

sellout crowd of 18,254—an excellent figure for an NIT game—streamed into the gleaming arena, and they saw a team possessed. The Gophers defense was all over the Sooners—a team that would be in the Final Four two years later—and they were led offensively by Lenard's 17 points and by McDonald, Tubbs, and Nzigamasabo, who combined for 30 points on 13-of-17 shooting. Final score: Minnesota 86; Oklahoma 72.

Minnesota fans again poured out to support the Gophers, packing the Met Center in Bloomington with 15,393 screaming fans, as Minnesota took on Southern California in their quarterfinal NIT game. Lenard continued to step up as a leader, pouring in 25 points to lead the Gophers; Walton added 12 points and Orr 11. But in this 76-58 victory, the Gophers star was again its defense. They held USC to 32.1 percent shooting, making their NIT defensive total a miserly 35.3 percent over the first three games against strong teams, all of which were very nearly NCAA Tournament picks.

"I remember that game at the Met Center the most," Orr says. "That was

the last basketball game ever played there, it was a sellout, and everybody was going crazy. The whole state was supporting us, and to win that game and take that victory lap around the court afterwards, that will always stick in my mind."

The Gophers traveled to New York City, whose Madison Square Garden is the traditional spot for the NIT final four. It might not have been the final four the Gophers wanted to be in, but they were determined to make the most of it nonetheless. And nobody more so than Voshon Lenard, whose legend grew every time he took the court in the NIT. For the Gophers' semifinal game against Providence, Lenard finished with 25 points, and he played the Gophers into the game after the Friars took a 53-42 lead with 13 minutes left, putting in 17 of his points in the second half.

It was on to Georgetown in the game to decide the NIT title. It looked like a championship game. Both teams—who were on missions to prove the NCAA selection committee wrong—played tough defense, with the Hoyas forcing 19 turnovers and the Gophers 16. Arriel McDonald led the Gophers with 20 points, and tournament Most

Valuable Player Lenard added 17. Those performances led the Gophers to a 62-51 lead with 4:27 left, but they never scored another point. The Hoyas put on a 10-0 run and closed to 62-61 with seven seconds left. Randy Carter blocked a shot, and Lenard intercepted a lob pass under the Georgetown basket with three seconds remaining, and the Gophers had won their first ever postseason championship.

They won by riding Lenard's scoring coattails and by playing dynamic defense. "That defense was a function of everybody helping everybody else out," says Orr. "It was the family love that we had developed over the past four years, where we all supported each other and helped out when we were needed."

Voshon Lenard rolled around on the Madison Square Garden floor. His teammates mobbed each other near center court. Seniors Nate Tubbs and Dana Jackson had been members of the Minnesota team that had come so close to the NCAA Final Four, but none of their teammates knew what it was like to play on a college basketball team that had managed to earn the respect of a nation. These Gophers—who had felt so slighted after their NCAA snub—

■ Randy Carter puts up a jumper in the 1993 NIT championship game against Georgetown.

nation. These Gophers—who had felt so slighted after their NCAA snub—had sought vindication, and they had earned it.

"It was a great feeling," Orr remembers. "We had the opportunity to play in a great place, against some very strong

from the lower deck to the upper, but they would be cheering the NIT champions, so most fans kept their grumbling to a minimum.

The Gophers started play in August far away from their newly remodeled home; they headed for Europe and an

■ *The Gophers bask in the glory of their NIT Championship at center court of Madison Square Garden in New York City.*

teams, and we gave the U its first national championship. We did a lot for the history of the University of Minnesota, and that meant a lot to us."

"We were very upset to have to settle for the NIT, and that motivation was a factor, but talent won out in the end," Haskins says. "I was very proud of the way those kids played."

Before the 1993-94 season began, the University needed to either make some major renovations to Williams Arena, or move the Gophers off campus to Target Center. The school chose the former, and as a result of the changes—the most visible of which were new entrance areas and contoured plastic seats instead of bone-numbing benches—the capacity of the Barn was reduced from 16,549 to 14,321. That meant that many of the newly resurgent Gopher season-ticket base of 12,600 were moved

eight-game exhibition schedule there, where they went 4-4. When they returned home to prepare for their regular season, the Gophers learned they were ranked 10th in the nation, having won the NIT championship and returning all five of their starters from the previous year.

Their tournament performance guaranteed that the Gophers would start the season in the Preseason NIT tournament. They opened that contest with two games at home, the first against Rice. Minnesota was battling a flu bug that had made its way around the locker room, and the Gophers got a scare from lightly-regarded Rice, but they recovered for a 70-61 win. They took on Georgia in the next round at Williams Arena, and this time the Gophers played well. Randy Carter had 20 points, and freshman John

broken his hand—stepped in to score eight points and pull in five rebounds and become a physical force under the basket in his first college game. The two led Minnesota to a 91-71 win over the Bulldogs, and earned the team a second trip to New York in only eight months.

Now it was time for the tough part. The Gophers first had to face Kansas, ranked sixth in the nation, and led by powerful seven-foot center Greg Ostertag. Even though the Jayhawks out-defended the Gophers and Voshon Lenard had an ineffective game because of an injured toe, the Gophers almost pulled off an upset, losing 75-71. But top-ranked North Carolina was next, and that was a different story. Minnesota walked away from Madison Square Garden feeling good about the way it

than North Carolina," says Orr. Had they beat Kansas, they would have faced Massachusetts in the championship game, rather than North Carolina in the consolation matchup. "But I still thought we were a good team and we deserved our preseason ranking. We lost to teams that were ranked above us. Still, those losses set the tone for the rest of the season."

Minnesota was due for an easy game, and on came Mississippi Valley State. The Gophers started the game with a 20-0 run, and finished with a 107-63 victory. Next was Middle Tennessee State on the road. This was where Clem Haskins had scored an Ohio Valley Conference record 55 points as a Western Kentucky sophomore, and while the Gophers had no one quite that prolific (Carter led the team with 27 points), they

■ *Another sellout crowd at the Barn waits for the opening tip in 1994.*

played, led by David Grim's 15 points off the bench, but still lost, 90-76. "We never recovered from those two games the whole year," Haskins says.

"Had we won that Kansas game, it would have put everything in a different light; we would have matched up much better against Massachusetts

still came away with a 90-76 victory. The Gophers came home to face Clemson, and they put together a brilliant run in the first 11 minutes—when they led by 18 points—on the way to a 73-54 win. Lenard had 19 points in that game, Carter had 14 points and 11 rebounds, and McDonald had 13 points.

The Gophers headed west to face San Jose State on Christmas Eve, and they got a nice gift when they shot 34 percent from the field, but still won, 66-53, largely on the strength of David Grim's 15 points. The holiday ended as the team travelled cross-country to face Virginia, which had been a Sweet 16 team the year before. Carter scored 10 points and grabbed 13 rebounds against the Cavaliers, but the rest of the Gophers' big men, Kolander, Nzigamasabo, and Thomas, scored exactly one point among the three of them. The result was a 62-57 Minnesota loss.

After that performance, Haskins ordered a series of two-a-day practices. That got his players' attention, and they responded with a better—if not perfect—game at home against James Madison. Jayson Walton had 16 points and 15 rebounds in a game in which the

■ *Arriel McDonald puts up a short jumper against Purdue.*

Gophers outrebounded the Dukes 51-32, including 23-9 in offensive rebounds, and Minnesota won, 73-68. The Gophers made their final preparation for the Big Ten season by beating Northeastern Illinois easily, 89-62, but they once again were strong defensively and inconsistent offensively.

The Big Ten opener for Minnesota was on the road, but fortunately that venue was Northwestern's Welsh-Ryan Arena, the only place the Gophers visited where they had put together any kind of a winning streak (they had won five straight going into this game). Despite a stronger-than-normal performance from the Wildcats, the Gophers won, 73-65, largely on the strength of 23 points from Lenard, 18 from Townsend Orr, and at least five rebounds from every starter.

"I know it was only Northwestern, but it was important for us to win that game on the road," Orr says. "After awhile, you get tired of hearing about not being able to win on the road, but it's easy for people to say it because they're not out there playing. Coming into my college career I thought I could play on Mars and win, but when you hear these things enough, eventually they rub off on you."

After that road win, things only got better at Williams Arena, where the 18th-ranked Gophers took on the 12th-ranked Wisconsin Badgers. The rankings would change after that game, as the Gophers creamed the Badgers, 90-53. Along the way, Lenard scored 23 points, Grim and Carter had 13 apiece, and McDonald had 12 points and a Minnesota-record 16 assists in only 31 minutes.

As good as the Gophers were against Wisconsin, they were that bad in Penn State's tiny arena. Chad Kolander scored 15 points, including 11 of 15 free throws, and Lenard had 20, but the Gophers shot only 33 percent from the field overall and committed 30 fouls. The end result was a 78-67 win, the Nittany Lions' first in the conference in 1993-94. The Gophers returned home to face a Michigan team playing with two of its best players, Juwan Howard and Jimmy King, out with chicken pox. In spite of a poor game from Lenard, the Gophers won, 63-58.

Senior Arriel McDonald won the next game, against Michigan State at Williams Arena. Other Gophers contributed, but McDonald scored 16 points,

including the final basket with two seconds remaining to give his team a 68-66 win. McDonald also added six assists and a career-high 10 rebounds to lead the Gophers. Minnesota made an unimpressive showing at Assembly Hall in Indiana, losing to the Hoosiers, 78-66, to give Indiana sole possession of the Big Ten lead at 5-1, while the Gophers were in a tie for third at 4-2. But Clem Haskins promised that when the Hoosiers travelled to Williams Arena a month later, the tables would turn.

Meanwhile, Purdue came to the Barn, and unfortunately Glenn Robinson came with them. The Big Dog, who would become the first pick overall in the NBA draft later that year, managed 27 points, 12 rebounds, four steals, and two blocks to almost single-handedly beat the Gophers, 75-72. Minnesota next travelled to Madison Square Garden one more time, this time to take on St. John's in a nationally televised game. While they were determined not to return to the Garden as part of the NIT this year, they made short work of St. John's, winning 92-64 behind 27 points from Lenard and 17 points and 12 rebounds from Carter. But they followed that with a disappointing loss in Iowa City, falling to the Hawkeyes, 92-88.

Northwestern came to Williams Arena without a Big Ten win, and they left the same way, as 79-65 losers. The game was most notable for Wildcat Coach Ricky Byrdsong, who turned over coaching duties to an assistant and spent much of the game roaming the stands, talking to Minnesota fans and even exchanging a high-five with one. At one point during the game, an usher kicked Byrdsong out of a season-ticket holder's seat. The next home game was against Ohio State, and Lenard and Carter pulled that game out for the Gophers, scoring a combined 46 points, including 26 of Minnesota's final 27, even though Carter played much of the game with a painful tendon injury. The Gophers squeaked by, 79-73.

Wisconsin was next on the road, and something about the Badgers continued to bring out the best in the Gophers. They routed Wisconsin, 109-78, scoring the school's highest point total ever in a road game and shooting 56.2 percent from the field, including five of six from David Grim. The Gophers returned home for "Play Hosea Night," a promotion designed to encourage Haskins to play Hosea Crittenden, the Gophers' popular, 5-foot-9 walk-on guard. Lenard had 30 points and Carter had 20

■ *Ernest Nzigasamabo celebrates the Gophers' 1994 two-point win over Michigan State.*

Lenard had 30 points and Carter had 20 points and 10 rebounds, and Minnesota's dominant play allowed Haskins to put Crittenden in for the final 99 seconds. To the frenzied crowd's delight, he buried a three-pointer with 43 seconds left to seal a 94-66 win.

That put Minnesota at 8-4 in the conference, two games behind Michigan as they traveled to Ann Arbor to face the

■ *Townsend Orr slips past two Northern Illinois defenders during the Gophers' 1990 NCAA Tournament victory.*

Wolverines. But they didn't come through, shooting only 38 percent and committing 21 turnovers to seal a 72-65 loss to all but bury the Gophers' Big Ten title hopes. Things got worse a few days later at Michigan State, when Minnesota put its NCAA Tournament hopes in jeopardy as well. Shawn Respert dis-

mantled the Gophers with 43 points, half of his team's production in an 85-68 Spartan win. Haskins was so disappointed by the performance of his starters in the first half that he kept Carter and Walton out of the game the entire second half to send a message to his team.

The message was received, and the result was one of the greatest games in Golden Gopher history. Bobby Knight brought his 12th-ranked Indiana team to the Barn, having beaten Minnesota in Bloomington earlier in the season, and the 20th-ranked Gophers destroyed the Hoosiers from the opening tip to the final buzzer. The Gophers led 56-24 at halftime. They shot 64 percent for the game and set school records with 32 assists and 11 three-pointers. Lenard scored 35, his career high, McDonald collected 10 assists, and Walton and Carter—the examples in the game before—both played strongly and scored in double figures. The final score: 106-56, a 50-point victory against a nationally-ranked team and a Big Ten power.

"It was just one of those things," Orr says. "We were playing very well that day, they were not playing very well at all, we were pumped up to be playing on national TV, and we had a lot of help from God. At Indiana we did everything right but win, so we had a revenge factor."

The up-and-down Gophers, after being up so high, came down again for the next game, at Purdue. Glenn Robinson had 31 points and 12 rebounds, and Chad Kolander and Jayson Walton both shot 0-for-5 from the floor. That combination could not overcome 17 points from Lenard, and the Gophers lost, 86-70. That put them at 19-10 overall, and 9-7 in the Big Ten. If Minnesota lost both its remaining conference games, they would again finish at 9-9 and be on the NCAA Tournament bubble. They were determined to win one of their remaining two games and eliminate any doubt as to whether they would receive an invitation to join the field of 64.

With that in mind, the Gophers welcomed last-place Iowa to Williams Arena for Senior Night, the last home game for Randy Carter, Arriel McDonald, and Ernest Nzigamasabo. Iowa smelled upset, and they played the Gophers tough for 40 minutes. So tough, in fact, that the score was tied at the end of regulation. At the end of the first with four seconds remaining when Lenard, who finished with 38 points, drained an off-balance, desperation three-pointer to send the game to a second overtime. Lenard was on the spot again with five seconds left; he was fouled and made his first free throw to tie the game at 92, but missed the second to force a third extra period. Minnesota's veterans, including Randy

I wasn't really in the game, but in the third overtime I decided I'd sat and watched long enough, and I told myself that if I had the opportunity I would go in and do something to help the team and end that game."

The Gophers lost their final game, on the road against Illinois, 90-75. But they still earned their place in the NCAA Tournament, gaining a sixth seed in the

Carter (19 points and 12 rebounds for the game) and Townsend Orr, stepped up in the third overtime and took control. Orr hit two key free throws and a three-pointer to give the Gophers a lead they never lost, and they finally wrestled away an exhausting 107-96 victory. It was more than a moral victory, too. It guaranteed the Gophers not only a winning conference record and almost assured them of an NCAA bid, but it put their overall record at 20-10, giving them the first back-to-back 20-win seasons in Minnesota history.

Milestones aside, the Gophers, including Orr, were just glad to get to the locker room after the game. "We thought that game would never end. For awhile

West Regional in Sacramento, California. There they faced Southern Illinois, and they played inconsistently again. But the good outweighed the bad—18 points from Lenard, 15 from McDonald, 12 from Kolander, and nine points and nine rebounds from Nzigamasabo, as well as dogged defense was the good; but the Gophers fell behind by 10 early in the game, and Walton was lost with a sprained ankle and a knee injury. Minnesota won, 74-60, and prepared to face Louisville, a considerably tougher opponent, but not an unbeatable one.

Against the Cardinals, the Gophers played well enough to win. They held Louisville's leading scorer, Clifford Rozier, to just two points; Lenard scored

■ *Clem Haskins watches Voshon Lenard direct the floor against Louisville in the 1994 NCAA Tournament.*

12 points in the final 9:05; and the Gophers led by 12 at halftime. But Louisville managed to battle back, and they made the most of 17 second-half Minnesota fouls and won, 60-55. "Jayson Walton didn't play in that game," Haskins notes. "You can't take 15 points and seven rebounds out and expect to win. But I felt good with the type of year it was for us."

"Everything had been going so great until then," Orr said, "that we thought if we had beaten Louisville, we could have gone to the Final Four. We just couldn't get it done against Louisville."

The Louisville game appeared to be Voshon Lenard's last as a Gopher. Against Haskins' advice, Lenard decided to pass up his senior season and enter the NBA draft. It was the first year of a new NCAA rule, that allowed a

player to declare himself for the draft, but return to school if he didn't like where he was selected, if a team chose him at all. Indeed, Lenard, who had been projected as a late-first round pick, did not go until the second round, to the Milwaukee Bucks. The Bucks had already taken two players in the first round, including Purdue's Glenn Robinson as the first player chosen overall, and Lenard didn't figure he would get much playing time, or money. After the Bucks offered him the NBA minimum salary for his rookie season, Lenard opted to return to the Gophers for 1994-95.

SECTION 8

The five players who entered the University of Minnesota as freshmen in 1991 were now seniors. Chad Kolander, Voshon Lenard, Townsend Orr, Jayson Walton, and Ryan Wolf had worked themselves and their team from a .500 record their freshman year to two straight 20-win seasons, an NIT championship, and three straight post-season appearances. Now, with junior forward David Grim; sophomore centers John Thomas and Trevor Winter; freshman guards Sam Jacobson, Darrell Whaley, Eric Harris, and Micah Watkins; and crowd favorite Hosea Crittenden, a walk-on junior guard, many said that the Gophers were the preseason favorite to win the Big Ten crown. Lenard was named a preseason candidate for both the Naismith College Basketball Player of the Year and the John Wooden Award, and he was on the preseason all-Big Ten team. Jacobson arrived amid a hubbub that generally surrounds a player expected to accomplish great things and achieve national prominence before his senior year is over— "He's as good as any freshman in the country," Haskins said before the season. "He will someday be one of the best players in America." In short, big things were expected of this team. Now, as the Minnesota Golden Gophers prepared to play their 100th season of college basketball, all they had to do was come through.

■ *Sam Jacobson dunks the ball over a Purdue defender.*

The freshmen got their chance to play early in a home exhibition against the U.S. Army's Fort Hood Tankers. The Tankers, apparently used to hand-to-hand combat, banged the Gophers at every turn. But that didn't stop Jacobson and Orr from scoring 15 points apiece; Kolander also put in 12 points and grabbed 10 rebounds, Whaley had 11 points, Thomas had 12 rebounds and eight points, and Winter had nine points and three rebounds. The result was a 102-59 Minnesota rout, and some quality playing time for some of the less experienced team members. The Gophers had a similar result in another exhibition, this one a 106-57 walk past the Croatian National Team, when Lenard scored 21 points, Jacobson had 13 points, Walton had 11 in his first game back from resting his bad knees, Whaley had nine points, and Harris had six points and six assists.

The exhibition games were easy; what came next would be very difficult. Minnesota traveled to Anchorage for the Great Alaska Shootout and the potential to play against some very strong teams on national television. The first was Arizona, ranked fifth in the nation. The Gophers earned a five-point victory to send them to the second round in the winners' bracket.

Next was No. 21 Villanova, and again the Gophers dominated the boards, winning that battle 52-32, and

■ *Clem Haskins keeps an eye on his Gophers during the 1994-95 season.*

■ *Micah Watkins chases a loose ball ahead of several Buckeyes.*

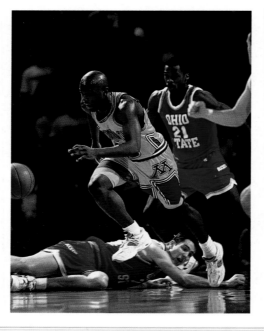

smothering the Wildcats defensively, allowing them only 32 percent shooting for the game, on the way to a 85-64 victory. Orr, the player of the game for the second time in a row, and Lenard each had 19 points and nine rebounds, Walton had his second straight double-double with 14 points and 10 rebounds, and Kolander had 10 points and six rebounds.

That sent the Gophers to the finals against Brigham Young, a tenacious opponent that made Minnesota work at least as hard as with its previous two

opponents, despite the Cougars' lack of a national ranking. But that didn't matter; the Gophers walked away with the Great Alaskan Shootout title with a 79-74 win. They did it thanks to Orr, who had 15 points despite playing in pain with a twisted ankle and who was named the tournament MVP; 24 points from Lenard; 13 from Grim; 11 points and 16 rebounds from Walton; and nine points from Kolander.

"Alaska was amazing, both for me and for the team," Orr says. "It was our chance to show we could play with top teams. As for me, I always said, the more freedom and opportunities I get, the better I play. Coach Haskins gave me some freedom, and I ran with it. I might make one or two mistakes, but I think I always do five or six good things to offset that."

After that heady early test, it was back to a more typical nonconference schedule for the Gophers, who were ranked 15th in the nation; they had consecutive home games against Sacramento State, Central Connecticut, and Rhode Island. Of the 302 Division I teams, Sacramento State was ranked 300th, and Central Connecticut was 301st. But Sacramento State came out fighting. The final scoreboard showed the Gophers with a 102-84 win behind 28 points from Lenard, 17 points and nine rebounds from Walton, and 15 points and seven rebounds from Jacobson — this despite the Hornets opening the game with a 10-3 lead and only trailing the Gophers by seven points with less than seven minutes to go.

The next game was different. The Gophers dominated Central Connecticut from beginning to end, with Lenard scoring 19 points in only 18 minutes, Orr adding 12, and Harris scoring 10. They ended with a 92-56 victory. They had similar success against Rhode Island, winning 90-65. In that game, Orr led the Gophers with 17 points, Walton added 12 points to his 16 rebounds, Thomas had 14 points and six rebounds, and Jacobson had 11 points.

The 11th-ranked Gophers entered their next home game, a nationally-televised contest against 17th-ranked Cincinnati, with a 6-0 record. But the Gophers shot only 42 percent from the field, including 28 percent combined from Lenard and Orr. The Bearcats came away with a 91-88 overtime win. Minnesota traveled to Oakland to take on undefeated California. The Gophers again shot less than 40 percent for the game, and Lenard still had trouble find-

■ *Hosea Crittenden was a fan favorite, partly because he always seemed to be smiling.*

ing his shot, putting in only 25 percent of his attempted field goals. So, despite 21 points, nine rebounds, and five assists from Orr, the Gophers lost to Cal, 82-75.

That was bad, but what followed was worse. Texas Southern, an underrated but talented team, came to

■ *Haskins brings the Gophers together before they break a timeout huddle and prepare to take the floor.*

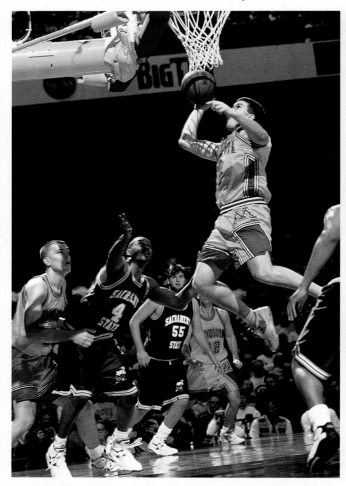

Williams Arena and clobbered Minnesota, 71-50. How could the Gophers get beat so soundly at home by a team everybody thought they would beat? Orr, Lenard, and Thomas were scoreless at halftime, Kolander had only two, and Minnesota was down 29-14 at the intermission. They shot 28 percent for the game, including only 19 percent in the first half. They never got closer than 13 points, and Walton led the Gophers with an anemic 10 points. "They played their best basketball, and we didn't play our best basketball," Orr says simply.

"We might have peaked too early," Haskins says of the Gophers' impressive early wins followed by the disappointing defeats. "The expectations might have become too great. People forget, the other teams are trying to win, too. Against Cincinnati and California we played well and lost, and we did play well against a good Texas Southern team at home. But we regrouped."

San Jose State had the misfortune of being next at the Barn and having to face a Minnesota team focused on taking out their frustrations over the previous game's embarrassment. The result was a 115-68 dismantling by the Gophers, who had 17 points from Orr, and 16 points each from Lenard, Walton, and Jacobson (who added 10 rebounds). Kolander and Winter had 12 points apiece, and Thomas added 11. The Gophers shot 52 percent, the first time they made more shots than they missed all season.

The Gophers traveled to Virginia to take on James Madison, which had already beaten Purdue that year and would present a more formidable test than did San Jose State. Lenard woke up and found his shooting hand again, scoring 15 points, 11 in the second half. He was helped by 16 points from Walton and 11 points and 10 assists from Orr on the way to a 74-68 win. The Gophers finished their nonconference schedule at 7-3 with an easy, 98-57, win over Middle Tennessee State. The main benefit of that game was that it was a confidence-builder; Lenard scored 25 points and hit six three-pointers, Thomas and Jacobson had 13 points apiece, and Harris and Winter each scored 11.

That was all fine, but it was not the Big Ten. That came next, beginning with Penn State at Williams Arena. The Nittany Lions had been all but pushovers

■ *Opposite page, clockwise from top left Ryan Wolf goes up for two points against Sacramento State; Townsend Orr tries for an assist against Cincinnati; David Grim comes from behind to block a seemingly sure Texas Southern basketball; Lenard tries to knock a loose ball to teammate Eric Harris.*

■ *Trevor Winter (below left) posts up against Northwestern. John Thomas bangs for the ball inside against Penn State.*

THREE POINT ATTEMPTS: 24
THREE POINTS MADE: 11
THREE POINT AVERAGE: 45 %

NORW

67   3:26   65
2

■ *Sam Jacobson rejects an Iowa shot as Voshon Lenard, Jayson Walton, Townsend Orr, and John Thomas watch.*

■ *Freshman guard Darrell Whaley tries to beat a Northwestern player to a loose ball.*

in their first two Big Ten seasons, but they were a different team in 1994-95. They showed that to the Gophers by leading 62-53 with only two minutes remaining. The Gophers put together a furious 8-0 run to cut the margin to one point, when David Grim hit a wide-open three-pointer in the corner to put the Gophers ahead 69-67, their final margin of victory. The Gophers were led by

Lenard's 21 points, and John Thomas continued warming to his role as a physical inside player, scoring 14 and holding Penn State's star center, John Amechi, in check all night.

The Gophers had to travel to Purdue for their next game, not something that would inspire confidence, considering they had lost 13 straight and 21 of their last 22 games, dating back to 1973, at Mackey Arena. This game was no different. Even though Glenn Robinson had moved on to the NBA, the Boilermakers were still too much to handle, and that was despite the Gophers taking 27 more shots than their opponents. Of course, Minnesota shot 40 percent while Purdue shot 50 percent, and the Boilermakers were 28-for-35 from the free-throw line to the Gophers' 3-for-8.

A home game against Northwestern, though, was a cure for all the Gophers' ills. They hit their first eight shots, led 20-0 after the first four minutes, shot 59 percent on the night, and they made an amazing two-thirds of their three-point shots (12-for-18). Lenard hit a school-record seven three-pointers and finished with 27 points, to go with 14 each from Orr and Kolander.

The final score was Minnesota 105, Northwestern 74.

But the Gophers just couldn't keep that momentum going. They headed for Madison to play a Wisconsin team that featured two certain future NBA first-round picks, senior forward Michael Finley and sophomore center Rashard Griffith. The Gophers managed to stop Griffith, but Finley and Darnell Hoskins picked up the slack on the way to a 74-67 Wisconsin win. It didn't help the Gophers any that they shot less than 36 percent, including 26 percent from Lenard, and forwards Kolander and Walton combined for a paltry four points.

Ohio State was supposed to be one of the doormats of the Big Ten that year, but with their up-and-down play the Gophers were taking nothing for granted. Haskins pulled Walton from the

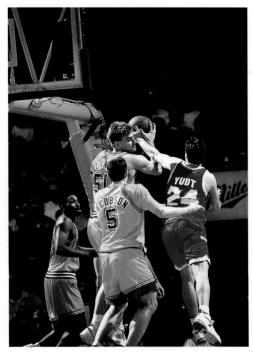

■ *Chad Kolander holds onto the ball despite Ohio State's Steve Yudt's best efforts.*

■ *Freshman Sam Jacobson goes up for a block against Ohio State.*

starting lineup and replaced him with Jacobson, sending a message that he would not tolerate the kind of sporadic play he had been receiving from his seniors. Walton responded with 11 points off the bench, and Lenard scored 14, but he hit only one of five three-point attempts. Still, Minnesota's bench outscored Ohio State's 33-4, and the Gophers left the Barn with an 81-61 win.

and determined to hold Spartan star Shawn Respert in check. They accomplished all that. They just didn't win the game. Instead, Michigan State came out on top of the ugly game, 54-53, as neither team could shoot better than 38 percent from the floor. Lenard led the Gophers with only 14 points. The loss sent Minnesota's record to 13-6 overall and 4-3 in the conference—certainly

■ *Jayson Walton battles Wisconsin's Rashard Griffith (left) for a rebound, while John Thomas and Sam Jacobson look on. Walton (right), arthritic knees and all, drives the lane for two.*

In their next home game, against Illinois, the Gophers came together as a team and played excellent all-around basketball for the first time since the Great Alaskan Shootout that opened the regular season. Kolander, who had been replaced in the starting lineup by Grim because of his poor play, came off the bench to score 14 points. Thomas had 10 second-half points. Orr scored all of his 18 points on three-point shots. As a team, Minnesota shot 59 percent and won, 77-66.

The Gophers traveled to East Lansing intent on controlling the pace of their game against Michigan State,

not good enough for first place (the Spartans held that mantle at 5-1), the Gophers felt they were in good position to make a strong run.

After the game, in which Orr missed a couple of key free throws down the stretch, he told reporters he was responsible for the loss. "I just didn't help the team the way I should have," he says upon reflection. "I just felt like if I could have given just a little more, we would have won. But we grew from that game at Michigan State. We didn't want that to happen again."

But it almost did three days later in Iowa City. Iowa came into the game averaging more than 80 points per game, so the Gophers were intent on slowing down the pace, turning the contest into a defensive struggle, and holding the Hawkeyes to as few points as possible. They succeeded, but they gave away a seven-point lead with 8:30 remaining, and with 13.2 seconds left, the score read 54-53 Iowa, the exact same score by which the Gophers had

basket. Thomas slammed the ball home with 3.7 seconds remaining to give Minnesota a 55-54 road win. Lenard scored 15 points in the game, all in the second half, Jacobson added 10 points, and Orr had eight assists.

"That was a great play and a great feeling," Orr says of his final assist to Thomas. "My only thought was just for us to get the hoop. I kept thinking,

■ *Kolander puts up a 15-footer against Iowa.*

lost the last game. But Thomas, who was warming to his role as a banging inside player, came to the rescue with the help of Orr and Lenard. Lenard dribbled upcourt, passed up a long jumper, and passed to Orr who penetrated into the lane as two defenders collapsed on him. He, too, passed up the shot and dished to Thomas who was left open under the

please, John, catch the ball. Just catch it and put it in."

The Iowa win gave the Gophers a confidence they intended to use for the rest of the season as they neared the halfway mark in the conference season. Michigan came to the Barn, and even though they had only two of their original Fab Five remaining—the rest hav-

■ *Haskins is not happy with an official's call during the Gophers' 74-70 loss to Iowa at Williams Arena in 1995.*

ing left school early to turn pro — the Wolverines were still a formidable opponent. No matter. Haskins had worked his team into an emotional frenzy, and they responded by dominating the game beginning with the opening tip. They opened with an 18-10 lead and rode a three-point flurry by Lenard to a 45-29 halftime lead. Michigan never got closer than 11 points after that, mainly because of 20 points from Orr, 19 from Lenard, and 11 points and 10 rebounds from Walton, whose arthritic knees were becoming more painful for him every game. The final score was 80-58, Minnesota's most convincing rout of Michigan since 1969.

The Michigan win put Minnesota at 6-3 in the Big Ten, good enough for third place, and 15-6 overall. The Gophers were shooting 44 percent as a team—not as good as they might like, but better than they had shot in past years. Their smothering defense was carrying the team; Minnesota's Big Ten opponents were shooting a combined 39.5 percent. The rest of their schedule included road games at 1-8 Northwestern and 0-9 Ohio State, as well as three home games. If they

could win four of their final nine games the Gophers would be 10-8 in the conference, a near-lock for an NCAA Tournament bid. And if they could win six of those games—a very realistic goal—they would be 12-6, and would be in the running for the conference championship.

Those goals became even more realistic after the Gophers traveled to Bloomington to take on Indiana. Assembly Hall is one of the toughest road venues in the conference, but Minnesota again dictated the pace of the game and came out the winner, this time 64-54. After 13 minutes of the first half, the score was tied at nine. The halftime score was 18-18. The Gophers shot 23 percent for the half, the Hoosiers 22 percent. The Gophers finally pulled away with an 19-8 run to end the game, as Lenard finished with 21 points and Walton—who promised to make Haskins "eat his words" when the coach said the senior's knees were too tender for him to play very much—added 10.

Iowa came to Williams Arena, and the Gophers looked upon that as one of the games they ought to win on their way to the Big Ten crown. But Orr sprained his foot, Grim bruised his arm, Trevor Winter aggravated an elbow injury, and Kolander was poked in the eye. The crucial backcourt combination of Lenard and Orr combined for 5-for-22 shooting, and the Gophers couldn't recover. They lost, 74-70.

As part of the celebration of the U's 100th season of basketball, the Department of Men's Athletics sponsored a fan vote to choose the best player of each decade and the Player of the Century. While the validity of such comparisons could be debated, and the emotions of passing time might have clouded some judgements, more than 80,000 fans nonetheless cast their ballots and registered their opinions. Their consensus:

1900s: George Tuck (Minnesota's first
    All-American in 1905)
1910s: Erling Platou (All-American
    in 1919)
1920s: Arnold Oss (All-American,
    1919 and 1921)
1930s: John Kundla (Team MVP in 1939
    and coach from 1959-68)
1940s: Tony Jaros (Team MVP in 1946)
1950s: Meyer "Whitey" Skoog
    (All-America, 1950, 1951)
1960s: Lou Hudson (All-American, 1965)
1970s: Mychal Thompson
    (All-American, 1977, 1978)
1980s: Kevin McHale (All-Big Ten and
    team MVP, 1979, 1980)
1990s: Voshon Lenard (Soon to be
    Gophers all-time leading scorer)
Player of the Century: Kevin McHale

As eighth-ranked Michigan State made its trip to Williams Arena, the Gophers felt they were in a must-win situation. The Spartans were leading the conference, but the Gophers wanted to. Once again, it was Minnesota's defense that provided the difference. Minnesota was the only team all season to hold Michigan State to fewer than 60 points, and it happened twice. This time the result was different, though; the Gophers came out on top, 66-57. Lenard scored 17, Walton continued his mission to prove Haskins wrong by putting in 14, Thomas had 12, and Jacobson added 10.

Voshon Lenard made history in the Gophers' next game, at Illinois. Lenard sunk a free-throw with 10 seconds left in overtime to give him 1,993 career points, passing Mychal Thompson's all-time mark that had stood since 1978. Lenard had 24 points on the night, including one of two free throws with 20 seconds left in regulation that tied the score at 73 and sent the game into overtime. But the Illini made all five of their field goal attempts in the final period and the Gophers went 1-for-5 in overtime from behind the three-point line, and Illinois won, 94-88.

Before the next game, at Ohio State, Haskins told the media he was worried about that game. "I'm scared to death," he told the *Star Tribune*. It sounded like the obligatory comments a coach makes about the next opponent, coming as it did about a team that was 1-13 in the Big Ten. But either Haskins was serious, or Ohio State put some ringers on the court, because the lowly Buckeyes upset the No. 22 Gophers, 73-65. Not only did the loss end any hope of a Big Ten title for the Gophers—who were 17-9 overall and 8-6 in the conference—but it made an invitation to the NCAA Tournament far less of a sure thing. The NCAA selection committee uses as one of its criteria a computer-generated power rating, which dropped the Gophers like a stone out of the top 30 in the nation to 51st after the Ohio State loss.

That game could have driven the Gophers to despair, but they managed to come out for Wisconsin at Williams Arena ready to play. Most ready was Jayson Walton, still out to show he could play on his bad knees. Walton had his seventh double-double of the season, scoring 19 points and bringing down 14 rebounds, and he had help with 22 points from Lenard and 15 from Orr, as the Gophers came out on top, 78-70. Their Big Ten record stood at 9-6, and they were 18-9 overall. That meant that one win would guarantee them the 10-8 conference record that usually means an NCAA berth, and two of their last three would give the Gophers an unprecedented third consecutive 20-win season.

The first step towards that goal would be a trip to Evanston to play Northwestern—an absolutely essential win if the Gophers were going to rate serious postseason consideration and keep their self-respect. With that on the line, Lenard put down 30 points, Walton continued his tear with 19 points and 11 boards, and Orr added 15 points and five assists. The result was their 10th conference victory, 82-70.

The next game was Senior Night, the final home game for Lenard, Orr, Walton, Kolander, and Wolf. They were

■ ***Following pages***
Townsend Orr goes up in the lane at Williams Arena against Wisconsin.

joined on the senior roster by Aaron Osterman, a standout wide receiver for the Gophers football team who walked on with the basketball team for the 1994-95 season. The Gophers were playing Purdue, which would clinch a share of the Big Ten championship with a win in the Barn. The Gophers were playing for their 20th win and a sure-thing NCAA bid. Minnesota outplayed the Boilermakers both offensively and defensively

that families do, like noticing who's sitting across from you on the plane, getting up and making sure your roommate was up in time for breakfast, just palling around. When I look back in 10 years, I know I'm going to realize how much I miss them."

But there was more basketball to play. The Gophers still were working on sealing themselves a trip to the big tournament, and they wanted to do it con-

■ *The Gopher bench cheers a teammate's three-pointer.*

in the first half, and went into the locker room with a nine-point lead. But the tables turned in the second half, as the Gophers shot just 26 percent in the half and let Cuonzo Martin bury them with jump shots. Purdue won easily, 72-59, but nearly every one of the 14,459 fans stayed for the postgame ceremony to pay tribute to the seniors that had combined for a 78-48 record over their four years, the third-best class in team history. One-by-one, the seniors walked from the Gopher bench to the free-throw line, met their parents, and walked to center court to greet Haskins and his assistants, Milton Barnes, Bill Brown, and Larry Davis. Then as a group they circled the raised, maroon and gold floor, waving as the still-full house gave them one last standing ovation.

"We were like a family, the five of us," Orr says. "We had those little things

vincingly, with a win at Penn State to close out the regular season. Walton had another big game, with 14 points, and Jacobson also had 14 points in one of his best performances of the season. But Lenard scored only two points, and Kolander had five. They let Nittany Lions center John Amechi have his way inside, and the result was a 69-60 Penn State win, and a few anxious days of waiting for the Gophers.

"The fans were disappointed with the way we ended our season, but I think they took it too hard," Haskins says. "We were disappointed, too, but people don't mention the injuries we had. Players couldn't practice, and if we can't practice and prepare, it's very difficult to win."

Minnesota felt it deserved to be in the tournament on the strength of a 19-11 overall record and a 10-8 Big Ten mark.

They beat such tough teams as Villanova, Arizona, BYU, Michigan State, Michigan, Indiana, and Iowa. But they also lost to Ohio State, Penn State, California, and Texas Southern and Cincinnati at home, and they finished with four losses in their last six games. The Big Ten was considered by many to be weaker than in previous years, and there was no guarantee that 10-8 was going to be good enough this time.

But it was. The Gophers got their invitation, and they prepared to head to the East Regional in Baltimore to take on St. Louis University. Gophers fans were ecstatic. Hundreds purchased package ticket-flight plans and packed their bags for Baltimore, fully expecting to stay for two games and see the Gophers take on top-seeded Wake Forest in the second round after they dispatched St. Louis. After all, the Billikens played in the Great Midwest Conference which, while it was a good league, was no Big Ten. And they had no regular player taller than 6-foot-6 and lived and died with the three-point shot. Besides, Haskins' Minnesota teams had never lost a first-round NCAA game in three tries.

But when game time finally came, the Gophers came out flat and the Billikens were charged up. Minnesota simply could not get started, missing its first 10 shots and falling behind 19-3. Throughout the game, the Gophers made only about one-third of their shots, while St. Louis scorched the nets with 8-for-16 three-point shooting in the first half and 11-for-23 in the game. The Gophers somehow fought back from second-half deficits of 16 and 10 points, and a Kolander layup tied the game with 10 seconds left and sent it into overtime. But all those comebacks had sapped the Gophers' energy, and they could not keep up with the Billikens, who won, 64-61.

"We just couldn't make a shot," Haskins says, offering no excuses for the way the Gophers fell behind early. "After that opening, we were just out of the ballgame. We tied it up with a chance to win it, but we just ran out of gas."

The ending may have been disappointing, but the Gophers maintained they had nothing to be ashamed of. Among the seniors, Lenard, who was named second-team All-Big Ten, averaged 17.3 points per game on the season. Orr, a third-team All-Big Ten

selection, had 13.0 points and 4.6 assists. Walton, who made honorable mention despite his painful knee condition, scored 10.9 points and pulled down 7.1 rebounds per game. Kolander averaged 6.0 points per game, and Wolf added 2.1 in limited playing time. Jacobson and Thomas formed the nucleus for the Gophers' future, and they each averaged more than seven points and four rebounds per game.

More importantly for this senior class, they became the first Gopher basketball players in the school's history to play in postseason tournaments four straight years, including two trips to the NCAA Tournament and an NIT championship. They helped Haskins improve his record at the school to 151-124, a .549 winning percentage. That included the dismal rebuilding years of 1986-87 and 1987-88, before the

■ *Voshon Lenard goes in for a layup against Northwestern; he'll be headed to the free throw line after that.*

trips to the Sweet 16 and Elite Eight of the NCAA Tournament.

"When I look at myself in the mirror, I feel good about what we have accomplished at Minnesota," Haskins says.

Overall for the first century of Gopher basketball, the school was 1,196-883-4, a winning percentage of .575 that stands as testament to the enduring legacy of men's basketball at the University of Minnesota. Included in those numbers are two national championships, eight Big Ten titles, six trips to the NCAA Tournament, and an NIT championship. It also encompasses more than 500 individuals who took the court as players or served as coaches during that century—the people who gave Gopher basketball its character beyond the won-loss records and deeper than any count of championships could show. They, along with tens of millions of fans who attended their games, watched them on television, listened to them on radio, or read about them in the newspapers, have given Golden Gopher basketball its soul, and they have helped create a legacy that will serve the game at the University of Minnesota in its second century, and beyond.

Note: Minnesota's score is in the left column of each game entry, and its opponent's score is in the right column.

1895-96 (4-7)
Coach: none
3 U of M Agric. School	13
2 U of M Agric. School	8
5 Company A	4
4 U of M Agric. School	7
3 U of M Agric. School	5
1 U of M Agric. School	3
6 Minneapolis YMCA	3
3 Minneapolis YMCA	6
3 Minneapolis YMCA	6
9 Hamline	3
9 Hamline	6

1896-97 (3-6-1)
Coach: none
1 U of M Agric. School	25
6 YMCA Triangles	18
3 U of M Agric. School	19
11 YMCA Triangles	5
6 YMCA Alphas	23
11 YMCA Goalites	7
5 YMCA Picked Team	5
6 YMCA Alphas	13
11 Macalester	9
5 YMCA Basketites	15

1897-98 (5-8-1)
Coach: L.J. Cooke
7 U of M Agric. School	8
12 Macalester	2
2 at Minneapolis YMCA	9
5 Macalester	13
13 Minneapolis YMCA	14
14 Faculty	6
3 at U of M Agric. School	22
6 at YMCA Triangles	18
11 YMCA Triangles	5
6 at YMCA Alphas	23
11 at YMCA Goalites	7
5 All-Stars	5
6 at YMCA Alphas	13
11 Macalester	9

1898-99 (5-5)
Coach: L.J. Cooke
6 Minneapolis YMCA	8
28 St. Paul YMCA	5
7 Macalester*	9
2 at Minneapolis YMCA	12
8 Macalester	9
7 U of M Agric. School	10
23 St. Paul YMCA	9
20 U of M Agric. School	9
2 Minneapolis YMCA	0
26 Faculty	6

*at St. Paul YMCA

1899-1900 (10-3)
Coach: L.J. Cooke
4 at Minneapolis YMCA	6
14 Central H.S.	8
27 Fargo YMCA	3
14 at St. Cloud Normal	7
30 Iowa	4
32 St. Cloud Normal	2
18 Wisconsin	15
11 at Superior Normal	26
15 at Superior Normal	19
8 Central H.S.	7
27 Superior Normal	7

13 Superior Normal	9
26 Faculty	22

1900-01 (11-1)
Coach: L.J. Cooke
31 Alumni	2
12 Carleton	3
27 Central H.S.	4
17 U of M Agric. School	4
37 St. Paul YMCA	19
23 W. Superior Normal	5
12 W. Superior Normal	14
38 Iowa	5
37 Fargo YMCA	7
26 Fargo College	5
24 North Dakota Aggies	5
42 Wisconsin	15

1901-02 (15-0)*
Coach: L.J. Cooke
44 Alumni	11
13 Sophomores	8
18 Seniors	1
2 South H.S.	0
32 Yale	23
44 East H.S.	4
22 Central H.S.	5
47 North Dakota Aggies	7
50 Fargo H.S.	4
56 Fargo College	24
22 Fond du Lac—Co. E	16
60 North Dakota Aggies	9
52 Nebraska	9
30 Wisconsin	10
49 Iowa	10

*named Helms Athletic Foundation National Champions

1902-03 (13-0)
Coach: L.J. Cooke
42 Faculty	4
42 Central H.S.	6
39 Grinnell	2
57 at Fargo College	11
41 at Fargo H.S.	20
31 North Dakota Aggies	13
37 at Superior Normal	10
44 at Superior Normal	6
37 at Anoka H.S.	4
60 Fargo College	6
46 Fargo College	7
38 Wisconsin	11
41 Nebraska	14

1903-04 (10-2)
Coach: L.J. Cooke
30 at Lewis Inst. (Chicago)	14
26 at West Side YMCA (Chicago)	36
32 at Purdue	22
28 at Crawfordsville (Ind.) H.S.	23
31 at Ohio State	18
28 at Rochester	17
46 at Cornell	18
16 at Washington Continental	21
10 Williams College	6
42 Nebraska	21
33 North Dakota Aggies	15
23 West Side YMCA (Chicago)	13

1904-05 (7-7-1)
Coach: L.J. Cooke
36 Alumni	18
61 Holcomb College	10
49 Iowa	17
21 Nebraska	22
25 Nebraska	28
41 at Rochester	12
27 at Washington Continental	35
15 at Columbia	27
18 at Co. E Schenectady	47
16 at Dartmouth	16
11 at Williams	32
27 at Ohio State	25
34 at Purdue	19
22 at Chicago	25
33 at Chicago	22

1905-06 (13-2, 6-1/1st)
Coach: L.J. Cooke
27 Central High	11
49 Macalester	9
47 Holcomb	12
47 Holcomb	13
27 Faculty	11
31 Illinois	19
26 Fargo Aggies	15
24 at Wisconsin	31
27 at Purdue	25
16 at Wabash	26
27 at Illinois	25
31 at Chicago	29
20 Chicago	17
16 Wisconsin	10
25 Nebraska	16

1906-07 (10-2, 6-2/1st)
Coach: L.J. Cooke
18 Wisconsin	11
42 Illinois	3
44 St. Thomas	6
25 All-Stars	12
20 Nebraska	19
20 Nebraska	18
37 at Purdue	26
36 at Illinois	29
24 Chicago	27
47 UW-Stout	28
20 Wisconsin	31
21 Chicago	10

1907-08 (11-7, 2-6/4th)
Coach: L.J. Cooke
40 Wisc.-Stout	12
52 St. John's (Minn.)	15
33 St. Thomas (Minn.)	12
9 Columbia	8
16 Columbia	11
32 at Iowa	12
16 at Wisconsin	37
19 Grinnell	25
33 Iowa	25
15 Illinois	16
23 Chicago	26
14 Wisconsin	34
43 Nebraska	12
32 Nebraska	10
34 at Purdue	25
20 at Illinois	22
12 Chicago	22
2 Purdue (default)	0

1908-09 (8-6, 3-6/5th)
Coach: L.J. Cooke
41 Ripon	7
18 Illinois	17
13 Wisconsin	16
20 at Illinois	21
24 Nebraska	17
39 Nebraska	21
2 at Chicago	27
21 at Northwestern	16
28 at Nebraska	26
29 at Nebraska	20
16 at Iowa	37
14 Wisconsin	37
15 Chicago	20
23 Iowa	18

1909-10 (10-3, 7-3/2nd)
Coach: L.J. Cooke
15 Chicago	10
15 at Chicago	18
14 at Wisconsin	24
16 Wisconsin	9
22 at Illinois	9
18 Purdue	10
15 at Purdue	17
20 Iowa	9
22 at Iowa	18
38 Wisc.-Stout	6
33 Nebraska	14
27 Nebraska	9
31 Northwestern	18

1910-11 (9-4, 8-4/1st)
Coach: L.J. Cooke
18 Illinois	19
25 Nebraska	10
40 Nebraska	15
17 Wisconsin	16
37 Iowa	7
12 at Illinois	22
21 at Wisconsin	13
18 at Northwestern	21
29 at Iowa	10
23 Purdue	14
19 at Purdue	15
13 at Chicago	22
23 Chicago	16

1911-12 (7-6, 6-6/4th)
Coach: L.J. Cooke
22 Illinois	16
12 at Wisconsin	22
39 at Iowa	17
40 Nebraska	15
16 at Purdue	30
10 at Illinois	13
34 Indiana	7
23 Chicago	13
12 Purdue	24
29 Iowa	10
26 Wisconsin	29
26 at Indiana	17
13 Chicago	27

1912-13 (3-8, 2-8/7th)
Coach: L.J. Cooke
11 Wisconsin	19
20 Nebraska	11
29 at Purdue	27
12 at Illinois	19
9 at Chicago	23

26 at Iowa 10
10 Illinois 20
11 at Wisconsin 29
16 Chicago 20
8 Purdue 23
9 Iowa 12

1913-14 (4-11, 4-8/6th)
Coach: L.J. Cooke
20 Northwestern 21
7 at Wisconsin 28
14 at Iowa 16
16 at Illinois 18
17 at Northwestern 21
15 Nebraska 21
9 Nebraska 14
30 Iowa 9
21 Purdue 17
16 North Dakota 18
11 Illinois 26
26 Indiana 23
9 Wisconsin 27
15 at Purdue 28
28 at Indiana 8

1914-15 (11-6, 6-6/4th)
Coach: L.J. Cooke
11 at Illinois 26
38 St. Olaf 8
19 Hamline IS
22 Nebraska 18
25 Nebraska 9
20 Wisconsin 23
29 Iowa 14
15 Chicago 16
26 at Northwestern 16
11 at Iowa 10
10 Illinois 20
18 Purdue 14
15 Chicago 19
7 at Wisconsin 31
35 Macalester 12
23 North Dakota 10
14 at Purdue 13

1915-16 (10-6, 6-6/4th)
Coach: L.J. Cooke
23 St. Olaf 18
39 UW-Stout 7
21 Hamline 3
20 UW-Stout 10
11 at Wisconsin 31
26 Iowa 11
25 Chicago 27
20 at Purdue 16
29 at Indiana 20
22 Illinois 27
21 at Iowa 13
29 Purdue 18
27 Indiana 20
14 Wisconsin 32
9 at Illinois 20
14 at Chicago 20

1916-17 (17-2, 10-2/1st)
Coach: L.J. Cooke
34 No. Dakota Aggies 15
49 Gustavus 3
53 St. Olaf 12
17 St. Thomas 11
36 Wisc.-Stout 11
44 Macalester 11
27 Wisc.-River Falls 15
33 Wisconsin 23
20 Illinois 11
22 at Northwestern 13
25 Ohio State 24
17 at Illinois 18
19 at Ohio State 10
20 at Chicago 18
39 at Iowa IS
19 Chicago 12
13 at Wisconsin 16
30 Northwestern 20
31 Iowa 19

1917-18 (9-3, 7-3/2nd)
Coach: L.J. Cooke
17 at Illinois 28
33 Iowa 18
28 at Michigan 13
25 at Chicago 23

21 at Iowa 25
49 Michigan 10
24 Chicago IS
35 Illinois 22
39 at No. Dakota Aggies 18
17 Wisconsin 18
19 at Wisconsin 11
49 Great Lakes T.C. 17

1918-19 (13-0, 10-0/1st)*
Coach: L.J. Cooke
40 Overland Aviation 18
50 Aviation Cubs 7
68 Wisc.-Stout 4
35 Indiana 13
38 Wisconsin 11
36 Illinois 17
28 at Iowa 18
36 Iowa 22
36 Purdue 24
20 at Indiana 14
26 at Purdue 21
23 at Wisconsin 12
26 at Illinois 9
named Helms Athletic Foundation National Champions

1919-20 (8-8, 3-9/8th)
Coach: L.J. Cooke
49 Wisc.-Stout 3
30 St. Thomas (Minn.) 11
49 Excelsior 14
26 Wisc.-River Falls 23
19 Northwestern 12
21 Iowa 19
19 at Illinois 31
24 at Northwestern 28
12 at Wisconsin 28
5 at Iowa 30
10 Chicago 35
20 Michigan 21
10 Illinois 26
32 Wisconsin 26
16 at Chicago 58
30 at Michigan 16

1920-21 (10-5, 7-5/4th)
Coach: L.J. Cooke
35 St. Olaf 14
28 UW-River Falls 13
19 North Dakota 18
24 Iowa 19
23 Indiana 25
22 Illinois 23
22 Wisconsin 21
17 at Chicago 19
17 at Iowa 14
20 at Illinois 24
26 at Northwestern 11
24 Chicago 19
12 at Wisconsin 18
29 at Indiana 25
29 Northwestern 13

1921-22 (5-8, 4-7/8th)
Coach: L.J. Cooke
11 Kansas 31
28 Northwestern 13
24 Iowa 16
17 at Wisconsin IS
19 at Indiana 16
25 Chicago 12
19 Indiana 23
28 Illinois 29
18 at Illinois 28
9 at Northwestern 21
22 at Iowa 39
17 at Chicago 23
20 Wisconsin 34

1922-23 (2-13, 1-11/9th)
Coach: L.J. Cooke
23 Hamline 17
11 Macalester 12
11 St. Olaf 15
11 Michigan 32
12 Wisconsin 24
16 Iowa 32
21 Illinois 24
14 at Chicago 28
18 at Michigan 34
20 at Indiana 33

18 at Illinois 25
21 Chicago 24
24 at Iowa 29
10 at Wisconsin 36
29 Indiana 25

1923-24 (9-9, 5-7/8th)
Coach: L.J. Cooke
22 Notre Dame 21
13 Notre Dame 19
17 Iowa State 12
38 Grinnell 17
25 Grinnell 19
36 Illinois 20
23 Indiana 29
27 Purdue 37
31 at Michigan 32
29 at Ohio State 33
25 at Indiana 39
37 at Purdue 40
27 Michigan 16
24 Northwestern 16
41 Ohio State 38
30 at Northwestern 20
19 at Illinois 31

1924-25 (9-7, 6-6/6th)
Coach: Harold Taylor
30 North Dakota IS
25 Notre Dame 12
29 Creighton 25
18 U.S. Naval Academy 24
19 at Iowa 27
16 Wisconsin 14
26 at Chicago 16
14 at Northwestern IS
25 at Wisconsin 14
20 Ohio State 32
36 Purdue 16
20 at Ohio State 26
15 at Purdue 27
20 Iowa 18
20 Northwestern 23
38 Chicago 17

1925-26 (6-10-1, 5-7/7th)
Coach: Harold Taylor
14 at Notre Dame 36
17 at Marquette 28
21 at Creighton 21
11 at Creighton 27
32 Iowa State 17
24 at Wisconsin 33
28 at Indiana 33
8 at Illinois 17
26 Chicago 24
14 at Iowa 21
22 at Michigan 33
28 Michigan 17
23 Indiana 41
28 at Chicago 23
31 Wisconsin 19
28 Illinois 21
15 Iowa 17

1926-27 (3-13, 1-11/9th)
Coach: Harold Taylor
27 North Dakota 26
26 Carleton 13
19 Notre Dame 24
21 Cornell 26
13 Illinois 27
20 Michigan 31
24 Indiana 37
28 at Purdue 32
20 at Michigan 32
20 at Ohio State 32
31 Ohio State 33
27 at Illinois 36
16 at Indiana 42
29 Northwestern 24
25 at Northwestern 33
28 Purdue 29

1927-28 (4-12, 2-10/9th)
Coach: Dave MacMillan
21 Cornell 25
42 North Dakota 28
18 Notre Dame 26
38 Marquette 22
33 at Iowa 32
26 Wisconsin 35

20 at Chicago 26
22 at Northwestern 25
40 Ohio State* 42
27 Iowa 30
18 at Wisconsin 38
36 Northwestern 41
30 Chicago 18
37 at Ohio State 46
27 at Purdue 45
24 Purdue 32
first game played at Williams Arena

1928-29 (4-13, 1-1 I/10th)
Coach: Dave MacMillan
24 North Dakota 25
21 at Drake 32
28 Carleton 21
33 Drake 25
29 Cornell 19
21 Wisconsin 29
36 Indiana 37
23 at Iowa 36
17 at Wisconsin 39
22 at Indiana 41
32 Illinois 35
18 Michigan 23
37 Iowa 22
25 at Chicago 33
19 at Michigan 28
23 Chicago 27
27 at Illinois 32

1929-30 (8-9, 3-9/7th)
Coach: Dave MacMillan
39 No. Dak. Aggies 16
34 North Dakota 25
46 Cornell 15
27 Montana 24
30 Grinnell 15
17 Michigan 32
27 Northwestern 32
19 at Ohio State 30
13 at Michigan 26
29 Ohio State 26
26 Illinois 21
22 at Illinois 26
17 at Northwestern 47
24 Purdue 42
22 at Purdue 50
25 at Indiana 31
34 Indiana 29

1930-31 (13-4, 8-4/2nd)
Coach: Dave MacMillan
59 South Dakota State 21
25 Grinnell 10
39 Beloit 18
25 Carleton 24
29 Iowa State 17
26 at Iowa 22
31 at Chicago 32
28 Wisconsin 26
30 Chicago 27
36 Iowa 14
26 at Northwestern 35
42 at Wisconsin 15
30 Purdue 26
22 at Ohio State 21
23 Northwestern 45
28 at Purdue 33
31 Ohio State 24

1931-32 (15-3, 9-3/2nd)
Coach: Dave MacMillan
31 North Dakota State 18
40 Oklahoma A & M 27
41 Cornell (Iowa) 20
32 Nebraska 24
19 Carleton 14
50 South Dakota 24
22 at Chicago 14
25 at Michigan 30
37 Indiana 35
30 Michigan 26
40 Chicago 27
24 Iowa 22
22 at Indiana 27
15 at Illinois 23
43 Wisconsin 17
27 Illinois 26
24 at Iowa 22
23 at Wisconsin 21

1932-33 (5-15, 1-11/9th)
Coach: Dave MacMillan

46	South Dakota	26
55	Grinnell	25
26	Pittsburgh	35
27	Nebraska	25
32	at Nebraska	22
32	Purdue	42
28	at Ohio State	43
16	at Purdue	40
22	at Notre Dame	30
22	Michigan	34
23	Ohio State	24
21	Carleton	31
22	at Indiana	32
25	at Northwestern	41
22	Illinois	26
25	Indiana	31
30	at Illinois	28
18	at Michigan	21
28	Northwestern	39
27	Notre Dame	31

1933-34 (9-11, 5-7/7th)
Coach: Dave MacMillan

24	St. Thomas	25
47	Cornell	23
23	at Pittsburgh	28
14	at DePaul	22
37	Nebraska	16
30	at Purdue	45
26	at Northwestern	33
39	Iowa	38
24	Ohio State	28
31	Northwestern	30
36	Chicago	18
41	at Ohio State	39
23	at Chicago	22
34	at Notre Dame	43
30	Wisconsin	31
30	Purdue	47
30	at Iowa	33
43	Carleton	29
23	at Wisconsin	24
43	Notre Dame	41

1934-35 (11-9, 5-7/7th)
Coach: Dave MacMillan

31	Hamline	24
28	St. Thomas	18
42	North Dakota State	13
34	Carleton	26
24	at Nebraska	26
44	at Superior Teachers	33
30	Notre Dame	28
31	Michigan	24
33	Iowa	39
42	at Chicago	33
31	at Wisconsin	38
36	at Iowa	35
35	Chicago	26
23	at Indiana	48
29	at Michigan	26
27	Wisconsin	28
34	Illinois	38
29	at Illinois	40
27	at Notre Dame	38
29	Indiana	38

1935-36 (7-17, 3-9/9th)
Coach: Dave MacMillan

35	Cornell	23
30	North Dakota State	22
26	Carleton	29
34	Nebraska	41
31	at Marquette	34
17	at DePaul	48
27	Notre Dame	29
21	Illinois	49
28	at Michigan	38
24	at Northwestern	45
31	Indiana	33
30	Northwestern	29
31	Michigan	26
42	at Ohio State	21
23	at Indiana	26
23	Ohio State	44
25	Purdue	39
33	at Illinois	35
29	at Notre Dame	34
17	at Notre Dame	35
40	Carroll	26

36	Drake*	19
30	at DePaul	36
27	at DePaul	33

at Chicago Distinct Olympic Tournament

1936-37 (14-6, 10-2/1st)
Coach: Dave MacMillan

41	Carleton	11
29	North Dakota State	33
36	Kansas State	37
24	at Nebraska	29
34	at Creighton	23
49	Iowa State	16
34	DePaul	25
30	Chicago	23
22	at Ohio State	23
36	at Northwestern	23
31	Ohio State	14
45	Purdue	41
37	at Wisconsin	32
43	at Iowa	37
33	at Purdue	34
44	Iowa	25
30	Wisconsin	17
34	Northwestern	33
33	at Chicago	23
18	at Notre Dame	44

1937-38 (16-4, 9-3/2nd)
Coach: Dave MacMillan

45	South Dakota	23
41	Grinnell	33
41	Carleton	30
33	at Nebraska	28
56	Long Island Univ.*	41
36	New York Univ.#	31
27	George Washington*	35
37	Notre Dame	25
28	Wisconsin	35
38	Indiana	39
16	Michigan	31
41	at Illinois	29
45	Chicago	29
28	Iowa	26
28	Illinois	25
29	at Michigan	26
37	at Indiana	36
38	at Chicago	27
30	at Iowa	29
35	at Wisconsin	28

at New York

1938-39 (14-6, 7-5/4th)
Coach: Dave MacMillan

46	South Dakota State	36
50	South Dakota	26
47	Carleton	24
47	Creighton	32
66	at Nebraska	37
39	at New York Univ.	32
38	Temple	35
38	Chicago	28
36	Iowa	29
34	at Michigan	21
31	at Northwestern	32
35	Illinois	33
33	at Notre Dame	55
34	at Chicago	27
30	Ohio State	31
20	Purdue	30
34	Wisconsin	32
37	at Indiana	49
25	at Wisconsin	35
54	at Iowa	43

1939-40 (13-8, 5-7/7th)
Coach: Dave MacMillan

47	North Dakota State	28
38	South Dakota State	30
29	Carleton	20
35	South Dakota	28
61	Nebraska	37
47	at Washington	41
28	at Washington	26
33	at Washington	37
32	Idaho	26
42	Iowa	34
38	Northwestern	46
46	Indiana	44
34	at Purdue	50
31	at Illinois	60
34	at Wisconsin	36

34	Iowa	29
32	Chicago	35
43	at Ohio State	48
43	Wisconsin	39
46	at Chicago	33
32	Michigan	43

1940-41 (11-9, 7-5/3rd)
Coach: Dave MacMillan

53	Carleton	16
36	Iowa State	37
32	Idaho	26
43	at Nebraska	36
32	at Creighton	37
51	at New York U.	54
43	at Geo. Washington	46
53	Montana	38
44	Wisconsin	27
34	Iowa	41
35	at Chicago	24
24	at Michigan	41
46	Ohio State	43
50	Illinois	38
34	at Indiana	44
55	at Northwestern	34
68	Purdue	50
56	Chicago	24
32	at Wisconsin	42
39	at Iowa	46

1941-42 (15-7, 9-6/5th)
Coach: Dave MacMillan

55	Millikan College	19
56	South Dakota	35
41	North Dakota State	32
44	Creighton	30
56	Nebraska	32
56	at Ohio State	42
38	at Northwestern	49
63	Indiana	43
41	Iowa	39
44	Michigan	32
34	North Dakota State	52
52	at Chicago	28
36	at Illinois	49
46	at Purdue	39
32	at Michigan	34
63	Ohio State	33
34	Purdue	27
37	Illinois	41
47	Great Lakes N.T.C.	39
45	at Indiana	54
47	Wisconsin	49
61	Northwestern	42

1942-43 (10-9, 5-7/6th)
Coach: Carl Nordly

35	Carleton	29
49	South Dakota	29
50	North Dakota State	34
62	South Dakota State	52
38	Dartmouth	47
46	at Iowa	45
41	at Iowa	48
46	Michigan State	32
42	Purdue	49
50	Purdue	48
47	Northwestern	46
33	at Wisconsin	54
47	at Chicago	25
35	Illinois	56
43	Illinois	67
39	at Indiana	51
28	at Indiana	40
41	Great Lakes N.T.C.	46
48	Wisconsin	34

1943-44 (7-14, 2-10/8th)
Coach: Carl Nordly

54	St. Mary's (Minn.)	32
59	South Dakota	31
34	Iowa Seahawks	54
41	Nebraska	23
31	Iowa State	28
32	Great Lakes N.T.C.	59
34	Iowa	37
29	Iowa	37
38	at Purdue	51
17	at Purdue	43
45	at Nebraska	32
30	Wisconsin	49
32	at Northwestern	57

38	at Camp Grant	53
48	Indiana	47
47	Indiana	48
38	at Wisconsin	52
49	Chicago	36
43	Great Lakes N.T.C.	73
32	at Illinois	50
27	at Illinois	53

1944-45 (8-13, 4-8/6th)
Coach: Weston Mitchell

50	South Dakota	28
41	at Iowa State	42
32	Iowa Seahawks	38
42	Great Lakes N.T.C.	46
55	at Nebraska	54
44	at Great Lakes N.T.C.	63
43	at Marquette	40
45	Lawrence College	30
34	at Iowa	41
49	Purdue	44
33	at Northwestern	52
37	at Wisconsin	46
46	Indiana	48
45	at Purdue	54
56	at Indiana	48
35	Illinois	57
43	Northwestern	37
48	at Illinois	49
48	Iowa	55
54	Wisconsin	50
30	Iowa Seahawks	49

1945-46 (14-7, 7-5/5th)
Coach: Dave MacMillan

71	South Dakota	27
78	South Dakota State	25
55	Nebraska	30
65	Iowa State	33
50	at Great Lakes N.T.C.	67
48	at Michigan State	50
69	North Dakota State	46
45	DePaul	36
46	at Wisconsin	45
59	at Indiana	48
71	Chicago	44
64	Great Lakes N.T.C.	49
56	Purdue	43
61	at Iowa	63
40	at Purdue	65
49	at Northwestern	72
52	at Chicago	30
50	Northwestern	52
52	Indiana	75
58	Iowa	47
58	Wisconsin	57

1946-47 (14-7, 7-5/4th)
Coach: Dave MacMillan

54	DePaul	39
65	South Dakota	33
75	North Dakota	34
40	St. Louis	36
51	at Iowa State	41
68	at Nebraska	58
47	at Washington	61
68	at Washington	72
41	at Ohio State	43
34	at Illinois	31
48	Michigan	37
64	at Iowa	77
73	Michigan State	58
59	Indiana	56
63	at Purdue	66
63	Northwestern	61
51	at Wisconsin	60
81	Purdue	69
59	Iowa	55
25	at Michigan	44
58	Wisconsin	55

1947-48 (10-10, 5-7/7th)
Coach: Dave MacMillan

42	at St. Louis	50
63	Nebraska	59
46	DePaul	44
47	Washington	37
49	Washington	55
60	at California	58
35	at California	59
50	at Wisconsin	59
41	at Michigan	43

59 Illinois 51
72 Iowa 56
43 at Indiana 65
69 Michigan State 63
68 Ohio State 55
51 Purdue 53
53 at Northwestern 51
38 at Purdue 54
45 Michigan 56
50 at Iowa 54
46 Wisconsin 41

1948-49 (18-3, 9-3, 2nd)
Coach: O.B. Cowles
68 Western Illinois 46
61 at Nebraska 52
67 at DePaul 50
47 Navy 40
52 St. Mary's (Calif.) 42
64 Dartmouth* 52
50 at Drake* 26
70 Colgate 46
45 Michigan 31
47 Wisconsin 33
67 at Purdue 52
61 at Iowa 44
35 Indiana 28
44 at Illinois 45
61 Northwestern 40
39 at Ohio State 48
54 Iowa 49
54 at Michigan 47
57 at Michigan State 47
58 Purdue 48
43 at Wisconsin 45
*Corn Bowl Tourn. at Des Moines

1949-50 (13-9, 4-8/6th)
Coach: O.B. Cowles
55 Loyola (Chicago) 51
60 Oregon State 44
67 Iowa State 44
55 at Washington 53
46 at Washington 53
51 at Oregon State 41
67 Stanford* 65
47 California* 45
74 Marquette 38
53 at Northwestern 60
67 Purdue 40
54 at Wisconsin 57
60 at Michigan 52
73 at Michigan State 56
58 Ohio State 63
57 Illinois 67
39 at Indiana 59
53 Michigan 48
62 Iowa 64
39 at Purdue 55
54 Wisconsin 60
64 at Iowa 49
*at Cow Palace (San Francisco)

1950-51 (13-9, 7-7/4th)
Coach: O.B. Cowles
55 Nebraska 41
66 Loyola (Chicago) 51
45 at Oklahoma 66
72 Pittsburgh 43
49 Oklahoma 42
74 Colorado* 68
62 Kansas* 51
62 Kansas State* 70
62 at Illinois 70
77 Ohio State 64
78 Purdue 55
66 Michigan 62
47 Iowa 69
26 at Indiana 32
44 Wisconsin 47
44 at Michigan State 50
61 Indiana 54
48 at Michigan 52
70 at Ohio State 56
78 at Purdue 81
73 at Northwestern 68
56 Michigan State 39
*Kansas City Tournament

1951-52 (15-7, 10-4/3rd)
Coach: O.B. Cowles
54 Bradley 58
63 at Nebraska 55
57 DePaul 64
61 Kentucky 57
51 Washington 55
63 Princeton* 57
75 Dartmouth* 62
73 Arizona# 61
43 Illinois 52
55 Michigan State 49
70 Michigan 60
59 at Iowa 76
58 at Ohio State 59
74 Northwestern 56
65 at Purdue 50
84 Ohio State 56
54 at Wisconsin 47
74 Indiana 61
52 at Michigan 44
60 at Michigan State 58
59 Purdue 56
52 at Indiana 68
*Michigan State Tournament
#at Milwaukee

1952-53 (14-8, 11-7/3rd)
Coach: O.B. Cowles
79 at Bradley 63
76 at Xavier 71
71 Nebraska 62
77 Illinois 73
64 Michigan State 47
59 at Marquette 70
65 Northwestern 71
64 Wisconsin 53
63 at Indiana 66
74 at Wisconsin 76
65 Iowa 58
82 Ohio State 64
77 at Purdue 72
60 at Michigan State 64
72 at Northwestern 69
74 Purdue 50
71 at Ohio State 81
90 Michigan 83
82 at Illinois 83
83 at Michigan 69
79 at Iowa 81
65 Indiana 63

1953-54 (17-5, 10-4/3rd)
Coach: O.B. Cowles
75 at Nebraska 64
62 Tulsa 60
57 Oklahoma A & M 56
74 Colorado 46
66 at Tulsa 63
91 Marquette 73
67 at Xavier 64
59 at Kentucky 74
84 at Illinois 72
63 Indiana 71
59 at Iowa 55
82 at Northwestern 78
80 Purdue 64
79 Michigan State 71
67 at Purdue 64
77 at Indiana 90
82 Iowa 86
78 at Wisconsin 68
73 at Ohio State 84
79 Michigan 70
81 Northwestern 69
78 Wisconsin 73

1954-55 (15-7, 10-4/2nd)
Coach: O.B. Cowles
93 at DePaul 94
94 DePaul 84
54 at Oklahoma A & M 62
89 SMU 72
77 Notre Dame 66
81 Wake Forest* 73
79 Duke* 73
84 North Carolina St.* 85
72 at Northwestern 74
81 at Iowa 80
88 Indiana 74
102 Purdue 88
75 at Michigan State 87

102 Northwestern 82
59 at Purdue 56
82 Ohio State 56
78 Illinois 71
80 at Indiana 70
74 at Michigan 65
71 at Wisconsin 69
70 Iowa 72
72 Wisconsin 78
*Dixie Classic (Raleigh, N.C.)

1955-56 (11-11, 6-8/6th)
Coach: O.B. Cowles
82 DePaul 78
81 So. Methodist 82
83 Notre Dame 75
65 at Kentucky* 72
90 Utah* 77
83 Wake Forest# 87
64 Oregon State# 60
70 Wyoming# 66
79 Michigan 81
77 Indiana 71
62 at Iowa 84
69 at Michigan State 80
83 Northwestern 67
84 Illinois 95
67 at Purdue 75
77 at Wisconsin 71
77 Michigan State 73
80 at Ohio State 91
73 Iowa 83
81 at Illinois 97
86 at Michigan 72
95 Ohio State 89
*Kentucky Inv. (Lexington, Ky.)
#at Raleigh, N.C.

1956-57 (14-8, 9-5/3rd)
Coach: O.B. Cowles
63 Vanderbilt 60
74 at Rice 79
84 at So. Methodist 91
80 Kansas State 72
84 Loyola (Chicago) 61
83 Xavier* 76
75 Canisius* 84
91 Illinois 88
66 at Iowa 89
73 at Ohio State 85
73 at Northwestern 62
99 Marquette 78
59 Michigan State 72
89 Michigan 79
82 at Michigan 62
72 at Indiana 91
74 Purdue 61
85 Wisconsin 53
65 at Michigan State 70
102 Iowa 81
86 at Illinois 75
76 Ohio State 69
*Queen City Tournament (Buffalo, N.Y.)

1957-58 (9-12, 5-9/8th)
Coach: O.B. Cowles
66 So. Methodist 52
67 Iowa State 66
89 at Vanderbilt 85
67 North Carolina* 73
58 at Kentucky* 78
74 Yale 53
83 Purdue 76
71 at Kansas State 72
64 at Indiana 85
79 at Ohio State 95
71 Iowa 73
76 at Northwestern 85
64 at Michigan State 88
69 Indiana 66
71 at Wisconsin 66
80 Michigan 69
75 Northwestern 76
87 at Illinois 94
79 at Purdue 88
71 Wisconsin 63
60 Ohio State 70
*Kentucky Inv. (Lexington, Ky.)

1958-59 (8-14, 5-9/9th)
Coach: O.B. Cowles
77 Vanderbilt 76
75 at Iowa State 81
45 Oklahoma 52
78 Nebraska 57
58 at So. Methodist 67
72 Stanford 61
63 at Washington 85
57 at Washington 73
79 Wisconsin 66
59 at Indiana 63
64 Purdue 62
71 at Northwestern 67
76 Michigan State 82
81 Illinois 70
80 at Ohio State 84
65 at Iowa 69
57 Indiana 62
69 at Wisconsin 50
62 Northwestern 79
55 at Purdue 67
66 Ohio State 68
66 at Michigan 68

1959-60 (12-12, 8-6/3rd)
Coach: John Kundla
60 So. Methodist 73
72 at Vanderbilt 59
66 at Nebraska 76
59 Oklahoma 57
80 Missouri 62
72 UCLA 73
59 Oklahoma 57
65 North Carolina* 72
72 Utah* 75
48 North Carolina St.* 57
70 Iowa 61
82 at Illinois 90
74 at Michigan 58
77 Illinois 70
61 at Northwestern 62
87 at Iowa 72
86 Wisconsin 72
63 at Michigan State 84
64 Northwestern 66
82 Michigan State 73
71 Purdue 69
87 Michigan 61
74 at Indiana 78
66 Ohio State 75
*at Raleigh, N.C.

1960-61 (10-13, 8-6/4th)
Coach: John Kundla
58 Bradley 62
56 at Oklahoma 60
60 at Missouri 56
53 Maryland 64
52 St. Mary's (Calif.) 54
60 at So. Methodist 63
52 Southern California* 75
49 California* 63
83 Michigan State* 77
46 at Iowa 71
64 Purdue 65
66 Northwestern 54
56 at Ohio State 75
89 Michigan State 70
66 at Northwestern 59
66 Indiana 58
60 Illinois 65
70 Michigan 53
75 at Michigan State 72
75 at Wisconsin 83
43 Iowa 61
85 at Illinois 76
73 at Michigan 70
*Los Angeles Classic

1961-62 (10-14, 6-8/7th)
Coach: John Kundla
56 DePaul 66
89 Memphis State 81
70 So. Methodist 56
69 at Maryland 75
47 at Bradley 80
70 Arizona State 68
63 at Marquette 69
66 Temple* 70
98 Miami of Ohio* 64
70 at Wake Forest 79

81 Purdue 67
104 Indiana 100
63 at Iowa 65
76 Ohio State 90
79 at Michigan State 84
104 at Indiana 105
88 Wisconsin 94
80 at Illinois 89
66 at Ohio State 91
73 Northwestern 64
80 at Purdue 94
92 at Wisconsin 90
98 Michigan State 91
102 at Michigan 80
*Hurricane Classic (Miami)

1962-63 (12-12, 8-6/4th)
Coach: John Kundla
78 Wake Forest 66
73 Kansas State 62
73 Bradley 63
74 at DePaul 76
70 at Memphis State 78
80 at So. Methodist 100
79 at Arizona State 98
62 at Wichita State 79
65 at Drake 67
87 Houston 68
76 at Ohio State 78
83 Iowa 58
66 at Michigan 63
82 at Purdue 73
59 Michigan State 61
69 at Wisconsin 68
80 Purdue 73
77 at Indiana 89
75 at Michigan State 70
72 Wisconsin 48
66 at Northwestern 71
70 Illinois 81
105 Indiana 73
65 Ohio State 85

1963-64 (17-7, 10-4/3rd)
Coach: John Kundla
76 at Kansas State 66
60 at Houston 58
61 Iowa State 50
107 South Dakota 62
75 at Bradley 78
65 Wichita State 71
64 Drake 51
89 Cornell* 77
69 St. Joseph's* 63
73 Villanova* 77
97 Purdue 93
73 at Ohio State 85
103 Michigan State 82
76 Northwestern 74
66 at Michigan 80
76 at Northwestern 82
111 Wisconsin 92
76 at Iowa 71
92 Illinois 81
89 Michigan 75
78 at Illinois 86
70 Iowa 63
105 at Wisconsin 96
90 at Indiana 89
*Holiday Festival Tourn. (New York)

1964-65 (19-5, 11-3/2nd)
Coach: John Kundla
101 South Dakota State 55
67 at Drake 60
63 at Iowa State 53
78 Marquette 59
88 Utah State 69
89 Loyola (Chicago) 75
77 Washington* 76
77 UCLA* 93
74 Iowa* 76
80 Detroit 66
81 Wisconsin 57
72 at Illinois 75
97 Ohio State 77
85 at Purdue 81
70 Northwestern 66
88 at Michigan State 79
105 Illinois 90
101 at Wisconsin 91
88 at Northwestern 77

78 Michigan 91
100 Indiana 88
78 at Iowa 70
85 at Michigan 88
85 Iowa 84
*Los Angeles Classic

1965-66 (14-10, 7-7/5th)
Coach: John Kundla
73 North Dakota 59
80 Iowa State 69
81 Drake 67
89 Creighton 77
92 at Detroit 88
72 at Utah State 97
84 Cornell* 82
66 St. Joseph's* 91
92 LaSalle* 87
69 at Loyola (Chicago) 82
65 at Michigan State 85
91 Indiana 82
85 at Michigan 97
91 at Purdue 75
86 Northwestern 76
66 Purdue 61
81 Michigan State 71
87 at Iowa 96
89 at Illinois 100
98 Ohio State 102
94 Illinois 92
96 at Indiana 90
89 at Ohio State 94
74 Wisconsin 87
*City Tournament (Philadelphia)

1966-67 (9-15, 5-9/9th)
Coach: John Kundla
60 at Kansas State 59
75 Houston 86
69 at Iowa State 87
71 Drake 68
71 Ohio University 67
61 at Marquette 74
60 at Oregon 67
88 at West Virginia 93
60 at Oregon State 54
63 Loyola (Chicago) 87
65 Ohio State 78
68 at Indiana 83
73 Purdue 86
67 at Ohio State 60
72 at Purdue 83
81 Indiana 82
93 Illinois 81
75 at Wisconsin 85
66 at Michigan State 67
88 Iowa 86
89 Michigan 86
71 at Illinois 84
86 at Northwestern 84
59 Michigan State 67

1967-68 (7-17, 4-10/9th)
Coach: John Kundla
85 South Dakota 52
63 at Drake 82
56 Kansas State 81
62 North Dakota 53
65 at Houston 103
65 at Creighton 82
73 Ohio University 63
55 UCLA* 95
65 Utah State* 73
65 USC* 78
59 at Indiana 74
60 Illinois 61
71 at Northwestern 77
70 at Iowa 82
62 Wisconsin 72
82 Indiana 75
101 at Michigan 113
62 at Purdue 89
85 Northwestern 80
83 Ohio State 79
92 Michigan 105
82 at Wisconsin 94
75 at Michigan State 68
72 Iowa 91
*Los Angeles Basketball Classic

1968-69 (12-12, 6-8/5th)
Coach: Bill Fitch
48 Iowa State 57
75 Marquette 73
76 at Loyola (Chicago) 71
65 at Notre Dame 69
77 North Dakota 64
51 UCLA 90
73 at San Diego State 60
48 Drake* 71
72 Mississippi* 58
85 Detroit 80
58 at Illinois 80
94 Michigan 67
61 at Wisconsin 68
68 at Iowa 89
79 Purdue 102
89 Northwestern 80
89 at Indiana 83
63 Wisconsin 69
41 at Ohio State 58
83 Indiana 79
79 at Michigan 83
70 at Northwestern 74
71 Iowa 65
78 Michigan State 65
*Dallas Classic Tournament

1969-70 (13-11, 7-7/5th)
Coach: Bill Fitch
75 Notre Dame 84
85 at North Dakota 71
71 UCLA 72
84 at Iowa State 89
79 Drake 76
51 at Marquette 67
79 San Diego State 68
70 Bowling Green* 68
65 Detroit* 64
71 at Ohio State 78
77 Indiana 65
84 at Wisconsin 90
85 Michigan State 78
77 Ohio State 76
85 Loyola (Chicago) 73
92 at Michigan State 87
77 at Iowa 90
82 Illinois 72
80 Northwestern 72
87 at Michigan 95
94 Purdue 108
73 at Illinois 75
93 Michigan 82
44 at Purdue 48
*Motor City Inv (Detroit)

1970-71 (11-13, 5-9/5th)
Coach: George Hanson
85 North Dakota 61
89 Iowa State 69
61 Marquette 70
82 at Loyola (Chicago) 62
95 Bradley 89
66 at Drake 83
77 at Evansville 73
56 at Virginia Cmmnwlth. 63
73 at Notre Dame 97
92 Niagara 87
76 Purdue 83
73 at Indiana 99
92 at Purdue 97
66 Ohio State 68
79 Michigan 97
78 at Illinois 93
97 Michigan State 86
88 Iowa 76
90 at Michigan 108
81 at Northwestern 79
80 Illinois 64
70 at Ohio State 84
104 Wisconsin 98
71 at Michigan State 73

1971-72 (18-7, 11-3, 1st)
Coach: Bill Musselman
68 North Dakota 49
72 at Iowa State 58
67 at Bradley 74
77 Butler 56
40 at Marquette 55
70 Drake 56
57 Temple* 60

83 Texas Christian* 57
84 Loyola (Chicago) 59
52 Indiana 51
84 Northwestern 60
65 at Wisconsin 59
67 at Michigan State 57
44 Ohio State 50
61 at Iowa 50
53 Iowa 52
42 at Indiana 61
78 at Northwestern 55
76 Wisconsin 73
52 at Michigan 64
48 Purdue 43
91 Illinois 62
49 at Purdue 48
56 Florida State** 70
77 Marquette** 72
*Rainbow Classic (Honolulu)
**NCAA Tournament

1972-73 (21-5, 10-4/2nd)
Coach: Bill Musselman
93 Cal-Irvine 71
111 Western Illinois 66
79 Wisconsin-Milwaukee 60
87 at Loyola (Chicago) 81
78 San Francisco State 38
67 Corpus Christi 53
41 Washington State* 35
59 Oregon* 49
83 Oregon State* 80
62 at Iowa 65
78 Wisconsin 54
64 Marquette 53
71 at Indiana 83
93 Michigan State 77
81 at Wisconsin 64
70 Purdue 53
80 at Ohio State 78
82 Indiana 75
82 at Illinois 73
98 Michigan 80
90 Northwestern 74
79 at Purdue 66
77 Iowa 79
74 at Northwestern 79
68 Rutgers** 59
65 Alabama** 69
*Far West Classic
**NIT

1973-74 (12-126-8/6th)
Coach: Bill Musselman
55 Cal-Davis 45
49 Furman 47
58 Loyola (Chicago) 54
50 at Marquette 68
65 at Niagara 79
70 at Butler 68
73 Bradley* 68
68 New Mexico* 102
82 Northern Michigan 59
55 at Iowa 66
52 Detroit 54
65 Michigan 66
77 at Ohio State 81
66 Michigan State 67
57 at Northwestern 54
64 Wisconsin 63
56 Ohio State 51
45 at Purdue 64
80 Illinois 61
56 at Michigan State 50
55 Indiana 73
72 at Illinois 52
56 at Michigan 79
50 Iowa 60
*Far West Classic (Portland, Ore.)

1974-75 (18-8, 11-7/3rd)
Coach: Bill Musselman
80 North Dakota State 47
78 Montana State 58
63 Northern Illinois 57
53 Stanford 52
66 at Loyola (Chicago) 53
66 at Furman 77
68 Navy 35
66 Clemson 52
61 at Wisconsin 46
54 Purdue 51

75	Illinois	47
67	at Ohio State	76
59	at Indiana	79
82	Michigan State	71
67	Michigan	58
44	at Iowa	53
70	at Northwestern	57
56	at Illinois	50
62	Ohio State	53
54	Indiana	69
81	at Michigan State	86
65	at Michigan	67
68	Iowa	67
66	Northwestern	58
65	Wisconsin	58
72	at Purdue	100

1975-76 (16-10, 8-10/6th)
Coach: Jim Dutcher

96	South Dakota State	74
74	North Dakota	60
68	Loyola (Chicago)	55
77	Marquette	73
83	at Montana State	75
89	at Stanford	84
86	Penn State	70
80	Creighton	74
110	Purdue	111
72	at Michigan	95
77	Illinois	68
68	Iowa	71
77	at Northwestern	85
96	at Wisconsin	84
76	Indiana	85
82	Ohio State	69
63	at Michigan State	75
72	at Illinois	62
58	at Iowa	65
69	Northwestern	75
98	Wisconsin	74
64	at Indiana	76
89	at Ohio State	73
71	Michigan State	61
81	Michigan	79
87	at Purdue	94

1976-77 (24-3, 15-3)#
Coach: Jim Dutcher

101	North Dakota State	68
104	at Detroit	80
96	Northern Michigan	50
66	at Nebraska	58
96	Vermont	61
66	at Marquette	59
62	Kansas State	60
84	Cornell	54
102	Montana	81
78	Iowa	68
83	at Illinois	69
64	at Purdue	66
82	Wisconsin	64
75	Michigan State	70
79	at Indiana	60
77	at Ohio State	67
79	Northwestern	53
80	Michigan	86
91	Ohio State	65
61	at Iowa	58
65	Indiana	61
99	at Michigan State	77
70	at Michigan	89
84	Purdue	78
72	Illinois	70
64	at Wisconsin	61
105	at Northwestern	82

#the NCAA declared all games from 1976-77 forfeits. The Big Ten doesn't recognize them as wins and has Minnesota 0-27, 0-18

1977-78 (17-11, 12-6/2nd)
Coach: Jim Dutcher

55	at South Carolina	62
61	Eastern Kentucky	59
66	at Loyola (Chicago)	70
44	Marquette	61
49	Nebraska	63
75	at South Florida	61
66	Air Force	50
88	Florida State	74
83	at Michigan State	87
65	at Michigan	69
75	Indiana	62
72	Ohio State	47
70	Illinois	66
61	at Wisconsin	51
64	at Purdue	72
69	at Northwestern	58
82	Iowa	71
80	Northwestern	69
64	Wisconsin	55
78	at Iowa	65
75	at Illinois	69
79	Purdue	72
72	Louisville	71
87	at Ohio State	94
47	at Indiana	68
84	Michigan	78
70	Michigan State	71

1978-79 (11-16, 6-12/8th)
Coach: Jim Dutcher

72	Idaho	57
48	at Nebraska	58
95	Loyola (Chicago)	90
62	at Kansas State	72
55	at Marquette	72
69	South Florida	54
53	South Carolina	57
80	Houston	67
57	Georgia Tech	56
75	at Michigan	88
62	at Michigan State	69
80	Indiana	63
60	Northwestern	58
80	at Ohio State	83
82	Wisconsin	72
61	Purdue	64
64	at Iowa	81
57	at Illinois	67
71	Iowa	97
74	at Wisconsin	72
57	Illinois	59
68	Ohio State	74
56	at Purdue	80
73	at Northwestern	71
46	at Indiana	71
63	Michigan State	76
78	Michigan	69

1979-80 (21-11, 10-8/4th)
Coach: Jim Dutcher

77	Eastern Michigan	56
65	Fresno State	49
87	North Dakota	60
75	Nebraska	58
64	at Tennessee	71
91	at Florida State	112
78	Kansas State	61
98	Rutgers	59
69	Texas A&M	63
67	at Michigan	71
93	at Michigan State	80
82	Wisconsin	76
79	Illinois	75
70	at Ohio State	75
67	Purdue	61
55	Indiana	47
73	at Iowa	80
74	at Northwestern	64
63	Iowa	74
56	at Purdue	58
72	Northwestern	55
74	Ohio State	70
54	at Indiana	67
58	at Illinois	60
55	at Wisconsin	70
87	Michigan State	73
68	Michigan	67
64	Bowling Green	50
58	Mississippi*	56
94	S.W. Louisiana*	73
65	Illinois*	63
55	Virginia*	58

*NIT

1980-81 (19-11, 9-9/5th)
Coach: Jim Dutcher

99	North Dakota State	64
79	Florida State	66
100	Loyola (Chicago)	83
84	Marquette	92
62	at Louisville	56
95	Yale	54
72	Texas Tech	56
74	USC*	67
76	North Carolina*	60
76	Wisconsin	60
67	Michigan	68
86	at Michigan State	77
76	at Illinois	80
63	Ohio State	76
60	at Iowa	48
53	Indiana	56
74	Northwestern	63
59	at Purdue	74
68	at Northwestern	62
58	Iowa	60
92	Purdue	72
82	at Ohio State	76
63	at Indiana	74
76	Illinois	59
92	Michigan State	89
67	at Michigan	83
58	at Wisconsin	60
90	Drake**	77
84	at Connecticut**	66
69	West Virginia**	80

*Winston Tire Classic (Los Angeles)
**NIT

1981-82 (23-6, 14-4/1st)
Coach: Jim Dutcher

88	San Francisco State	69
90	Dayton	74
61	at Loyola (Chicago)	60
80	Drake	55
76	at Marquette	54
52	at Kansas State	62
79	Army	37
91	Arizona	62
75	Long Beach State	67
47	at Ohio State	49
64	at Michigan State	58
61	Iowa	56
67	Michigan	58
78	at Wisconsin	57
57	Illinois	64
61	at Northwestern	53
69	at Indiana	62
73	Purdue	50
55	Indiana	58
71	Wisconsin	60
53	at Purdue	52
76	Northwestern	66
65	at Illinois	77
61	at Michigan	50
57	at Iowa	55
54	Michigan State	51
87	Ohio State	75
62	Tenn.-Chattanooga*	61
61	Louisville*	67

* NCAA Tournament

1982-83 (18-11, 9-9/6th)
Coach: Jim Dutcher

83	North Dakota State	61
78	at Iowa State	80
70	at Drake	65
87	U.S. International	72
71	at Dayton	65
100	Marquette	66
62	at Jacksonville	48
120	Indiana State	82
62	Montana State	45
75	Illinois	49
54	Purdue	48
58	at Michigan	63
69	at Michigan State	67
52	Iowa	68
68	Northwestern	53
63	at Wisconsin	58
89	at Ohio State	80
51	at Indiana	76
59	Indiana	63
69	Ohio State	74
49	Cincinnati	46
78	Wisconsin	71
66	at Northwestern	83
71	at Iowa	69
67	Michigan State	79
88	Michigan	75
62	at Purdue	68
67	at Illinois	70
73	at DePaul*	76

*NIT

1983-84 (15-13, 6-12/8th)
Coach: Jim Dutcher

93	South Dakota State	77
96	Indiana State	70
60	at Marquette	77
65	Oregon	49
52	Jacksonville	50
78	North Dakota	73
60	at Detroit	56
55	at Montana State	52
66	Iowa State	64
53	at Illinois	80
69	at Purdue	72
62	Michigan	66
69	Michigan State	61
56	at Iowa	49
50	at Northwestern	52
75	Wisconsin	62
54	Indiana	67
83	Ohio State	61
62	at Ohio State	73
72	at Indiana	74
68	at Wisconsin	67
65	at Cincinnati	61
63	Northwestern	57
50	Iowa	62
62	at Michigan State	83
50	at Michigan	51
41	Illinois	53
62	Purdue	63

1984-85 (13-15, 6-12/8th)
Coach: Jim Dutcher

75	Wisconsin-Green Bay	71
61	Connecticut	60
85	Montana State	71
46	Princeton	44
86	at Indiana State	94
57	at Oregon	53
88	at Arizona	79
46	at Arkansas	56
67	Detroit	77
70	Marquette	62
60	Illinois	58
65	Purdue	74
65	Iowa	57
56	at Michigan	97
81	at Michigan State	75
72	Wisconsin	62
51	Northwestern	56
62	at Ohio State	76
66	at Indiana	89
65	at Iowa	70
73	Michigan State	64
64	Michigan	66
74	at Northwestern	48
61	at Wisconsin	65
68	Indiana	79
77	Ohio State	78
67	at Purdue	79
56	at Illinois	82

1985-86 (15-16, 5-13/8th)
Coach: Jim Dutcher**

120	W. Virginia State*	106
79	Middle Tenn. State*	92
87	Brigham Young-Hawaii*	80
95	San Francisco State	63
66	South Dakota	57
87	Eastern Illinois	69
83	Detroit	71
71	Arkansas	64
62	Colorado State	59
63	at Marquette	74
69	Connecticut	70
71	Oklahoma State	59
110	Alcorn State	72
57	at Illinois	76
61	at Purdue	68
62	at Iowa	75
73	Michigan	63
76	Michigan State	71
67	at Wisconsin	65
	at Northwestern-forfeit (loss)	
70	Ohio State	65
54	Indiana	62
65	Iowa	60
56	at Michigan	92
66	at Michigan State	76
60	Northwestern	65
64	Wisconsin	70
63	at Indiana	95

55 at Ohio State 68
63 Purdue 64
64 Illinois 73
*National Airlines Tournament. (Honolulu)
**Jimmy Williams served as interim head coach for final nine games.

1986-87 (9-19, 2-16/9th)
Coach: Clem Haskins
70 North Dakota State 53
72 at Houston 86
75 Eastern Michigan 59
69 Chapman College 67
66 at Oklahoma State 77
64 Austin Peay 73
76 at Detroit 68
91 Wichita State 66
92 Tennessee Tech 69
78 Murray State 64
69 Wisconsin 67
60 Northwestern 53
57 Iowa 78
59 at Purdue 86
58 at Illinois 80
78 Ohio State 93
53 Indiana 77
65 at Michigan 92
60 at Michigan State 72
47 at Iowa 78
67 Illinois 79
73 Purdue 81
70 at Indiana 72
73 at Ohio State 88
70 Michigan 95
67 Michigan State 77
52 at Wisconsin 69
71 at Northwestern 72

1987-88 (10-18, 4-14/9th)
Coach: Clem Haskins
67 Drake 70
84 Western Illinois 52
75 Toledo 83
61 at Colorado State 80
65 Houston 60
75 at Ball State 67
89 Marquette 65
94 Beathune-Cookman 50
106 Grambling 82
68 at Wichita State 78
61 Illinois 65
71 at Michigan 103
74 Purdue 82
61 at Northwestern 65
76 Ohio State 85
59 at Michigan State 56
51 at Iowa 76
63 at Indiana 92
71 Wisconsin 62
50 at Illinois 86
82 Northwestern 67
78 Michigan 82
86 Iowa 107
70 at Wisconsin 81
74 at Ohio State 77
62 Michigan State 61
85 Indiana 91
66 at Purdue 93

1988-89 (19-12, 9-9/5th)
Coach: Clem Haskins
57 Ball State 63
97 Youngstown State 64
112 Maryland-E. Shore 68
99 Florida International 75
52 at Drake 66
83 at Marquette 67
93 Detroit 69
93 at Northern Illinois 74
99 Denver 54
67 at Wisconsin 75

72 Kansas State 67
83 at Michigan 98
80 Iowa 78
76 Purdue 66
67 at Northwestern 75
69 Illinois 62
64 at Michigan State 73
76 Ohio State 73
62 at Indiana 66
59 Wisconsin 58
88 Michigan 80
61 at Iowa 99
63 at Purdue 78
62 Indiana 75
58 at Illinois 63
78 Northwestern 59
77 Michigan State 61
78 at Ohio State 70
86 Kansas State* 75
80 Siena* 67
70 Duke* 87
*NCAA Tournament

1989-90 (23-9, 11-7/4th)
Coach: Clem Haskins
64 at Cincinnati 66
85 Chicago State 62
85 at Toledo 70
98 Iowa State 82
89 at Detroit 61
69 at Kansas State 68
77 Washington 60
81 Northern Illinois 62
97 Youngstown State 57
116 Rider 48
91 Illinois 74
78 at Purdue 86
83 at Michigan 87
97 Northwestern 75
83 Ohio State 78
75 at Wisconsin 77
84 Iowa 72
108 Indiana 89
79 at Michigan State 74
72 at Illinois 99
73 Purdue 72
73 Michigan 77
90 at Northwestern 72
68 Wisconsin 67
102 at Iowa 80
75 at Indiana 70
73 Michigan State 75
83 at Ohio State 93
64 Texas-El Paso* 61
81 Northern Iowa* 78
82 Syracuse* 75
91 Georgia Tech* 93
*NCAA Tournament

1990-91 (12-16, 5-13/9th)
Coach: Clem Haskins
74 Robert Morris 61
90 Augusta 60
65 Northern Illinois 37
84 at Iowa State 70
73 Santa Clara 63
64 Oregon State 53
64 Cincinnati 72
61 at Washington 72
72 Virginia 79
95 at Youngstown State 77
62 at Wisconsin 72
66 at Illinois 67
79 Iowa 77
59 Purdue 56
64 at Michigan State 73
70 Ohio State 80
85 at Northwestern 68
62 Michigan 66
66 Indiana 77
74 Illinois 94

69 at Iowa 82
82 at Purdue 89
62 at Ohio State 63
72 Michigan State 74
88 Northwestern 70
60 at Michigan 68
59 at Indiana 75
80 Wisconsin 70

1991-92 (16-16, 8-10/6th)
Coach: Clem Haskins
83 Arkansas* 92
89 Providence* 82
69 Arizona State* 37
95 Howard 54
98 Youngstown State 59
86 Akron 59
80 at Alabama-Birmingham 86
68 Detroit Mercy 66
62 at Memphis State 65
92 Weber State 52
89 Oregon** 64
80 Oregon State** 92
73 Iowa State 76
50 at Indiana 96
73 Michigan 64
49 at Wisconsin 48
70 Michigan State 66
69 at Ohio State 72
54 Illinois 53
92 Northwestern 50
70 at Iowa 87
57 at Purdue 65
57 at Northwestern 55
71 Indiana 67
58 at Illinois 74
70 at Michigan 95
64 Iowa 79
76 Wisconsin 57
58 Purdue 68
57 at Michigan State 66
63 Ohio State 94
70 at Washington State# 72
*Maui Invitational
**Far West Classic
#National Invitation Tournament

1992-93 (22-10, 9-9/5th)
Coach: Clem Haskins
108 So. Ill.-Edwardsville 64
88 Middle Tennessee State 65
93 Texas-San Antonio 75
92 Bethune-Cookman 50
92 Tennessee-Martin 63
87 at UC-Santa Clara 63
65 at Iowa State 99
70 Memphis State 55
74 Alabama-Birmingham 59
64 Michigan State 57
81 Purdue 60
77 at Iowa 84
70 at Wisconsin 79
73 Michigan 80
70 Northwestern 55
57 at Indiana 61
95 Penn State 67
63 at Michigan State 75
69 at Purdue 75
91 Iowa 85
85 Wisconsin 71
69 at Michigan 84
79 at Northwestern 60
75 Indiana 86
67 Illinois 65
67 at Penn State 41
58 at Ohio State 69
74 Florida# 66
86 Oklahoma# 72
76 USC## 58
76 Providence### 70
62 Georgetown### 61

#NIT (at Target Center, Minneapolis)
##NIT (at Met Center, Bloomington, Minn.)
###NIT (at Madison Square Garden, New York)

1993-94 (21-12, 10-8/4th)
Coach: Clem Haskins
70 Rice* 61
91 Georgia* 71
71 Kansas** 75
76 North Carolina** 90
107 Mississippi Valley State 63
90 at Middle Tennessee St. 76
73 Clemson 54
79 Western Carolina 61
66 at San Jose State 53
57 at Virginia 62
73 James Madison 68
89 Northeastern Illinois 62
73 at Northwestern 65
90 Wisconsin 53
67 at Penn State 78
63 Michigan 58
68 Michigan State 66
66 at Indiana 78
72 Purdue 75
92 at St. John's (N.Y.) 64
88 at Iowa 92
79 Northwestern 65
79 Ohio State 73
109 at Wisconsin 78
94 Penn State 66
65 at Michigan 72
68 at Michigan State 85
106 Indiana 56
70 at Purdue 86
107 Iowa (3 OT) 96
75 at Illinois 90
74 Southern Illinois# 60
55 Louisville# 60
*NIT Pre-Season Tournament
**NIT Pre-Season Tournament (at New York)
#NCAA Tournament (at Sacramento, Calif.)

1994-95 (19-12, 10-8/4th)
Coach: Clem Haskins
72 Arizona* 70
85 Villanova* 64
79 Brigham Young* 74
102 Sacramento State 84
92 Central Connecticut State 56
90 Rhode Island 65
88 Cincinnati 91
75 at California 82
50 Texas Southern 74
115 San Jose State 68
74 at James Madison 68
98 Middle Tennessee State 57
69 Penn State 67
60 at Purdue 68
105 Northwestern 74
67 at Wisconsin 74
81 Ohio State 61
77 Illinois 66
53 at Michigan State 54
55 at Iowa 54
80 Michigan 58
64 at Indiana 54
70 Iowa 74
66 Michigan State 57
88 at Illinois 94
65 at Ohio State 73
78 Wisconsin 70
82 at Northwestern 70
59 Purdue 72
60 at Penn State 69
61 St. Louis# 64
*Great Alaskan Shootout
#NCAA Tournament

Index

*Italicized page numbers indicate
a photo on that page.*